Interpreting Plato Socratically

J. Angelo Corlett

Interpreting Plato Socratically

Socrates and Justice

 Springer

J. Angelo Corlett
Department of Philosophy
San Diego State University
San Diego, CA, USA

ISBN 978-3-319-77319-3 (hardcover) ISBN 978-3-319-77320-9 (eBook)
ISBN 978-3-030-17105-6 (softcover)
https://doi.org/10.1007/978-3-319-77320-9

Library of Congress Control Number: 2018936606

© Springer International Publishing AG, part of Springer Nature 2018, First softcover printing 2019
This work is subject to copyright. All rights are reserved by the Publisher, whether the whole or part of the material is concerned, specifically the rights of translation, reprinting, reuse of illustrations, recitation, broadcasting, reproduction on microfilms or in any other physical way, and transmission or information storage and retrieval, electronic adaptation, computer software, or by similar or dissimilar methodology now known or hereafter developed.
The use of general descriptive names, registered names, trademarks, service marks, etc. in this publication does not imply, even in the absence of a specific statement, that such names are exempt from the relevant protective laws and regulations and therefore free for general use.
The publisher, the authors and the editors are safe to assume that the advice and information in this book are believed to be true and accurate at the date of publication. Neither the publisher nor the authors or the editors give a warranty, express or implied, with respect to the material contained herein or for any errors or omissions that may have been made. The publisher remains neutral with regard to jurisdictional claims in published maps and institutional affiliations.

Printed on acid-free paper

This Springer imprint is published by the registered company Springer International Publishing AG part of Springer Nature.
The registered company address is: Gewerbestrasse 11, 6330 Cham, Switzerland

For my mother

Preface

> It's easy to figure out that 'justice' (*dikaiosunē*) is the name given to the comprehension of the just (*dikaiou sunesis*), but the just itself is hard to understand. It seems that many people agree with one another about it up to a point, but beyond that they disagree—Socrates, *Cratylus* 412c-d[1]

This book is a sequel of sorts to my book, *Interpreting Plato's Dialogues* (Corlett 2005), which was my attempt to render dubious the Mouthpiece Interpretation of Plato's dialogues. While "the attempt to understand and develop Plato's philosophical views has a lengthy history, beginning with Aristotle and Plato's institutional successors in the Academy toward the end of the fourth century BC" (Brittain 2008: 526),[2] I made my focus in that book contemporary attempts to

---

[1] Unless stated otherwise, throughout this book translations of Plato's works shall be used from Cooper and Hutchinson (1997).

[2] Charles Brittain goes on to state of the Mouthpiece Interpretation that it contains "controversial assumptions." (Brittain 2008: 528) Brittain adds that the history of Platonism discredits the idea that there was a strand of Platonic orthodoxy that is reliably Plato's own set of views. (Brittain 2008: 530f.) Hence his statement that "The Platonic tradition is remarkably heterogeneous…" (Brittain 2008: 527) So as far back as one can trace the history of Plato scholarship, there are a variety of ways of approaching Plato's works that seemed reasonable to a variety of interpreters. Moreover, "…the idea that Plato's dialogues already presented a well-defined, comprehensive, and essentially correct philosophical *system* seems not to have arisen until the first century BC." (Brittain 2008: 526) Thus one ought to resist the temptation to think that, historically speaking, there is one best way to interpret Plato because that particular approach traces its roots back to Plato or thereabouts. The Mouthpiece Interpretation, no matter how popular it is among philosophers these days, enjoys no such privileged position.

justify that approach to Plato's dialogues. Since the publication of that book, more has been written in defense of the Mouthpiece Interpretation and against the Anti-Mouthpiece Interpretation. This book devotes a significant amount of space to addressing such discussions. But more than that, it seeks to do what *Interpreting Plato's Dialogues* did for the concept of mimetic art in some of Plato's dialogues, except for the most part with various concepts of justice within the Platonic corpus.[3]

Much has been written by philosophers on the subject of Socrates' views of justice, though most of it pertains to his views on a limited number of concepts related to distributive justice and how the ideal state ought to be structured. I devote a chapter of this book to concepts of distributive justice in the Platonic corpus. But since few philosophers have devoted their energies to what Plato's Socrates and other characters in Plato's writings articulate about criminal justice and punishment, on the one hand, or compensatory justice, on the other, much of this book is devoted to a philosophical exploration of what mainly Plato's Socrates had to say about matters of what is known today as corrective justice, and with some surprising results.

After the publication of *Interpreting Plato's Dialogues*, there were concerns raised, not about the plausibility of my critique of the Mouthpiece Interpretation of Plato's works, but about some of what I argued in support of the Socratic Anti-Mouthpiece Interpretation. Most of that book addressed attempts by some leading philosophers of Plato to justify the mouthpiece approach to the Platonic Question. The Platonic Question consists in the cluster of questions about how Plato's works ought to be approached in light of their literary style and contents. Should Socrates or some other character be considered to be the mouthpiece for Plato's beliefs, doctrines, or theories, as mouthpiece interpreters insist? Or is there insufficient reason to suppose that this approach is warranted? If so, what alternative approach might there be that might better answer the Platonic Question? Why did Plato write mostly in more or less aporetic dialogue form? Was it to convey to readers of his dialogues his views about certain matters,

---

[3] The exception is Appendix II to this book wherein the concept of art is discussed. It is included in order to serve as an updating of sorts to the treatment of the subject found in Corlett (2005).

Preface ix

or was there another reason?[4] While there are a variety of approaches to Plato's dialogues, I shall direct my primary attention to the most prominent one among contemporary philosophers of Plato (the Mouthpiece Interpretation) before I present and defend my alternative approach: the Socratic (Anti-Mouthpiece) Interpretation.

Chapters 2 and 3 address these concerns directly as a further defense of my approach to Plato's works against concerns raised at the 2006 American Philosophical Association session devoted to the book by Lloyd Gerson, Gerald Press, Charles Young, David Gallop, and some of those who have reviewed *Interpreting Plato's Dialogues* in some academic journals, as well as some of those who have written on the Platonic Question but were not discussed in the previous book. But as Nicholas D. Smith informed me during one of our many discussions about how Plato's dialogues ought to be approached, "the proof is in the pudding." He urged that it is one thing to successfully render problematic the Mouthpiece Interpretation. However, it is quite another thing to support my Socratic Anti-Mouthpiece Interpretation by way of plausible textual exegesis. While a lengthy chapter in *Interpreting Plato's Dialogues* is devoted to precisely that aim in terms of the concept of mimetic art in Plato's dialogues, this book seeks to expand the textual interpretive evidence in favor of the Socratic Anti-Mouthpiece Interpretation by explicating what Socrates has to say about certain justice concepts according to this approach. The results of my studies, I believe, will prove philosophically significant.

For example, the relatively few philosophers who have studied Socrates on criminal justice and punishment construe him as one who holds to some kind of moral education theory of punishment. But I will argue that this view is misleading. While it is true that there are a few passages, celebrated as they are by anti-retributivists, wherein Socrates expresses that some criminals ought to receive a moral education for their wrongdoings, the far majority of passages in which Socrates addresses issues of punishment are retributivist in character, based on considerations of desert, not moral education or social utility. Indeed, there are even pericopes in Plato's works wherein Socrates seems to express a view which favors the compensation by wrongdoers

---

[4] For a taxonomy of approaches to the Platonic Question, see Corlett (2005: 3f.). For purposes of this book, I shall not repeat the variety of positions propounded on the Platonic Question.

to their victims. This paints an entirely different picture of Socrates on criminal wrongdoing than what we are led to believe by those who have influenced philosophical thinking about these matters. For the sake of the history of philosophy, then, it is important to attempt to set the record straight about Plato's Socrates and criminal justice, *assuming for the sake of the Mouthpiece Interpretation, of course, that the character Socrates sincerely assents to the views he expresses in Plato's dialogues*. It will not do to allow one's own rather personal views on justice to affect how one interprets a select passage or two on justice from Plato's writings as if that constituted proper philosophical method in approaching Plato's works. One must do what one can to search throughout Plato's works to find each and every passage therein pertaining to justice and treat each such passage according to the category of justice to which it pertains, and then to permit Plato's characters to speak for themselves on the matter. When it comes to Socrates and criminal justice, what we find is that some who think they know about "Plato's theory of justice" are quite far off the mark when it comes to what Socrates actually argues about criminal justice and punishment, for instance. The history of philosophy in general, and Plato studies in particular, demands that we are more careful about what is attributed to either Plato or Socrates. Again, this assumes for the sake of the Mouthpiece Interpretation that it is legitimate to attribute any view whatsoever to either Plato's Socrates or Plato himself. The first chapters of this book undermine any attempt to ascribe to Plato either a belief, doctrine or theory at all. But if one is to engage in such an ill-founded interpretation of Plato's dialogues, then one ought to avoid misattributing to either Plato's Socrates or Plato himself particular beliefs, doctrines, or theories about justice that are sometimes ascribed to them.

Moreover, this book not only seeks to explicate what Socrates says but does not necessarily believe about criminal justice in some of Plato's works, it also directs attention to the discussions of justice (more broadly than either the notions of retributive or compensatory justice, δικαιοσύνη) in various of Plato's works. I attempt this aim at the expense of some well-respected mouthpiece interpreters who have misattributed certain theories, dogmas or beliefs about justice to Plato. I untangle this confusion and provide what seems most clearly to be the justice-related beliefs reasonably attributable to Plato's Socrates if it were justified to ascribe to him beliefs about such matters.

I thank Thomas C. Brickhouse, Gallop, Jay Kennedy, John J. Mulhern, David Murphy, Press, Smith, Burleigh Wilkins, and Charles Young for their incisive comments on some or all of what eventually became this book. All references and quotations from Plato's works are taken from the translations in Cooper and Hutchinson (1997) unless otherwise indicated. Chapter 7 is a revised version of "Punishment and the Socratic Roots of Retributivism" which appears in J. Ryberg and J. A. Corlett, Editors, *Punishment and Ethics* (London: Palgrave MacMillan, 2010), pp. 1–15. A version of part of Chapter 2 was presented at a special author-meets-critics session of the American Philosophical Association devoted to my book, *Interpreting Plato's Dialogues*, Portland, Oregon, 24 March 2006. A version of Chapter 6 was presented at the Department of Philosophy, Aristotle University of Thessaloniki, Thessaloniki, Greece, on 8 October 2013. I thank the audience at that lecture for helpful comments.

San Diego, CA, USA　　　　　　　　　　　　　　　　　J. Angelo Corlett

References

Brittain, Charles. 2008. Plato and platonism. In *The Oxford handbook of Plato*, ed. Gail Fine. Oxford: Oxford University Press.
Cooper, John M., and D. S. Hutchinson (Eds.). 1997. *Plato: Complete works.* Indianapolis: Hackett Publishing Company.
Corlett, J. Angelo. 2005. *Interpreting Plato's dialogues.* Las Vegas: Parmenides Publishing.

Contents

1 **Introduction** 1
   References 12

2 **Interpreting Plato Socratically** 15
   The Socratic Interpretation of Plato's Dialogues. 20
   References 32

3 **Defending the Socratic Interpretation
of Plato's Dialogues** 33
   Does the Socratic Interpretation Make Plato a Skeptic? 33
   The Mouthpiece Interpretation and Developmentalism 36
   What Is the Philosophical Significance of the Socratic
Interpretation? 38
   Does the Socratic Interpretation Imply
the Impenetrability of Plato's Dialogues? 41
   Does the Fact That There Are Degrees of Aporicity
in Plato's Dialogues Pose a Problem for the Socratic
Interpretation? 43
   What Is the Importance, If Any, of the *Seventh Letter*
for the Platonic Question? 44
   Complex Features of Plato's Writings. 56
   Is Aristotle a Witness to the Substantive Philosophical
Beliefs, Doctrines or Theories of Plato? 59
   The Origin and Development of the Platonic Corpus
and the Mouthpiece Interpretation. 66
   The Platonic Question and the Burden of Argument. 73

	Are There Not Some Philosophically Substantive Beliefs Which Are Attributable to Plato?	81
	Do Elements of Style Within the Dialogues of Plato Provide Clues to Plato's Beliefs, Doctrines, or Theories?	84
	References	93
4	**In Defense of Socratic Studies**	97
	The Case for "Socratic Studies"	99
	The Socratic Interpretation of Plato's Dialogues and the Socratic Question	112
	Objections to the Socratic Anti-mouthpiece Interpretation, and Replies	116
	References	119
5	**Socrates and Distributive Justice**	121
	Socrates on Freedom and Rights	124
	Equality	127
	References	131
6	**Legal Obligation in Plato's *Crito***	133
	Legal Obligation in the *Crito*	136
	The Role of the *Nomoi* in the *Crito*	143
	Objections and Replies	158
	References	165
7	**The Socratic Roots of Retributivism**	169
	References	186
8	**Socrates and Compensatory Justice**	187
	Compensatory Justice in Plato's *Gorgias*	188
	Compensatory Justice in Plato's *Laws*	191
	Concerns with the Socratic View of Compensatory Justice	195
	References	197

Conclusion	199
Appendices	203
Selected Sources	233
Index	241

About the Author

J. Angelo Corlett, PhD, is Professor of Philosophy and Ethics at San Diego State University and the author of more than 150 books and articles on philosophy. His books include: *Analyzing Social Knowledge* (Rowman & Littlefield, 1996); *Responsibility and Punishment* (Kluwer, 2001, 2003, Springer 2004 and 2014); *Race, Racism, and Reparations* (Cornell, 2003); *Terrorism: A Philosophical Analysis* (Kluwer, 2003); *Interpreting Plato's Dialogues* (Parmenides, 2005); *Race, Rights, and Justice* (Springer, 2009); *The Errors of Atheism* (Continuum, 2010); and *Heirs of Oppression* (Rowman & Littlefield, 2010). Many of his articles have been published in journals such as *Analysis*, *American Philosophical Quarterly*, *The Classical Quarterly*, *International Journal for the Philosophy of Religion*, *The Journal of Ethics*, *Journal of Social Philosophy*, *Philosophy*, and *Public Affairs Quarterly*, among others. He is the Editor-in-Chief of *The Journal of Ethics: An International Philosophical Review*. *Interpreting Plato Socratically* is his second book on the Platonic Question.

Chapter 1
Introduction

> *Justice is said—and well said—to be the daughter of Respect.*
>
> Plato, Laws 943e.

In my book, *Interpreting Plato's Dialogues*, I provide a critical assessment of numerous arguments proffered by Julia Annas, Terence Irwin, Richard Kraut and some others in favor of the philosophically prominent[1] Mouthpiece Interpretation of Plato's dialogues (also referred to by some as the "dogmatic" approach to Plato's dialogues) according to which it is justified to ascribe to Plato some or all of the informational contents of what this or that character in Plato's dialogues states beyond mere elements of philosophical method such as

---

[1] The prominence of the Mouthpiece Interpretation is implied in the following statement: "There is, of course, also a historical precedent for denying that the Platonic dialogues advance positive doctrine—a non-dogmatist (or 'sceptical') tradition that goes back to the New Academy of Arcesilaus and Carneades. But it has always been a minority opinion. Dogmatism and (for the last two centuries) developmentalism have dominated Anglo-American Platonic scholarship." (Beversluis 2006: 86) The equation of the non-dogmatic or Anti-Mouthpiece Interpretation, on the one hand, with the skeptical tradition of Plato scholarship, on the other hand, is a common mistake among mouthpiece interpreters, as we shall see in Chapter 2. Moreover, as we shall see in that chapter, some mouthpiece interpreters tend to use the prominence of the Mouthpiece Interpretation as a reason why it ought to be adopted, thereby committing a kind of fallacy of appeal to authority when in fact that authority is what is precisely in question when it comes to serious consideration of the Platonic Question.

argumentation and analysis. The name for this approach to Plato's dialogues can be found in some of the writings of Gregory Vlastos,[2] among others. According to one of its recent proponents, "The idea is not that Plato held views *dogmatically*, but that he held *views* (δόγματα) which he advanced in the dialogues." (Beversluis 2006: 85)[3] After exposing the fallacies in the reasoning in support of the Mouthpiece Interpretation and thereby rendering dubious that approach to the dialogues (Corlett 2005: Chapter 2), I articulate and defend what I call the "Socratic Anti-Mouthpiece Interpretation" according to which Plato's employment of the dialogue form itself either intentionally or unintentionally prohibits readers' abilities to discern the substantive philosophical mind of Plato himself. Instead, the informational contents of Plato's dialogues ought to be studied as the philosophically profound works that they are in encouraging us to think analytically about the nature of justice, art, knowledge and education as we read the *Republic*, of knowledge and reality as we read the *Theaetetus*, of compensatory justice as we read the *Gorgias*, of law and punishment as we read the *Laws*, etc.. For even if one were to assume the controversial authorship of the *Seventh Letter* as do many proponents of the Mouthpiece Interpretation,[4] there is inadequate direct textual evidence from the Corpus Platonicum that Plato purports to somehow expound his positive substantive philosophical beliefs, doctrines or theories in his dialogues, and secondary evidence from one or more of his students in the Academy (most notably, Aristotle) is problematic.[5] My Socratic Interpretation of Plato's dialogues is a species of the Anti-Mouthpiece Interpretation, also called the "non-dogmatic" approach by some, and the Anti-Mouthpiece Interpretation is misleadingly referred to as the "dramatic" approach by others. While the full name I have given my approach to Plato's

---

[2] See, for example, Vlastos (1960: 508), where Vlastos, in discussing the concept of justice in Plato's *Republic*, writes: "For what is his mouthpiece, Socrates, trying to accomplish?"

[3] In later chapters, I shall clarify what is meant by "dogma" and "doctrine" and their cognates.

[4] Mouthpiece interpreter-critics of the authenticity of the *Seventh Letter* are represented most recently in Burnyeat and Frede (2015).

[5] Corlett (2005: Chapter 3). Also see Chapter 2 of this book for a discussion of this issue that supplements my earlier discussion.

dialogues is the "Socratic Anti-Mouthpiece Interpretation," I shall hereafter refer to it by its abbreviated name: the "Socratic Interpretation."[6]

By "theory" and its cognates is meant a systematic account of doctrines or beliefs to which Plato sincerely assents in his dialogues, ones which answer specific questions that a theory must answer regarding, say, the nature of something (art, justice, knowledge, reality, etc.), its justification (moral or epistemic, for example: knowledge), an explanation of why it is important, etc.. By "doctrine" (δόγματα) and its cognates is meant a conceptual aspect of a theory of Plato's to which Plato sincerely assents. In this sense, doctrines are parts of theories in the way that a concept of truth is part of a theory of knowledge according to standard justified true belief theories of knowledge and epistemic justification. And doctrines are beliefs one accepts through a rigorous justificatory process such that they cohere with important aspects of one's theory of this or that. By "belief" and its cognates is meant the Kripkean notion of a proposition to which one sincerely assents without ambiguity concerning the nature of the proposition and the extent to which one holds it. (Kripke 1979)[7] Unlike a doctrine, a belief need not in order to qualify as a belief importantly cohere with one's overall system of propositions one accepts that constitute one's theory of this or that. Indeed, a belief need not satisfy the rigors of accepted propositions wherein such claims are made one's own subsequent to somewhat rigorous consideration or even as the result of reflective equilibrium. In other words, while what we accept is a considered judgment, a belief need not be. But each is a proposition to which one sincerely assents. So it is the claim of the Socratic Interpretation that Plato's choice of the dialogue form in which he wrote most of his works prohibits us, neither in principle nor in an *a priori* manner, from extracting his beliefs, doctrines or theories from them. Rather, it is that there is a fundamental lack of epistemic justification in light of the available evidence to subscribe to the Mouthpiece Interpretation which seeks to attribute substantive philosophical

---

[6] The Socratic (Anti-Mouthpiece) Interpretation is not to be confused with the Socratic Mouthpiece Interpretation, as we will see below. The former approach denies what the latter affirms, namely, that Plato puts into the mouth of the character Socrates his own beliefs, doctrines or theories.

[7] For a discussion of Kripke's puzzle, see Corlett (1989).

beliefs, doctrines or theories to Plato based on what this or that character in his dialogues expresses. In light of this lack of justification on behalf of the Mouthpiece Interpretation, it constitutes a fundamental attribution error to assert that "Plato says" this or that in his dialogues. Instead, one ought to state more accurately and less problematically that, for instance, "In the *Republic*, Socrates says....." or "In the *Theaetetus*, Socrates argues...," etc.. To infer from what any character in Plato's dialogues expresses to what "Plato says" without adequate justification amounts to something akin to what John J. Mulhern refers to as the "Plato says fallacy." (Mulhern 1971) It is to confuse a character's stating something, no matter how strongly and repeatedly, with Plato's endorsement of it.[8] When it comes to Plato's dialogues, this is a dubious inference to make (that is, the inference from Plato's Socrates' stating something to Plato's believing it).

As an example of how mouthpiece interpreters often assume either without argument or without adequate argument the Mouthpiece Interpretation and then proceed to create their own puzzles about what they presume Plato believes, one might refer to a particular discussion of the concept of justice in Plato's corpus between some leading mouthpiece interpreters. Raphael Demos discusses some paradoxes in the discussion of the ideal state in Plato's dialogues, most notably in Plato's *Republic*. (Demos 1957) According to Demos, an important paradox emerges when "Plato populates his heaven with the forms of just individuals no less than with that of the just state." Demos continues: "But if there be no just citizens, (except perhaps for the rulers) how can there be forms of just men? The paradox seems all the more acute because Plato launches his project of constructing the ideal city for the express purpose of making the ideally just man more visible. Yet, when the edifice has been built, there are no just individuals to be seen within its walls." (Demos 1957: 164) Beside the facts that Demos has begun his discussion of some of Plato's dialogues with locutions such as "Plato populates his heaven" and "Plato launches his project," and even admitting later on that "The theory I have proposed does not agree with all the evidence in the text, but perhaps it agrees better with such evidence than alternative theories" (Demos 1957: 173),[9] he goes

---

[8]A similar view is found in Nails (1995: 230).

[9]After all, "It is not a question of decisive proof but of probability." (Demos 1957: 173)

1   Introduction   5

on to conclude that "The parallelism between justice in the individual and justice in the city is part of a more grandiose scheme in Plato's thought." (Demos 1957: 174) Thus from beginning to end Demos has presumed the legitimacy of the Mouthpiece Interpretation, as most contemporary philosophers of Plato do. Yet if the Socratic Interpretation is plausible, then the very paradox that Demos sees as belonging to Plato's alleged "grandiose scheme" dissolves. For in that case, Plato has no such scheme, much less a grandiose one, in his dialogues. Rather, he writes brilliant dialogues wherein Socrates and his interlocutors are discussing the plausibility of an ideal state that they have in some cases "constructed." But it takes no convoluted reading of Plato's works to see that Socrates and even some of his interlocutors fail to approve of the product of such thinking, as it possesses many flaws.

Furthermore, in his discussion of the concept of justice and the individual in Plato's *Republic*, R. W. Hall argues for a different interpretation of the problematic aspects of what is argued therein. He concludes,

> With this distinction between justice in the individual and justice in the state in mind, it seems that a plausible case can be made for an alternative interpretation of the relation between the individual and the *polis* in Plato's thought. Instead of interpreting the relationship as a ruthless subordination of the individual's well being to the good of the state, or as the individual's discovery of his true good in service to the state, I suggest that the individual has his own good: "personal" justice. The individual's good is neither opposed to, nor quite that of the *polis*. Rather the two goods, the justice of the individual and that of the state, exhibit a relation of mutual dependence. Only in the just state can citizens acquire personal justice; but only if they are personally just can the citizens adequately perform their social function and so bring about the justice of the *polis*. (Demos 1957: 158)

However, while Hall's interpretation of the passages in question might be plausible, what is unsupported is his unargued for ascription of the entire idea to Plato. Similar examples of the mouthpiece error on this particular matter in Plato's writings are found.[10] The philosophical

---

[10] See, for example, a discussion of the respective views of R. Demos and R. W. Hall in Skemp (1960). Also see a discussion of the views of Demos and Hall in Mulgan (1968). For a discussion of the views of Demos, Hall, Skemp and Vlastos, see Hall (1972). In each case, some version of the Mouthpiece

significance of this embarrassing mouthpiece presumption is that what they attribute to Plato as being "unpalatable" (Mulgan 1968: 86) or "distasteful" (Mulgan 1968: 86) amounts to an attribution error that misunderstands the content of "Plato's overall view" (Mulgan 1968: 87)—whatever that is. While those such as Gregory Vlastos might do well to rescue Plato's *Socrates* from the wreckage into which he gets himself, say, with regard to this issue of the concepts of individual and collective justice (Vlastos 1960), this is hardly the same thing as rescuing *Plato* from the same absent some plausible argument that would ground the Mouthpiece Interpretation in the first place. Yet it is Vlastos himself who believes that he has actually rescued *Plato* from such poor reasoning about the concept of justice in the ideal state. For Vlastos concludes: "…Plato is completely exonerated of the charge leveled against him in recent years: that he committed the colossal *ignoratio elenchi* that would be involved in undertaking to prove that *justice* (i.e., justice$_1$) pays by merely proving that psychic harmony (the resultant of justice$_2$) pays." While it makes good press for one's own thesis to be able to infer, if one can, that one has figured out what Plato was really up to here or there in his dialogues, or to actually resolve a puzzle set out therein, it is unjustified to do so all the while never addressing the fundamental question of how to even approach the dialogues the meanings of which one is seeking to unlock. Thus accuracy of the history of philosophy is at stake here, and those of us who are concerned with it must face the fact that we must either provide sound arguments for the Mouthpiece Interpretation, or admit that there are none, and then live with the philosophical implications of that position. Vlastos has provided no reason for our thinking that "Plato is completely exonerated" of certain charges in that, first, those making the charges themselves are making the Platonic presumption, and secondly, the Platonic presumption requires sound support if

---

Interpretation is presumed, and locutions such as "Plato believes" abound therein. It should be noted, however, that Hall's version of the Mouthpiece Interpretation is more subtle than the others, though phrases such as "the theory of justice in the *Republic*" are found in his argument. (See Hall 1972: 7, 16) Perhaps, then, Hall's take on the problem of justice in the *Republic* is best categorized as a version of the "Theoretical Interpretation" of Plato's dialogues. (Corlett 1997: 423–437)

these sorts of discussions are to be justified and taken with legitimate seriousness.

Recently, Annas seeks to provide a description of "Plato's account" of the relation of virtue to law, more specifically, how "Plato's account" "developed from the *Republic* to the *Laws*." She writes:

> My own position is that Plato consistently, throughout his intellectual life, held to a very general thesis about political and social life, namely that the only good society, one worth living in, is one which has the unified overall aim of making its citizens happy, and that this can be achieved only by having them educated and formed to develop the virtues and so to live happily…. *Republic* and *Laws* are two ways in which Plato worked out his vision of how the good society can be achieved. (Annas 2017: 8)

While Annas might well have a "position" on this matter, her reasoning about the Platonic Question which underlies her "position" as it is expressed directly in some previous works has been found to commit various logical errors. (Corlett 2005: 31–33) So her continued commitment to the Mouthpiece Interpretation of Plato's dialogues is unwarranted absent adequate philosophical and textual justification.

What such mouthpiece thinkers have done is to put the philosophical cart before the horse, as it were. Instead of taking seriously the meta-philosophical Platonic Question, they seem to ignore it (or give it rather short shrift) in favor of assuming their particular take on particular passages within the works of Plato. Then they set about trying to wrestle with this or that concept or problem in Plato's dialogues. While struggling with a concept in Plato's works is itself important, actually attributing a belief, doctrine or theory to Plato is problematic. It is a misattribution error that requires correction. A primary difficulty with Plato studies, of course, is that the very dialogical style of writing that Plato employs does not lend itself to straightforward interpretation in order to apprehend his ideas. So one must be ever careful to not presume this or that about what is in Plato's mind insofar as substantive philosophical views are concerned.

The Socratic Interpretation does not hold that it is impossible to extract from the dialogues, say, implicit methodological ideas to which Plato might have adhered, such as his obvious respect for reason understood in general terms of philosophical argument and analysis. What stands between the Socratic and mouthpiece interpretations is not the fact that the author of Plato's dialogues respects reason in the pursuit of wisdom, but rather that mouthpiece interpreters routinely and without adequate justification attribute all manner of positive substantive philosophical beliefs, doctrines or theories to Plato, such as a theory of forms, a theory of art, a theory of justice, a virtue ethic, a metaphysic, etc.. Socratic interpreters find inadequate justification for such ascriptions.

Consonant with Socrates' statement in *Charmides* 161c about philosophical inquiry more generally, the real issue at hand when discussing the Platonic Question is not which character says this or that and which one allegedly speaks for Plato, but rather whether or not this or that claim made by the character, including Socrates, is true. The Socratic Interpretation asks readers of Plato's dialogues to follow his mentor Socrates' advice in studying Plato's works instead of interpreting Plato's works through the mind of one or more of his students. For it is more plausible to think that Plato was more influenced by his mentor than he was by his students. Moreover, given the fact that nowhere does Socrates, so far as the textual evidence suggests, systematically set forth and defend his own beliefs, doctrines or theories, it is unjustified to attribute such beliefs, doctrines or theories to Plato. Indeed, as I shall argue Chapter 4, it is not even adequately justified to attribute such words to the historical Socrates! The most important question before us in investigating the Platonic Question is not whether or not Plato subscribes to this or that belief, doctrine or theory found in his dialogues. What is most important is whether or not, or to what extent, this or that belief, doctrine, argument or theory (should there exist any theories) presented in the dialogues is plausible, and why. To lose sight of this point is to lose sight of one of the most fundamental facets of Plato's works. It is to misunderstand the basic intent of Plato in choosing the dialogue form. It is to misunderstand at least part of the very essence of what Plato is attempting to do in his works. And this holds true even though there is some degree of aporetic disparity between the dialogues, from one period of Plato's writings to another.[11]

---

[11] Of course, such aporetic disparity might be due wholly or in part to the work of scribes or redactors of the extant Platonic corpus. So one ought to be mindful of not assuming that such aporetic disparity from earlier to middle to later dialogues is a sign of the maturity or development of Plato's thought as characterized in his dialogues.

In light of this important clarification of the primary point of the Platonic Question, it remains puzzling why devotees of the Mouthpiece Interpretation go to such lengths to attempt to prove what is by Socrates' own lights an insignificant question (or at least not the main point of philosophy), implying that the answer to what I refer to as the Platonic Question is a skeptical one at best. And for those interested in how to best fit Plato into the history of Western philosophy, perhaps it is best to describe Plato as the Socratic Interpretation does, namely, as a philosopher who chose to not propound his own philosophically substantive views in his writings, but who rather sought to engage readers in the mutual quest for wisdom on a variety of important topics. Of course, one of the many virtues of the Socratic Interpretation is that Plato turns out to be a rather modest philosopher. But again, I take this to be a good-making feature of this approach to Plato rather than as a weakness as it makes more sense to think that Plato was influenced more by his humble mentor than he was by one of his students as mouthpiece interpreters so often want to suggest or imply.

The Socratic Interpretation does not commit itself to the hyperbolic notion that Plato was a skeptic in general, or even a local skeptic with regard to this or that philosophical concern under discussion in this or that of his dialogues. Indeed, that would amount to a self-contradiction as the Socratic Interpretation disallows us the privilege to know to what Plato's substantive philosophical views amount. Of course, this does not mean that we cannot surmise some of Plato's positions about his philosophical method and style, whether or not he is committed to a respect for the law of non-contradiction, philosophical analysis and argumentation, etc.. But ascribing these kinds of general claims to Plato is not akin to ascribing to him all manner of specific beliefs, doctrines or theories about substantive philosophy. This is a point that some mouthpiece interpreters for whatever reason fail to grasp or refuse to accept in their approach to Plato's works. For them, Plato is either a "dogmatist" or "theoretician" (on the one hand), or he is a skeptic (on the other).[12] For them, Plato's dialogues are to be approached either as works containing Plato's views, or they are to be approached relativistically making him out to be a skeptic. But such

---

[12] An example of this view is found in Annas (1992: 64), as discussed in Corlett (2005: 31–33).

mouthpiece interpreters provide us with a false dilemma, a bifurcation fallacy. For neither one of these extreme approaches is one we either ought to adopt or one that is defended by me. Instead, the Socratic Interpretation sees Plato neither as a skeptic nor a relativist, neither as a dogmatist nor a theoretician insofar as his aim in composing dialogues is concerned. His aim is rather to take readers on a philosophical, analytical journey with Socrates and his interlocutors in investigating various important problems, and we as readers are to continue the argumentation and analyses wherever they lead.

In this book, I set out to expose some further errors of the Mouthpiece Interpretation, such as the one wherein contemporary philosophers follow the lead of M. M. Mackenzie (MacKenzie 1981) in thinking without adequate textual support that Plato was anything but a retributivist concerning the moral justification of punishment. I also assess Thomas C. Brickhouse and Nicholas D. Smith's latest attempt to address what I refer to as the "Socratic Question" insofar as it might be thought that Plato's Socrates might represent the mind of Plato. (Brickhouse and Smith 2010) And I continue my exposition of various Platonic themes in line with the Socratic Interpretation of Plato's dialogues. Indeed, the chapters of this book on Socrates and justice are intended to demonstrate that it is possible to provide a Socratic Interpretation of Plato's dialogues, one that refuses to commit the fundamental attribution error of ascribing to Plato various substantive philosophical theories, doctrines or beliefs.

In closing these introductory remarks, it is important that I clarify some key assumptions I make throughout this book. First, I assume that there exists sufficient genuineness in the apocryphal and pseudopygraphal writings of Plato to consider them as legitimate sources to cite, and that there is not substantial reason to rule out any of them as not being sufficiently reflective of Plato's genuine corpus of writings. Second, I wish to clarify a distinction, implicit in *Interpreting Plato's Dialogues*, that there are strong and weak versions of the Socratic Interpretation: (1) that it is impossible even in principle to find Plato's beliefs, doctrines or theories in Plato's dialogues (stronger version); (2) that it is possible but has yet to be adequately proven that Plato's beliefs, doctrines or theories are extractable from his dialogues (weak version). I subscribe to the weaker version of the Socratic Interpretation according to which it is possible in principle to prove the Mouthpiece

Interpretation. However, given the weakness of the arguments and paucity of evidence adduced in favor of it, it is unjustified (or at best only weakly justified) to accept it as a viable approach to Plato's dialogues.

Briefly, this book proceeds as follows. Chapters 2–3 seek to answer further previously unaddressed questions about the viability of the Socratic Interpretation, and to clarify issues along the way. They also refute arguments against the Socratic Interpretation (or ones that might be raised against it) that have heretofore been unaddressed. When coupled with my previous work on the Platonic Question, I am hopeful that no significant philosophical stone is left unturned in attempting to address what has been or might be said to cast doubt on the Socratic Interpretation. Chapter 4 is devoted to an analysis of Brickhouse and Smith's defense of Socratic studies. I seek therein to extend the Socratic Anti-Mouthpiece Interpretation to an approach to Plato's works that attributes what Plato's Socrates says to the character Socrates. While this seems counter-intuitive to some, the analysis set forth has important implications for both Socratic studies and Plato studies. Chapter 5 considers some of what Socrates says about certain concepts of distributive justice, dealing with such justice concepts as equality, freedom, rights, etc.. Chapter 6 provides an in-depth Socratic Interpretation of the concept of legal obligation in Plato's *Crito*, resulting in a unique answer to the age-old cluster of questions about Socrates' words in the *Apology* and the *Crito* on such matters, including why Socrates chose death when he had alternatives presented to him that would have prolonged his life. Chapter 7 considers and refutes the popular idea that Plato had a theory of punishment that amounts to a "moral education" theory of punishment. In fact, Plato had no theory of punishment. But what Socrates said about punishment hardly amounts to such a view. Instead, most of what Socrates expresses in Plato's works is consistent with a retributive notion of punishment, embracing standard retributivist ideals of responsibility, desert, and proportionality. Chapter 8 pertains to what Socrates said concerning compensatory justice, to my knowledge a topic never before addressed by philosophers of Plato or by contemporary philosophers of law. The results might shock the moral senses of most contemporary philosophers who are bent on utilitarian-based accounts of "justice" that tend to either discount or deny the moral legitimacy of compensatory justice because it tends to create inequalities amongst citizens. Appendix I serves as a defense of Harold Cherniss' critique of the use of Aristotle as a witness to Plato's beliefs, doctrines or theories against Lloyd Gerson's critique of Cherniss' critique. In the end, the attempt of Gerson to bolster the Mouthpiece Interpretation of Plato by a resurrection of the use of Aristotle for such purposes fails miserably. Finally, Appendix II is a critical discussion of a recent attempt to interpret the concept of mimetic art in Plato's *Republic* in mouthpiece terms.

This book seeks to add to the increasing numbers of works on justice in Plato and Socratic studies. But in the end, it is a vindication of how the Socratic Interpretation can and does serve as the most plausible approach to Plato's dialogues. If the proof is in the pudding, this pudding has the right consistency, and the right taste.

References

Annas, Julia. 1992. Plato the sceptic. In *Oxford studies in ancient philosophy*, ed. James C. Klagge and Nicholas D. Smith, Supplemental volume, 43–72. Oxford: Oxford University Press.
———. 2017. *Virtue & law in Plato & beyond*. Oxford: Oxford University Press.
Beversluis, John. 2006. A defence of dogmatism in the interpretation of Plato. In *Oxford studies in ancient philosophy*, ed. David Sedley, vol. 31, 85–112. Oxford: Oxford University Press.
Brickhouse, Thomas C., and Nicholas D. Smith. 2010. *Socratic moral psychology*. Cambridge: Cambridge University Press.
Burnyeat, Myles, and Michael Frede. 2015. In *The pseudo-Platonic Seventh Letter*, ed. Dominic Scott. Oxford: Oxford University Press.
Corlett, J. Angelo. 1989. Is Kripke's puzzle really a puzzle? *Theoria* LV: 95–113.
———. 1997. Interpreting Plato's dialogues. *The Classical Quarterly, New Series* 47: 423–437.
———. 2005. *Interpreting Plato's dialogues*. Las Vegas: Parmenides.
Demos, Raphael. 1957. Paradoxes in Plato's doctrine of the ideal state. *The Classical Quarterly, New Series* 7: 164–174.
Hall, R.W. 1972. Egalitarianism and justice in the *Republic*. *Apeiron* 6: 7–19.
Kripke, Saul. 1979. A puzzle about belief. In *Meaning and use*, ed. A. Margalit, 239–283. Dordrecht: Reidel.
Mackenzie, M.M. 1981. *Plato on punishment*. Berkeley: University of California Press.

References

Mulgan, R.G. 1968. Individual and collective virtues in the *Republic*. *Phronesis* 13: 84–87.

Mulhern, John J. 1971. Two interpretive fallacies. *Systematics* 9: 168–172.

Nails, Debra. 1995. *Agora, academy, and the conduct of philosophy*. Dordrecht: Kluwer Academic Publishers.

Skemp, J.B. 1960. Comment on communal and individual justice in the *Republic*. *Phronesis* 5: 35–38.

Vlastos, Gregory. 1960. Justice and psychic harmony in the *Republic*, 505–521. LXVI: *The Journal of Philosophy*.

Chapter 2
Interpreting Plato Socratically

Amplifying the concise taxonomy of approaches to Plato I provide in the Introduction and elsewhere discuss in considerably more complexity (Corlett 2005), I would like to clarify that, though I shall herein focus my attention on the general mouthpiece and anti-mouthpiece interpretations of Plato, each of these approaches has several versions. There is the Socratic Mouthpiece Interpretation which states that the views placed in Socrates' mouth by Plato reflect either the character or the historical Socrates' own views. This is not to be confused with the Socratic (Anti-Mouthpiece) Interpretation which not only denies what the Socratic Mouthpiece Interpretation affirms, but is referred to as "Socratic" not because "Socratic" identifies the character expressing Plato's views, but because of the values and method of Plato's Socrates. So even the adjective "Socratic" in each case carries different meanings between the two approaches to Plato's dialogues.

Theoretical mouthpiece interpreters hold that Plato's works contain the theories of Plato and/or Socrates, while dogmatic interpreters believe they contain their doctrines, and doxastic interpreters aver that the works of Plato contain Socrates' and/or Plato's beliefs. Anti-mouthpiece interpreters deny that there is sufficient reason or evidence to accept these claims. Dramatic anti-mouthpiece interpreters hold that the works of Plato are for the most part dramas and do not contain theories, doctrines or beliefs of Plato's, while the Socratic Anti-Mouthpiece Interpretation argues that the works of Plato are mostly dialogues and readers are urged to use their contents as dramatic devices to continue the philosophical quest for truth and avoidance of error. Again and more specifically, the Socratic Anti-Mouthpiece Interpretation might assume either a strong or weak version. The strong version holds that it is impossible, no matter what the evidence, to extract Plato's philosophically substantive beliefs, doctrines or theories from his dialogues, while the weak version not only admits the possibility of extracting such beliefs, doctrines or theories from the dialogues, it admits that basic analytical philosophical method can be ascribed to Plato based on the constant use of reasoning by most, if not all, of the characters throughout Plato's writings. As in my previous work on the Platonic Question, I subscribe to the weak version of the Socratic (Anti-Mouthpiece) Interpretation. It is the position I have adopted subsequent to considering the many arguments in favor of the Mouthpiece Interpretation by some of the most distinguished and devoted of its adherents, and after considering the plausibility of their reasoning offered against views that conflict with the Mouthpiece Interpretation that the kinds of theories, philosophies, doctrines or beliefs commonly attributed to Plato are not adequately justified. At best, they might be "personally" or subjectively justified, but not also "verifically" justified.[1]

Within this taxonomy of approaches to Plato's works is the tendency of several philosophers to interpret the contents of Plato's works as having unity or development of certain theories, doctrines or beliefs that many ascribe to Plato. Versions of unitarianism and developmentalism can be found in either the Mouthpiece Interpretation or the Anti-Mouthpiece Interpretation, but they are most prevalent among mouthpiece interpreters. While global unitarians see the unity of certain theories, doctrines or beliefs throughout most or all of Plato's works, global developmentalists assert that theories, doctrines or beliefs develop throughout his works. And while moderate unitarians believe that certain theories, doctrines or beliefs are congruent with one another amongst some of Plato's works, moderate developmentalists construe certain theories, doctrines or beliefs to evolve from some of Plato's works to others. And while local unitarians see the unity of this or that theory, doctrine or belief in a particular work of Plato's, local developmentalists see incongruence or change therein.

---

[1] These terms are borrowed from the coherentist epistemology of Keith Lehrer as it is expressed in Lehrer (2000).

Of course, there is possible a kind of global, moderate, or local unity and development in all, most, or some of Plato's works: where there is unity there can also be development. That is, where there is unity of the concept of mimetic art in the *Republic*, for example, there can also be development of the concept of justice therein. In this way, we find local unity and development, it might be argued, especially within some of the major and more philosophically complex of Plato's dialogues.

While some mouthpiece interpreters eschew developmentalism in Plato's corpus of writings, Anti-Mouthpiece interpreters can concur with this observation. For instance, Debra Nails writes of the development of ideas in Plato's dialogues that "The reason for so many fresh beginnings in the dialogues, the reason we find inconsistencies and contradictions, is not that Plato was evolving intellectually, refining and rejecting doctrines and methods as he developed, but that no doctrine or method was ever deemed infallible." (Nails 1995: 235) But this statement is problematic for at least two reasons. First, it implicitly assumes that there are "inconsistencies and contradictions" in the Platonic corpus as if one or another of such positions was, say, Plato's own or "belonged to" (represented the beliefs of) a particular dialogical character, something that makes more sense on a Mouthpiece Interpretation than on an Anti-Mouthpiece Interpretation. Yet as we shall see, Nails is considered by some to be a proponent of an extreme version of the Anti-Mouthpiece Interpretation, wherein viewing the informational contents of Plato's dialogues as "doctrines" that might ever be in conflict with one another as advanced or endorsed positive doctrine would be inconsistent with the very point of the Anti-Mouthpiece Interpretation. Secondly, the statement as it reads appears to imply a false dilemma: either what appear to be inconsistencies and contradictions in Plato's dialogues represent the development of Plato's mind, or Plato believed that "no doctrine was ever deemed infallible." However, why cannot both of these alternatives be true? Why cannot it be the case both that in Plato's dialogues we find *prima facie* implicit indicators that his thinking on various matters was developing (though, if the Socratic Interpretation is correct, we seem to lack sufficient evidence as to the nature of his views) *and* that he believed that no belief, doctrine or theory was infallible? Indeed, might not his being a fallibilist explain his evolution as a philosopher, so much so that it might also explain why he wrote in dialogue form rather than in treatise form, and why Plato, so far as we know, chose not to set forth and defend his own views in his writings? Of course, all of this assumes the general (though of course not absolute) reliability of the extant documents comprising the Corpus Platonicum, an assumption I make throughout this book and my previous work on the Platonic Question.

Again, I shall discuss the merits of the more general versions of the mouthpiece and anti-mouthpiece interpretations, ignoring for the moment the nuances just mentioned. For my task herein is to critically assess each of these general approaches to Plato's works. While there are variants of each of these approaches to Plato's dialogues, the mouthpiece and anti-mouthpiece interpretations as I discuss them herein represent the most widely held approaches to Plato's writings and are the focus of this chapter.

Both the Mouthpiece Interpretation and the Socratic (Anti-Mouthpiece) Interpretation share at least the following ideas in common:

> (a) Textual evidence shows that Plato wrote several dialogues, but no treatises; (b) There are certain views propounded by certain dialogical characters in the Platonic corpus; (c) Plato wrote dialogues for a purpose, or a set of purposes, one of which is to guide readers to the search for their own philosophical enlightenment; (d) Plato may have had philosophical views; (e) There are better and worse ways to read Plato's works; and (f) It may or may not be true that the words of the characters of Plato's dialogues actually represent those of the historical persons they sometimes seem to represent.[2]

But what separates these two approaches to Plato's dialogues is that the Mouthpiece Interpretation holds that the works of Plato contain, and were meant to contain, Plato's (and/or Socrates') own beliefs, doctrines or theories, and that Plato's (and/or Socrates') beliefs, doctrines or theories are found in the ideas expressed by some of the interlocutors in Plato's dialogues, while the Socratic Interpretation denies these claims.

---

[2] (a)–(e) are also found in Corlett (2005: 24). An alternative listing of commonalities between different approaches to the Platonic Question is found in Nails (1995: 32 f.).

Rather than reconsider the dubiousness of previously addressed arguments for the Mouthpiece Interpretation, it is important to provide new reasoning for its rejection. I make the assumption that Plato no doubt had high respect for his mentor, Socrates, and I argue that even though Thomas C. Brickhouse and Nicholas D. Smith are correct in arguing that there is no formal Socratic method (Brickhouse and Smith 2002: 155), there are nonetheless certain aspects of the ways in which Socrates is depicted in Plato's dialogues as doing philosophy which are noteworthy. I argue that this is *part* of what is central to what Plato wants to convey in his dialogues, namely, how philosophy ought to be conducted. I then argue that the aporetic nature of many the dialogues renders further dubious the Mouthpiece Interpretation's attempt to attribute to Plato this or that view therein. Of course, only about six or so of the dozens of Plato's works are indeed aporetic in the strict sense, though various others are aporetic in a looser sense (or are aporetic to a lesser degree). Moreover, as Christopher Gill argues, the early and middle dialogues are elenctic, yet later dialogues such as the *Philebus* and *Sophist* are not. (Gill 1996: 292 f.) It would be problematic, then, to argue that the aporetic nature of the contents of some dialogues is a good enough reason to think that the dialogues as a whole are aporetic and all that this implies for how one ought to approach the corpus of Plato's writings. Thus I construe the aporetic nature of various, but not all, of Plato's dialogues, and the fact that not all of his works were indeed dialogues, as strong evidence for the Socratic Interpretation rather than as evidence found in every work of Plato's.

However, even though *aporia* does not find itself in every work of Plato's, to the extent that it does occur it poses significant problems for the Mouthpiece Interpretation. This view admits that *aporia* in the Platonic corpus is a matter of degree, and that it may appear to be more prevalent in the early and middle dialogues than in the later ones. Of course, that there is a great deal of *aporia* throughout most of Plato's works does not suggest that there is also not the reconsideration of characters' own views in light of the way the discussion is proceeding, or that interlocutors are not able to change their minds and shift perspectives on issues. (McCabe 2008: 103) Moreover, what Mary Margaret McCabe refers to as "detachment" also occurs in the dialogues wherein some interlocutors begin to see a problem from more than one standpoint. (McCabe 2008: 104) It is a kind of active reflective engagement (what McCabe refers to as "a position of detached reflection"[3]) that is not only experienced by some of the characters of Plato's dialogues, but by readers of the same.

But these factors still work in favor of the Socratic Interpretation and against the Mouthpiece Interpretation. For in the later dialogues where it is thought by some to be where Plato begins to engage his own contemporaries in philosophical dialectic, it hardly follows that there is sufficient evidence of Plato's views therein and that there is no degree of *aporia* present in even those dialogues. Furthermore, the fact that the latter works in question are *dialogues* prohibits any ascription of their doxastic, doctrinal or theoretical contents to Plato with reasonable confidence. Once again, consistent with *Charmides* 161c, it is not important so much who believes what in the dialogues so much as whether or not what is said is true, and why. It is, moreover, quite possible to interpret Plato's dialogues without committing what John J. Mulhern refers to as the "Plato says" fallacy. (Mulhern 2000: 223) The Socratic Interpretation provides a good reason for not committing this fallacy, this fundamental attribution error.

The Socratic Interpretation of Plato's Dialogues

More precisely, the Socratic Interpretation of Plato's dialogues takes seriously the depth of Socrates' influence on Plato in Plato's composing the dialogues and in Plato's very choice to employ the dialogue form for most of his works. Instead of construing Plato's works as having the purpose of teaching us his own beliefs, doctrines or theories as the Mouthpiece Interpretation insists, the Socratic Interpretation understands Plato's works as conveying the manner in which the examined life ought to be achieved, namely, by way of philosophical investigation. And what better way of communicating this than by employing the dialogical method in his writings and placing Socrates (paradigmatic of the philosophical method) as the main character in

---

[3] See McCabe (2008: 104–106), where McCabe also notes various passages from the *Sophist*, the *Statesman*, the *Theaetetus*, and the *Phaedo* to support her point.

most of them? In light of the Mouthpiece Interpretation's lack of a sound argument in its favor, the Socratic Interpretation refuses to accept absent adequate justification the claim that Plato's works reveal, or even attempt to reveal, Plato's beliefs, doctrines or theories.

The philosophical profundity of Plato's works lies not in the misascriptions of this or that belief, doctrine, or theory to Plato, but rather in the philosophical enlightenment that readers derive from a careful study of Plato's works, and in our further developing incomplete or unclear arguments and analyses found in them. As A. D. Woozley writes of the *Crito*:

> ...I believe that the dialogue...was intended to be a substantially faithful representation of the actual Socrates, but even more because the purposes of the book do not demand that the authorship of this view or that, even if it could, should be established. The views are presented, and the reasons advanced for them, are what here matter; it is more important that they be correctly interpreted and fairly assessed than that they be properly attributed to 'Socrates' rather than to Socrates, or *vise versa*. (Woozley 1979: 5)

Moreover, part of the philosophical depth of Plato's works is that they not only contain certain arguments and analyses which are problematic or not, as the cases may be, but that those who study them are urged to consider the problems they raise for themselves and, in taking up the torch of philosophical investigation, attempt as best they can to resolve them. As John M. Cooper writes, "It was characteristic of philosophy before Socrates and Plato that philosophers usually put themselves forward as possessors of special insight and wisdom: *they* had the truth, and everyone else should just listen to them and learn." (Cooper and Hutchinson 1997: xix) But as we know, throughout many of Plato's works Socrates makes claims to his own ignorance.[4] While some have made attempts to construe Socrates' words here (and often elsewhere) to be ironical (Vlastos 1991), it is also plausible to take them at their face value.

Now the facts that there is no formal Socratic method, on the one hand, and Socrates' insistence on his own ignorance, on the other, together support (though in themselves do not adequately justify) the

---

[4] As Anthony Kenny writes: "The man who is, as it were, the patron saint of philosophers, Socrates, claimed that the only way in which he surpassed others in wisdom was that he was aware of his own ignorance." (Kenny 2006: 13)

Socratic Interpretation's idea that the philosopher who had most influence on Plato was one who hardly fits the description of one who propounds one's own beliefs, doctrines or theories as both many of Socrates' predecessors and his contemporaries did. However, we ought not to expect, nor should we attempt, to locate Plato's own views in his dialogues. This is especially true in light of the various features of what we might informally refer to as Socrates' method of doing philosophy, including open-mindedness (*Euthyphro* 14c; *Phaedo* 82d; *Laws* 667a; *Protagoras* 349c–d; *Gorgias* 506c), persistence[5] and courage (*Euthyphro* 15c; *Phaedo* 84a; *Theaetetus* 155d; *Republic* 450e; *Phaedo* 83e, 90e; *Statesman* 260b), sincerity (*Protagoras* 331c; *Republic* 349a; *Protagoras* 348c; *Gorgias* 357e–358a, 489d, 515b–c; *Theaetetus* 151d, 191a; *Second Alcibides* 150e; *Republic* 535d–e; *Phaedo* 67d–68b, 82c), humility (*Apology* 21d, 29b; *Theaetetus* 150c; *Meno* 86b, e; *Cratylus* 428d, 436d, 440d; *Theages* 128b; *Phaedo* 107b), and justice (*Theaetetus* 167e–168a). In light of these factors, the informal Socratic method is a common search for truth and wisdom. And if it is true, as the Socratic Interpretation states, that Plato, in writing the dialogues and other works of the Platonic corpus, was influenced primarily by his mentor Socrates, then it would make good sense to think that Plato was in turn influenced by Socrates' "method" of philosophical inquiry, which is not dogmatic or theory-laden. If this is true, then it makes inadequate sense to think, as mouthpiece interpreters do, that Plato wrote dialogues in order to communicate to readers his own views. And if this is true, then it seems to follow that the primary purpose of Plato's works is not to communicate his own views, but to encourage readers to engage in philosophical dialectic as did Socrates, and to attempt to utilize philosophical method to attain truth, avoid error, and to become better persons in the process so that we may be better for the rest of our lives. (*Euthyphro* 16)

Indeed, the Socratic Interpretation embraces McCabe's description of what she refers to as "identification" of readers with views held by certain interlocutors in the Platonic corpus:

---

[5]What I refer to as Socratic open-mindedness and persistence is called "double open-endedness" in Nails (1995: 20).

For those cases where philosophical discussion is directly and richly portrayed—the *Meno*, for example, or the *Phaedo* or the *Philebus*—we might think we should *imagine ourselves as* one of the characters in question: should sympathize with their positions, should take up the point of view they espouse. So we might share Cebes' worries about whether the soul is immortal, while sympathizing with his earnest desire that it be so, indeed (*Phaedo* 88aff.). The arguments that follow, then, would engage with that position and show us where it should be modified and resolved. Or we might imagine ourselves as Meno, or Laches—and feel for them as their less than rigorous collections of beliefs are subjected to Socratic argument, feel with them the sense of puzzlement (of *aporia*), of frustration and irritation, or just sheer embarrassment (*Meno* 80aff.; *Laches* 194aff.; and compare Protarchus' more robust response, *Philebus* 20). We may feel some sympathy, even, for rebarbative characters such as Protagoras or Critias (*Protagoras* 333–34; *Charmides* 166). And we can empathize with the characters thus just because they are portrayed in vivid ways, such that we can clothe ourselves, as we read, with their character and attitudes. But we then find the attitudes and views that we thus adopt subjected to dialectical scrutiny, and this serves a direct philosophical purpose. So—we could say—the point of having these characters represented to us is that the representation is somehow transparent, available for us to identify with the characters on the dialogue's stage and to suffer their philosophical fate. . . . So in our imaginative engagement with the dialogue, our views are transformed. (McCabe 2008: 92–93)[6]

. . . For as we read, we identify with different positions, and then—also as we read—we are shocked out of that identification into a position of detachment, of reflection *on* the positions with which identification is possible. (McCabe 2008: 108)

Now in concurring with these words on the identification and detachment of readers with part or all of what is expressed in Plato's dialogues, it is important to note that it is no feature of the Socratic Interpretation that reading Plato's works is a matter of subjective

---

[6] The Socratic Interpretation disagrees, however, with McCabe's reading of the condemnation of *mimêsis* or imitation as ways of doing philosophy by way of reading the dialogues of Plato. (McCabe 2008: 94) To think that just because the mimetic arts are condemned by a character (no matter which one) is a good reason to think that readers cannot and should not follow the arguments and analyses of the dialogues in order to learn how to do philosophy and to further each particular argument and analyses as best one can is a misunderstanding. Reading Plato's dialogues may include certain aspects of passive learning. But it also, insofar as the Socratic Interpretation holds, bids us to engage the contents of the dialogues as active learners, as active philosophical participants.

interpretation of where the arguments/analyses lead the reader. Moreover, that the nature of the dialogues obscures attempts to discover Plato's own views and that the aim of the dialogues is to engage readers in a dynamic way in no way rules out the possibility of doing philosophy analytically and without adopting some strong form of skepticism. In particular, it does not rule out the possibility that a student of the *Theaetetus* might discover the most plausible analysis of human knowledge, or that a reader of the *Republic* might arrive at the truth about the nature of justice. Nor does the Socratic Interpretation deny that Plato had beliefs of his own with philosophical content. What it denies is that extant primary and secondary textual evidence is sufficient evidence of Plato's thought in any philosophically substantive sense as mouthpiece interpreters seem to think. For there are many passages throughout Plato's dialogues that "militate against the thought that what we have here are somehow references to a single body of fixed doctrine, underpinning all the dialogues." (McCabe 2008: 111) Of several passages from various of Plato's dialogues, McCabe concludes: "Nothing here requires us to suppose. .. that we have here merely a vehicle for Platonic doctrine or. .. to suppose that the dialogues repudiate positive views altogether.. ... But in writing the way he does, he engages his readers, too, in active scrutiny of what is said.. ." (McCabe 2008: 111) It seems as though McCabe has provided even more reason to hold to the Socratic Interpretation and to repudiate the Mouthpiece Interpretation.

The Socratic Interpretation also enjoys, intentionally or not, the support of the recent work of Sandra Peterson. While the dominant mouthpiece tradition holds both that the Socrates of Plato's dialogues is Plato's instrument for expressing Plato's own views and that Plato's views develop throughout the dialogues (a position Peterson refers to as "Plato-centric"), Peterson offers an "interlocutor-centered hypothesis" according to which Socrates, who says he knows nothing great, conducts different kinds of examinations with different interlocutors (Peterson 2011: xv), and that there is inadequate evidence to suggest that Socrates, as depicted by Plato, ever held the views, doctrines or theories so often ascribed to him by most contemporary Plato scholarship. (Peterson 2011: xvi) What many scholars of Plato seem to have confused is the difference in philosophical examining from some dialogues (such as the *Apology*) to others (such as the *Phaedo* and the

Republic) with what they hastily conclude is the development of "Plato's thought" between those dialogues. (Peterson 2011: 2–3)

Peterson argues that differences in Socratic philosophical style notwithstanding between various of Plato's works, "the Socrates in any of Plato's dialogues is examining his interlocutor and so engaging in the central component of the complex activity, philosophizing..." (Peterson 2011: 4) And she assumes with Gregory Vlastos and other mouthpiece interpreters both that the character Socrates in Plato's dialogues has a special status of serving as the best available clue to whatever Plato's own views happen to be (Peterson 2011: 5), and that "Plato's 'overriding concern is always the philosophy'." (Peterson 2011: 15) She also assumes that Plato had philosophical views and that the character Socrates does indeed convey convictions of Plato's. (Peterson 2011: 233) But Peterson does not think that such doctrines are "big" or substantive. Peterson also observes that the dialectic of the aporetic dialogues fails to reveal a Socrates who sets forth his own views. Moreover, Plato is a capable reasoner and is unlikely to hold positions that are refuted in the dialogues. (Peterson 2011: 11) Based on these observations, she is skeptical of the Mouthpiece Interpretation's attempt to ascribe to Plato seemingly all manner of doctrines or theories that can be found in the mouth of Socrates. Instead, she argues, what we find in the mouth of Socrates are not his own (or Plato's) convictions, but rather views Socrates is examining of his interlocutors therein. (Peterson 2011: 15)

Peterson's take on the philosophical commitments of Plato's Socrates "reduce to few": Socrates' claim to ignorance, his abhorrence of philosophical arrogance [so much so that "wise" is taken as slanderous by Socrates when he himself is labeled as such (Peterson 2011: 19–24) in that it implies that Socrates makes the worst error possible of not being thoughtful and is in a position to do the worst possible harm to others (Peterson 2011: 33–36)], and his "method" of philosophical examination. (Peterson 2011: 15, 233)[7] And it is such

---

[7]To this short list might be added the general point that Socrates, perhaps even Plato, ". . . commits himself—in his ways of writing—to a substantial philosophical position: that there is no line of demarcation between the constraints of logic and those of ethics, of psychology or metaphysics, or epistemology." (McCabe 2008: 108) However, that this amounts to a substantive philosophical belief, doctrine or theory of Plato's is unclear. I would think that is it actually

examination that readers of Plato's works are supposed to critically see themselves in the interlocutors' discussions with Socrates. (Peterson 2011: 16) The Socrates of the *Apology* (23b) is not cognizant that he is wise (Peterson 2011: 42), and this includes the understanding that he "knows nothing big." (Peterson 2011: 43) Peterson refers to this as Socrates' general agnosticism (Peterson 2011: 53) about philosophically substantive matters. To be sure, whatever Socrates seems to know is something "small," nonsubstantive (Peterson 2011: 55), or rather general: for instance, that we ought to care about how to live our lives well and that we ought to continue to examine ourselves (Peterson 2011: 57, 261) as the unexamined life, says Plato's Socrates, is not worth living. While "Socrates knows a few things," … "his knowing them is consistent with his not knowing anything big." (Peterson 2011: 58) This point of Peterson's addresses the concern of McCabe that in various dialogues this or that position is refuted or denied. (McCabe 2008: 95–96) That, for instance, justified true belief is found to be insufficient for human knowledge hardly tells us what Plato's or even Socrates' analyses of human knowledge amount to. The point of the Socratic Interpretation is not that Plato's dialogues are more or less "open-ended" and skeptical in their various "conclusions." Rather, it is that because most of them end in some degree or another in *aporia*, it is not plausible to think that one can extract Plato's substantive philosophical views from them.

Peterson then devotes energy to the possible challenge to her thesis that the Socrates of the corpus of Plato's dialogues is significantly different than the Socrates presented in the *Apology*. For it is common to think that Socrates is portrayed throughout the dialogues in rather different ways, suggesting, it is thought, that it is a mistake to believe that there is a particular and singular portrayal of him throughout Plato's works. As McCabe states: "This figure of Socrates is often unattractive and always difficult to interpret; it might properly deter us from looking for a single Socrates persisting through the dialogues. For its Socrates may be particular to each dialogue and may both remind us of the other Socrateses and discourage us from supposing that any portrait aims for verisimilitude." (McCabe 2008: 92)

---

one of the smaller ideas of which Peterson might well attribute to Socrates and Plato.

Peterson's answer to this challenge is that Socrates is the same throughout all of Plato's dialogues, thereby rebutting Gilbert Ryle's famous statement to the contrary. Ryle made the comment that the digression in the *Theaetetus* 172–177 is "quite pointless." While there is plenty of informative analysis and argument throughout the dialogue's focus on the question of the nature of human knowledge,[8] the digression in question lacks such qualities altogether. In the end, however, Peterson is convinced that the digression in question fails to demonstrate that there is a kind of changing of Socrates throughout Plato's dialogues to justify a developmentalist thesis concerning the philosophical content of Socrates' words therein.

Nor does the strangeness of various views articulated by Socrates in the *Republic* imply that there is a development of Socrates' views throughout Plato's dialogues. Peterson devotes considerable energy to this problem wherein she argues that what we find on the lips of Socrates are not his own views, but those of others. What is clear to the non-question-begging interpreter of Plato's works is that in such passages we find the same Socrates as we find in the *Apology*, one who examines others and finds that their professed wisdom is seemingly nowhere to be found.

Another piece of alleged evidence in favor of the Mouthpiece Interpretation of Plato's dialogues is that there are certain doctrines that Plato places in the mouth of Socrates. One such example is Socrates' discussion and apparent embracing in the *Phaedo* of the doctrine of the immortality of the soul. But Peterson argues that Socrates does not straightforwardly subscribe to the words placed in his mouth by Plato. That Socrates discusses a topic does not mean that he embraces what he expresses about it. For the Socrates of the *Apology*, Peterson states, is still alive in the other dialogues such as the *Phaedo*. It is Socrates who examines others for the sake of making himself and others better for the rest of their lives (*Euthyphro* 16): Socrates begins where his interlocutors are, philosophically. He then leads them through a critical examination of what they believe, allow-

---

[8] In fact, some have seen the remainder of the dialogue as the strong precursor of what has later become known as the "Gettier problem" even though it is questionable that E. Gettier added anything new and philosophically interesting to what perhaps ought more accurately to be known as the "Socratic problem of knowledge."

ing the intellectually honest among them to eventually grasp for themselves what is problematic regarding their positions that effect their lives so importantly. (Peterson 2011: 195)

Peterson further argues that various interlocutors' conceptions of the nature and function of philosophy do not belong to Socrates, but to them, wherein her focus is on Plato's *Euthydemus*, the *Rival Lovers*, and the *Sophist*, respectively. All in all, she reasons that there is inadequate evidence to show that the Socrates presented in these dialogues on the topic of the nature and function of philosophy would dissuade the reasonable person from seeing that Socrates is the same in these contexts as he is in the *Apology*. (Peterson 2011: 215)

Moreover, Peterson presents more general argumentation for the claim that Socrates remains the same throughout Plato's corpus of writings: "The totality of the dialogues featuring Socrates show that Plato thought that philosophizing as Socrates claims it in the *Apology* was the best practice in which to spend one's life." (Peterson 2011: 250) That is, Peterson's cautious view is "at least as likely as the alternative hypothesis that Socrates speaks doctrine of a developing Plato." (Peterson 2011: 216) This view of Peterson's has important implications for the Mouthpiece Interpretation's popular beliefs, doctrines, and theories that its adherents so continually and predictably attribute to Plato. For it is a denial that their interpretive method is justified by not only the very dialogical form in which Plato composed almost all of his works, but it is a denial that the very dialogical style and content of the corpus of his writings justifies the ascriptions of a theory of forms, a theory of mimetic art, a doctrine of the immortality of the soul, etc. to Plato as if he were writing treatises.

According to Peterson, throughout Plato's corpus of writings is found a consistent method of Socratic philosophizing: disclosing to his interlocutors what they believe or allowing them to reveal their beliefs, and the critical examination of said beliefs. What we have, argues Peterson, is not Vlastos' and other mouthpiece interpreters' Plato-centric writings, but rather interlocutor-centered ones. For "certain views commonly taken to be doctrines of Plato's we have only reason to believe that they attach to Socrates' interlocutors. We do not have reason to attach the views to Socrates." (Peterson 2011: 217) Thus the merely apparent doctrinal or theoretical Socrates, states Peterson, turns out to be the examining Socrates. (Peterson 2011:

218–219) So it is implausible to think that there is a developing of doctrines within Plato's writings such that he or even Socrates matures from the early to the middle to the late dialogues, as developmentalist mouthpiece interpreters assert.

As if her exegesis of various passages of many of Plato's dialogues were not sufficient to prove her thesis, Peterson points to an unappealing general implication in the approach of Vlastos, Charles Kahn and some others, namely, that it denies that in composing his later dialogues Plato took seriously the message of the Delphic oracle of which Socrates speaks so passionately in the *Apology*. (Peterson 2011: 221) And while Kahn resorts to imaginative questioning of why Plato might have abandoned the Socratic mission (Peterson 2011: 222), Peterson provides plausible answers to the making of such alleged "creativity" (Peterson 2011: 223), including the explanation that "It would be worthy of Plato's creativity for him to spend his writing career depicting discussions of widely different kinds with widely various kinds of people to further subject to examination Socrates' minimal but central conviction of the *Apology* that he failed to know the greatest things." (Peterson 2011: 223–224)

Peterson also asks of mouthpiece interpreters why Plato wrote dialogues in which he is never a character. (Peterson 2011: 230) That Plato wanted to avoid self-promotion is not an adequate answer to this important question. In fact, just the opposite may well have been the case: Plato wanted to not stand out as he wanted to disappear from his writings ["As Socrates disappears into his conversations with his interlocutors Plato disappears into his writing" (Peterson 2011: 235)]. They were for the most part about Socrates and his method of critically examining the views of others. (Peterson 2011: 231, 234)

Peterson provides valuable information concerning various passages about some of the alleged doctrines of Plato's, and about Socrates' purpose in doing philosophy. And her argument addresses a central underlying matter in studying Plato: the Platonic Question. While most mouthpiece interpreters seemingly want to disregard this problem or provide poor reasons why it is not a problem for their own methodological approach to Plato's corpus, Peterson has shed plausible new light on the issue.

Peterson might have been more direct in discussing the implications of her arguments for the Platonic Question, as there seem to be a few passages in her work wherein her words belie a possible confusion. One example is where Peterson assumes that Plato had doctrines and that Socrates conveys Plato's views. On the other hand, she states that ascribing this or that theory or doctrine to Plato is misplaced [see her point about the alleged theory of forms (Peterson 2011: 254)]. It is unclear whether her assumption that Socrates was Plato's mouthpiece is meant to alienate her from mouthpiece interpreters who do more than assume such, or whether she considers herself to be a mouthpiece interpreter of sorts. Evidence against the latter interpretation of her words is found in her rejection of the "Plato says" fallacy that is rampant in the writings of mouthpiece interpreters: "Most strictly speaking the phrase 'what Plato says…' must amount to 'what Socrates and others say…'" (Peterson 2011: 255),[9] a point made by various interpreters of Plato.[10] In the end, Peterson provides important additional internal textual evidence in favor of the anti-mouthpiece interpretation of Plato's *oeuvre*. Thus Peterson's work serves as a confirmation of the Socratic Interpretation as it is stated and defended herein and in *Interpreting Plato's Dialogues*. Or, at the very least, her work is not inconsistent with the Socratic Interpretation.

I assume neither an antiquarian nor an anachronistic model of how Plato's corpus of writings ought to be interpreted. For the task of the Plato interpreter is to develop an appreciation of and engagement with the analyses and arguments of the contents of his dialogues. The understanding of the contents of Plato's dialogues is crucial, but equally or even more important is our critically engaging the analyses and arguments therein. Further, it may involve rational reconstruction wherein the informational contents of Plato's dialogues becomes the starting point of further philosophical reflection about the philosophical ideas and arguments found therein and wherein such reflection is referred to as "Platonic" in the sense that the informational contents of Plato's dialogues inspired the extra dialogical philosophical investigations. But all the while, the Plato interpreter must not fall prey to the temptation to attribute to Plato this or that view found in the dialogues, especially since, as noted earlier, there is inadequate evidence

---

[9] Contrast, however, Peterson (2011: 14–15) where Peterson holds a version of the Mouthpiece Interpretation, albeit a moderate one.
[10] See Cooper and Hutchinson (1997: xviii–xxv); Corlett (2005: 84–85, 90, 93, and 97); and Mulhern (1971).

or reason to think that Plato anywhere writes or "speaks" in his own person. Again, the only primary textual evidence that we possess along these lines is the explicit support for the Anti-Mouthpiece Interpretation found in the *Seventh Letter* the authenticity of which, however, has been called into question by some scholars.[11] There is nothing necessarily wrong with rational reconstructive interpretations of Plato's dialogues as long as they are not presented as containing Plato's own views. The Mouthpiece Interpretation understands Plato's dialogues as texts that represent Plato's views, yet it lacks sufficiently good reason for ascribing such views to Plato.

Now all of this ignores the Problem of Discernability in the Interpretation of Texts, which is the epistemic problem of *how it might be known* when an interpreter has an author "right," all relevant things considered. Consistent with the commonalities between these approaches noted above, the Socratic Interpretation shares with the Mouthpiece Interpretation the descriptive interpretive goal of deciphering the meanings of what Plato wrote. Indeed, they also agree with one another that it is important to go beyond what Plato wrote and make evaluative judgments about the analyses and arguments found in Plato's writings. But whereas mouthpiece interpreters continually ascribe this or that view found in the dialogues to Plato, Socratic interpreters do not, as again there is insufficiently good reason to do so. So the point is *not* that those who are serious about the history of philosophy in general and about Plato in particular ought to consign themselves to merely describing what is in Plato's dialogues. That would be to commit the error of antiquarianism in its failing to grasp the significance of the contents of Plato's writings for *us*. Nor is

---

[11] It is worth noting that many of the reasons provided to deny the authenticity of the *Seventh Letter* have been debunked [See, for instance, P. Deane's undermining of the Levinson, et al. "attempt to demonstrate on stylometric grounds that the *Seventh Letter* was certainly not by Plato and was possible written by Speusippus" in Deane (1973)]. However, as noted in the Preface to this book, even if the *Seventh Letter* is spurious, it would not follow without further argument and solid evidence that it is unreliable in depicting Plato's denial that he has set any of his substantive views in writing. For a writing can be inauthentic insofar as Platonic authorship is concerned, yet remain reliable in containing or depicting the general aim of an author (in this case, Plato). It would appear, then, that it is an open question as to whether or not the *Seventh Letter* is authentic and/or depicts Plato's aims in composing dialogues.

the Socratic Interpretation committed to the fallacy of interpretive skepticism in thinking that interpretation of Plato's dialogues is impossible. On the contrary, Plato's dialogues ought to be studied carefully on their own terms, both to understand the analyses and arguments therein, but also to critically evaluate them for plausibility as we push them forward in our search for truth and wisdom.

References

Brickhouse, Thomas C., and Nicholas D. Smith. 2002. The Socratic *Elenchos*? In *Does Socrates have a method?* ed. Gary A. Scott, 145–157. University Park: Pennsylvania State University Press.
Cooper, John M., and D.S. Hutchinson, eds. 1997. *Plato: Complete works*. Indianapolis: Hackett Publishing Company.
Corlett, J. Angelo. 2005. *Interpreting Plato's dialogues*. Las Vegas: Parmenides Publishing.
Deane, P. 1973. Stylometrics do not exclude the *Seventh Letter*. *Mind* 82: 113–117.
Gill, Christopher. 1996. Afterword: Dialectic and the dialogue form in late Plato. In *Form and argument in late Plato*, ed. Christopher Gill and Mary Margaret McCabe, 283–311. Oxford: Oxford University Press.
Kenny, Anthony. 2006. *What I believe*. London: Continuum.
Lehrer, Keith. 2000. *Theory of knowledge*. 2nd ed. Boulder: Westview Press.
McCabe, M.M. 2008. Plato's ways of writing. In *The Oxford handbook of Plato*, ed. Gail Fine, 88–113. Oxford: Oxford University Press.
Mulhern, J.J. 1971. Two interpretive fallacies. *Systematics* 9: 168–172.
———. 2000. Interpreting the platonic dialogues: What can one say? In *Who speaks for Plato?* ed. Gerald A. Press, 221–234. Lanham: Rowman & Littlefield Publishers.
Nails, Debra. 1995. *Agora, academy, and the conduct of philosophy*. Dordrecht: Kluwer Academic Publishers.
Peterson, Sandra. 2011. *Socrates and philosophy in Plato's dialogues*. Cambridge: Cambridge University Press.
Vlastos, Gregory. 1991. *Socrates: Ironist and moral philosopher*. Ithaca: Cornell University Press.
Woozley, A.D. 1979. *Law and obedience: The arguments of Plato's Crito*. London: Duckworth.

Chapter 3
Defending the Socratic Interpretation of Plato's Dialogues

Having in Chapter 2 outlined and clarified some of the main points of my argument for the Socratic Interpretation of Plato's dialogues, I now turn to some concerns that have been or might be raised about it.

Does the Socratic Interpretation Make Plato a Skeptic?

One worry about the Socratic Interpretation is that it implies Platonic ignorance and Pyrrhonian (or extreme) skepticism. This position is expressed by many a mouthpiece interpreter. But Lloyd Gerson seems to capture it best when he states of the Anti-Mouthpiece Interpretation (what he refers to as the "nondogmatic" interpretation) that "for them a nondogmatic Plato is a Plato who either has no belief whatsoever regarding, say, the immortality of the soul or has a belief on this matter but has striven to conceal it." (Gerson 2002: 218) But this amounts to an implicit bifurcation fallacy and is a misunderstanding of the Anti-Mouthpiece Interpretation. Although it would be problematic to argue that because Socrates in some dialogues claims to be ignorant that this is insufficient reason to think that this can ground general Socratic ignorance throughout Plato's works, the Socratic Interpretation does not logically imply that either Socrates or Plato is a skeptic of any strong variety. Plato may well have had substantive philosophical views about this or that subject. That is hardly in dispute, contrary to what Gerson's statement implies. Nor is Gerson correct in misattributing a straw man position to anti-mouthpiece interpreters when he states of its take on whether or not Plato is committed to views in his dialogues that "a false model is being here applied according to which everything is up in the air until there is closure." (Gerson 2002: 223)[1] For it is not a component of the Anti-Mouthpiece Interpretation, except perhaps in its extreme forms, that Plato as the author of the dialogues in question is not committed to anything at all—even tentatively. Surely Plato is committed to the importance of reason, for instance. Rather, the issue at hand is whether or not one is epistemically justified in attributing to Plato this or that philosophically substantive belief, doctrine or theory beyond mere methodological ones based on the informational contents of the dialogues. Nor, contrary to Gerson's assertions (Gerson 2002: 219–220), does it matter whether or not one can justifiably distinguish between the ideas of Socrates and those of Plato. For that possibility does not address the issue at hand either. Whether or not their views can be separated from each other has nothing to do with whether or not it is justified to attribute to Plato what he has written in dialogue form.

But even if it turned out that the Socrates of Plato's dialogues was a skeptic of, for instance, even the Pyrrhonian variety, this would say nothing about what we are permitted by textual evidence to attribute to *Plato* given his use of the dialogue form itself and in absence of some direct textual evidence containing Plato's statement that some or all of the dialogues convey, in one way or another, his beliefs, doctrines or theories. Nor is it true that Socrates is indifferent to his own claims and arguments throughout Plato's works, or that Socrates is in a state of total ignorance (How could Plato's Socrates refute the assertions of his interlocutors out of complete or universal ignorance?). I believe neither of these claims about Socrates. I prefer "tentative" to describe the statements made and conclusions reached in Plato's works. For to whatever it amounts, Socratic ignorance is not the same

---

[1] Similar claims amounting to straw man arguments against a singular construal of the Anti-Mouthpiece Interpretation (as if all versions of it were the same in substance) are made in Gerson (2000). If my arguments against the Mouthpiece Interpretation are correct, then ironically it is mouthpiece interpreters (like Gerson) themselves who have absconded with Plato in the sense that they have absconded with the dialectician Plato and sought to replace him with a dogmatic "Plato."

as total ignorance or indifference,[2] and it is certainly not the same as his being a Pyrrhonian skeptic.

This factor seems to go a long way toward answering the question of why Plato would put into the mouth of Socrates arguments that Plato thought were not good ones. One possibility here is that at least in some cases, Plato might, for whatever reasons, not have believed them to be bad arguments or that they were arguments based on some of the beliefs of some of his contemporaries which Plato believed warranted philosophical examination. Another is that Plato composed the dialogues as dramatic devices to provide readers with a means to investigate such matters philosophically whether or not they represented views of some of his philosopher or social or political contemporaries. If such dialogical contents are tentative, then the possibility is left open for readers to analyze terms and arguments and push the arguments forward here and there, where genuine philosophical progress might be made. But this is a far cry from Plato's writing the dialogues in order to convey his own substantive philosophical views about this or that. We know that Plato's dialogues engage readers in the process of philosophical argument and analysis and encourage readers to take up the task of furthering philosophical dialogue for the aim of making philosophical progress on this or that issue or problem. On this point also both mouthpiece and anti-mouthpiece interpreters can agree. And again in light of this, adds the Socratic interpreter consonant with *Charmides* 161c, it matters not what Plato himself thinks, but what is true or false, and why. So if Plato's intentions are other than as the mouthpiece theorists take them to be, this does not change the fact that there are distinctions, hypotheses, and arguments (both positive and negative) in the text. But while it is correct to insist that "…an *aporia* at the end of a Platonic dialogue cannot be used as conclusive evidence of the absence of doctrine throughout that work," it hardly follows, as Gerson thinks it does, that discernible "…doctrine underlies the failed search for definitions." (Gerson 2002: 220) While this might be true of many other philosophers, we have inadequate evidence that it is true of Plato.

The aporetic nature of some of Plato's dialogues and Socratic ignorance serve as important, though are in themselves insufficient, pri-

---

[2] See Chapter 2 of this book wherein Sandra Peterson makes this point.

mary textual evidence for the claim that Plato was a skeptic in more than a mild sense of the term. But an even more important point here should not be overlooked, namely, that even in light of this delimiting of the evidence in question as it relates to the undermining of the Mouthpiece Interpretation and the grounding of the Socratic Interpretation, neither point truly addresses the fact that *the very dialogue form Plato adopts does not permit us without sound and independent argumentative support to attribute to Plato any statement in the dialogues.* This renders question-begging Gerson's statement of Plato and his dialogues that "…the most plausible one to whom to attribute this philosophy is the author of the dialogues in which these claims are made." (Gerson 2002: 224) Gerson's statement betrays either an ignorance or a denial (or both) of what is really at stake concerning the Platonic Question, and what counts as adequate evidence for one position or another regarding its most plausible answer. Whichever the case, Gerson begs the question against the Anti-Mouthpiece Interpretation in his attempt to refute it. Moreover, in failing to recognize the variants of the Anti-Mouthpiece Interpretation, Gerson appears to address them as if they each fall equally prey to his question-begging attempts to render them implausible. In fact, his criticism of what he construes as the Anti-Mouthpiece Interpretation fails entirely to address the Socratic version of it as it is articulated in Chapter 2 of this book.

The Mouthpiece Interpretation and Developmentalism

It must be kept in mind, moreover, that the Mouthpiece Interpretation still suffers from several problems, ones that have yet to be answered. (Corlett 2005: Chapter 1)[3] And it must be borne in mind that whatever

---

[3] One frequently employed tactic of some mouthpiece interpreters is to resort to the refutation of straw man arguments and then to attribute the straw man position to anti-mouthpiece interpreters, and to think that it follows from that that the Anti-Mouthpiece Interpretation is flawed. Another tactic that some mouthpiece interpreters employ is the use of *ad hominem* insults to impress those who are predisposed to that form of "argumentation" as opposed to reason. An example of this method of doing philosophy is found frequently in the writings of Gerson on this topic. One such instance is his insult of Anti-Mouthpiece inter-

imperfections might exist for the Socratic Interpretation are in no manner factors that somehow justify the Mouthpiece Interpretation. Again, the Mouthpiece Interpretation must bear its own argumentative burden, though it has done so rather poorly.

Perhaps the most thorough defense of the Mouthpiece Interpretation comes in the form of John Beversluis' criticisms of particular versions of the Anti-Mouthpiece Interpretation. His reasoning is important because it provides an implied set of arguments in favor of the Mouthpiece Interpretation that underlie his objections to certain versions of the Anti-Mouthpiece Interpretation, versions of the Anti-Mouthpiece Interpretation which he considers to be "extreme."

While it is true that developmentalism between concepts and arguments expressed throughout much of the Platonic corpus is relevant to the establishment of this or that version of the Mouthpiece Interpretation (Beversluis 2006: 86–88), it is unclear whether it pertains to the Platonic Question as just mentioned in the context of my replies to Gerson's objection regarding developmentalism in Plato's works. For

---

preters found in the following statement: "The nondogmatic interpretation of the dialogues has little use for developmentalism. It is an interpretive stance that, like the Alzheimer's patient, makes new friends every day." (Gerson 2002: 222) But not only is this set of claims an *ad hominem* abusively fallacious insult to anti-mouthpiece interpreters and insensitive to millions of patients suffering from Alzheimer's disease, not only is it statistically false in that it mistakenly infers that there are many detractors of the Mouthpiece Interpretation when comparatively (in philosophy) mouthpiece interpreters far outnumber anti-mouthpiece interpreters as anyone who is familiar with contemporary Plato studies would readily understand, but it is false that the anti-mouthpiece interpreters have little use for developmentalism. Indeed, as a Socratic interpreter I make much of the development of this or that concept in Plato's works. As I state below, however, the development thereof neither refutes the developmentalist Mouthpiece Interpretation nor uniquely supports the Anti-Mouthpiece Interpretation. It is false for Gerson to claim that developmentalism in Plato's works has no interest to the Anti-Mouthpiece Interpretation. Indeed, development of ideas and arguments is part and parcel of what sometimes is found in the Platonic corpus. So once again we find in Gerson misunderstandings, not only of the real issues involved in the Platonic Question, but of the Anti-Mouthpiece Interpretation more specifically. Perhaps such misunderstandings and misattributions are based on Gerson's inability or unwillingness to engage in a charitable understanding of the position he seeks to render dubious. In either case, it is clear that Gerson has done nothing to render seriously problematic the Socratic Anti-Mouthpiece Interpretation.

an anti-mouthpiece interpreter such as myself can and does accept the fact that many concepts and arguments are expressed in slightly different ways throughout parts of Plato's dialogues: earlier, middle and later. But again, this says nothing about whether or not such concepts or arguments are legitimately attributable to Plato. And this is true even if it were the case, contrary to fact, that we possess autographs of Plato's works. For it might very well be the case that Plato as the author of the dialogues sought not to communicate his own conceptions of justice, knowledge, art, etc. therein, but rather to attempt different ways in which to inspire readers to engage in philosophical dialectic concerning such problems. Given the differences in dating between the dialogues, it is also possible that Plato was somewhat dissatisfied with how some ideas and arguments were expressed by particular characters in some earlier dialogues and sought to make them less confusing, ambiguous, or otherwise problematic as he composed the middle and later ones in order to better clarify or pose a particular philosophical conundrum. Thus what many mouthpiece interpreters construe as the development of Plato's views on this or that might just as cogently, if not more cogently, be interpreted as his way of changing the manner in which he has various characters of his dialogues express this or that concept or argument. So mouthpiece interpreters must come to see that what they construe as the development of Plato's ideas in his corpus of writings can just as plausibly be seen as *the development of Plato's way of expressing certain philosophical problems in the dialogues by this or that character*. And this is true even if we assume, as I do, that Socrates is the most important character in most of the dialogues, not merely one among several other characters as some might have us think.[4]

What Is the Philosophical Significance of the Socratic Interpretation?

Moreover, it might be argued that there seems to be no philosophical significance to my criticism of the Mouthpiece Interpretation and defense of the Socratic Interpretation. To this claim I would reply that

---

[4] This assumption is challenged in Nails (1995: 40).

the accuracy of the very history of philosophy is at stake. And if for no other reason, we ought to have enough respect for the history of philosophy to attempt to get it right. And this means, among other things, refraining from question-beggingly ascribing a view to a philosopher which we have inadequate reason to attribute to him or her. It is also a matter of precision in scholarship. To do as mouthpiece interpreters often do and use locutions such as "Plato says…" "Plato believes…" "Plato's doctrine…" "Plato's theory…." and the like without providing sound arguments for doing so is, if my objections to the arguments given for the Mouthpiece Interpretation are plausible, akin to attributing a belief to a philosopher without a sufficiently good reason. The Platonic Question, then, is not an issue having little or no consequence for philosophical studies, unless, of course, one cares little or nothing about sound scholarship and accuracy of attributions in the history of philosophy. And it is vital that we begin to get Plato right, instead of misconstruing what his dialogues are about. What is not true, I believe, is the claim that if Socrates is not Plato's mouthpiece, then all or most of the mouthpiece scholarship on Plato is "logically flawed, methodologically inappropriate, or just plain wrong." (Press 2000: 6)[5] For much can and has been learned from mouthpiece interpreters' often insightful exegeses of various pericopes of Plato's works, even though a kind of translation must occur from the language of mouthpiece interpreters to that of anti-mouthpiece interpreters. For instance, a better rendering of a passage in Greek by a mouthpiece interpreter might very well reveal a new insight into what that passage actually means, regardless of whether or not it is attributable to Plato. Thus not only is there philosophical significance regarding my Socratic Interpretation of Plato's dialogues, but that importance embraces the many textual gains (absent, of course, the many "Plato says" fallacies committed therein) that have been made by the history of otherwise excellent mouthpiece interpreters. For example, it is hyperbolic to dismiss Julia Annas' book[6] on the *Republic* because she is a mouthpiece interpreter. For while she mistakenly attributes several beliefs, doctrines and theories to Plato, her book is a plausible rendering of the basic contents of various passages from the *Republic* on matters of

---

[5] Note that John Beversluis concurs with the logic of Gerald Press' statement.
[6] Annas (1981).

justice, art, education, and the myths of the sun, line, and cave, etc.. Similar things can be expressed of the excellent works of Terence Irwin on Plato's ethics,[7] and a host of other works by various mouthpiece interpreters. The problems with some of what they had expressed that I treated in *Interpreting Plato's Dialogues* pertained to their weak arguments in favor of the Mouthpiece Interpretation and against the Anti-Mouthpiece Interpretation with regard to the Platonic Question. I had nothing negative to express therein about the quality of their exegetical work beyond matters of the Platonic Question. So it is problematic to think that just because one might be wrong about how to generally interpret or approach Plato's dialogues that one is necessarily wrong or altogether wrong about how to interpret the informational contents of particular passages therein. For an interpreter can get it right concerning what the character Socrates says in this or that dialogue, while committing a fundamental attribution error in ascribing that thought to Plato.

Not only, however, is the Socratic Anti-Mouthpiece Interpretation significant with regard to the history of philosophy, it also serves to emphasize the very philosophical method employed throughout most of Plato's works. The dialectical form of analytic reasoning employed by Socrates and his interlocutors sets the history of philosophy in motion, as it were. In a real sense, Plato's works for the most part exemplify what philosophy is about, that is, how it works. And this holds true whether or not philosophy is done by way of Plato's dialogues. The consideration of claims, objections to them, replies, etc., form the very basis of the nature of philosophy. The Socratic Interpretation places this fact at the center of its approach to Plato's corpus of writings. So to the extent that the Socratic Interpretation is plausible, its philosophical significance is that it accentuates analytic philosophical method as the very essence of philosophy.

Thus the objection that there is no philosophical significance to my criticisms of the Mouthpiece Interpretation and my defense of the Socratic Interpretation is wrongheaded. Significance abounds therein. It is vital to both avoid the fundamental attribution error with regard to Plato and the informational contents of his dialogues and to do our best to understand the informational contents of the dialogues them-

---

[7] Irwin (1995).

selves so that we might carry forward what Plato started into greater depths of philosophical analysis and argument.

Does the Socratic Interpretation Imply the Impenetrability of Plato's Dialogues?

Another possible concern for the Socratic Interpretation is that it effectively makes Plato's dialogues impenetrable.[8] Whether or not Plato holds this or that theory, doctrine or belief is not available to us because of the dialogical form in which he chose to write. So it is not that we cannot figure out the informational content of what is written in the dialogues. Rather, it is that we cannot, if the Socratic Interpretation is correct, discern which, if any, views belong to Plato. This clarification ought to go a long way toward addressing the concern that the fact that Plato wrote dialogues makes them "impenetrable." I do not mean to suggest that the very content of the dialogues themselves is impenetrable. Again, that would court a kind of interpretive skepticism that the Socratic Interpretation eschews. Rather, it is that *Plato's own views* as expressed in the dialogues are impenetrable.

A related concern with the Socratic Interpretation is that just as we can infer from our reading of Shakespeare that Shakespeare believed some particular theory or doctrine about this or that, we can in a similar manner attribute to Plato this or that theory or doctrine that we find in the Platonic dialogues. Moreover, we are justified in attributing to Plato the belief that it is better to be Socrates than anyone else in the dialogues just as we are justified in ascribing to Shakespeare the belief that it is better to be Hamlet than anyone else in the play, *Hamlet*. Why? Because just as Hamlet is the obvious hero in the play, despite any personality flaws Hamlet may have that led to his downfall, Socrates is the philosopher-hero of the Platonic dialogues, despite some of the flaws in his reasoning. Since the Socratic Interpretation does not permit the attribution of any beliefs to Plato, it is, on this view, problematic.[9]

---

[8] I owe this point to Charles Young.
[9] I owe this point to Young.

But even if one thought that Shakespeare favors Hamlet as a character over others in the play *Hamlet*, this does not necessarily mean that any particular words of Hamlet are held to be truer than the words of other characters in the play. Nor does it entail that Shakespeare believes that particular words of Hamlet's express a theory or doctrine to which Shakespeare himself subscribes. That is, just because Hamlet states:

What a piece of work is a man!
How noble in reason!
How infinite in faculty!
In form, in moving, how express and admirable!
In action how like an angel!
In apprehension how like a god!
The beauty of the world!
The paragon of animals!
And yet to me, what is this quintessense of dust?

does not entail that Shakespeare himself deems humans to be meaningless bits of earthen material. Although we seem to be justified to infer that Shakespeare believes that it is better to be Hamlet than anyone else in the play, *Hamlet*, when we make attributions to Shakespeare regarding more specific and complex claims, we are doing so unsupported by sufficient evidence. And the same thing is true of Plato and his dialogues. Plato might believe that the way Socrates does philosophy is the best way to engage in it, and that Socrates, being his mentor, is quite the philosopher and the hero of the dialogues, and other such general claims. But this is a far cry from mouthpiece interpreters' ascribing seemingly all manner of substantive philosophical beliefs, doctrines and theories to Plato because they are placed by him in the mouth of Socrates.

Furthermore, many might not see how the Socratic Interpretation yields interesting and worthwhile things to say about the dialogues.[10] But leaving aside the issue of whether or not the Socratic Interpretation has anything of interest to say about Plato (it does if one does not insist that the Mouthpiece Interpretation is correct), this concern seems to imply that interpreters of Plato ought to accept that view of Plato which we prefer. It appears to be akin to a religious person's

---

[10] I owe this point to Young.

claiming that her belief in an afterlife is preferable to its denial because a belief in an afterlife makes her life more "interesting and worthwhile."

However, philosophers ought not to be in the business of choosing between views on the basis of which one strikes them as being most interesting or worthwhile. Rather, we must follow the best arguments wherever they lead, as Socrates implores us. So if the Socratic Interpretation makes the mouthpiece interpreter feel uncomfortable, so be it! *It is time that mouthpiece interpreters are challenged to either adequately support their longstanding approach to Plato, or recant it for a more rationally supported one.* Furthermore, any request for a Socratic interpreter to "Show us that Plato in the *Republic* does not believe…" is the last ditch effort of the mouthpiece interpreter to attempt, without success, to shift the burden of argument to the Socratic interpreter. But this effort fails, as it is the sole burden of mouthpiece interpreters to provide support for their own position. Moreover, to demonstrate that Plato believes or does not believe this or that based on the content of a dialogue is precisely what I argue is highly unlikely in light of the dialogue form in which Plato writes. This objection begs the question in favor of the Mouthpiece Interpretation rather than providing an independent argument in its favor. It asks the Socratic interpreter to deny her position in order to support the Mouthpiece Interpretation, which is absurd given the solid objections raised to the myriad of fallacious arguments given for the Mouthpiece Interpretation, detailed both in *Interpreting Plato's Dialogues*, and in this book.

Does the Fact That There Are Degrees of Aporicity in Plato's Dialogues Pose a Problem for the Socratic Interpretation?

Why, one might ask, should we think that all of the dialogues should be approached in the same way?[11] While it is correct to point out that some dialogues are less aporetic than others, this serves as inadequate grounds for the Mouthpiece Interpretation. That this or that character, leading or not, in this or that dialogue seems to articulate whatever counts for a "belief" is hardly sufficient reason to ascribe that belief to

---

[11] I owe this point to Young.

Plato. The Socratic Interpretation makes it clear that the dialogue form in which Plato wrote is crucial in determining which approach is best to interpret Plato's body of work. So even if there are different kinds of dialogues amongst the corpus of Plato's works, as McCabe notes (McCabe 2008: 88), they are, nonetheless and for the most part, *dialogues*. And mouthpiece interpreters owe us a sound argument for why one might be justified in holding the Mouthpiece Interpretation in light of this fact.

Further reasons why Plato composed dialogues include that he wanted to memorialize his mentor, that he thought that writing dialogues might lead others to take an interest in philosophy and to engage in philosophy themselves, and it might well have been an indication of Plato's humility. These reasons are not inconsistent with Plato's commitment to whatever the dialogues are committed. But I do not see how this is an argument exclusively for the Mouthpiece Interpretation. It means that the Mouthpiece Interpretation shares some things in common with the Socratic Interpretation, as mentioned in Chapter 2 of this book.

What Is the Importance, If Any, of the *Seventh Letter* for the Platonic Question?

In the *Seventh Letter* 341c, we read:

> So much at least I can affirm with confidence about any who have written or purpose to write on these questions, pretending to a knowledge of the problems with which I am concerned, whether they claimed to have learned from me or from others or to have made their discoveries for themselves: it is impossible, in my opinion, that they have learned anything at all about the subject. There is no writing of mine about these matters, nor will there ever be one. For this knowledge is not something that can be put into words like other sciences; but after long continued intercourse between teacher and pupil, in joint pursuit of the subject, suddenly, like light flashing forth when a fire is kindled, it is born in the soul and straightaway nourishes itself.

If Plato is the author of these words, then it is clear that the Mouthpiece Interpretation is implausible based on the relevant primary textual evidence alone. So it is no wonder that so many mouthpiece interpreters reject the *Seventh Letter's* authenticity. If it is authentic or reliable, then there is primary textual evidence in favor of the Anti-Mouthpiece Interpretation and against the Mouthpiece Interpretation insofar as it contains a clear denial that Plato expressed his own views in writing: "There is no writing of mine about these matters, nor will there ever be one." Indeed, as McCabe argues, if, as the author of the *Seventh Letter* states, "writing is somehow unreliable, why—if we are searching for wisdom—should we read the dialogues?" (McCabe 2008: 98) This poses a potential difficulty for the Socratic Interpretation, though it does so simultaneously for the Mouthpiece Interpretation as each approach to Plato's works assumes that it is Plato's desire, as author of the dialogues in question, to read them in their respective ways. This puzzle is indeed a philosophical one, though I believe that McCabe herself points us in the right direction on this matter in arguing of the *Seventh Letter's* words on writing philosophy that "... in challenging its own mode of presentation, it asked how the search for wisdom should proceed, and this question, itself a philosophical one, is provoked by, and so reflective on, the written dialogue itself." (McCabe 2008: 98) Furthermore, I would add, the puzzle here seems to also entail that for future generations writing philosophy might be the only available mode of communicating both the nature and importance of the search for wisdom. And the best way of accomplishing that task is by way of doing it orally. Both the dialogues of Plato and the *Seventh Letter* concur on this vital point. Thus the statement in the *Seventh Letter* concerning the unreliability of writing at least for purposes of doing philosophy has been exaggerated. That the medium of writing is a problematic form of discourse hardly disqualifies it from our legitimate purview. What remains then? Speaking only? Yet it is obvious where that lands one, both in Plato's dialogues and in our own philosophical pursuits as they are riddled with the imprecision present in writing. The skepticism expressed in the *Seventh Letter* must not be overstated, as no other available medium of communication fares much better, if it fares better than writing at all. For while it is obvious that oral communication lends itself to the interrogation of interlocutors, more often than not less care is taken in the communication of ideas "on the spot," orally, compared to the significantly more time and care one typically sets aside for written and published discourse. In the end, each medium of communication is fraught with troubles, and the caution in question should not be taken to suggest that there is a real quandary as to why Plato composed dialogues. For "The paradigm of philosophical activity, then, is dialectical discussion; this is portrayed and reflected on by the dialogues.. .." as "The conditions for philosophical discourse,. .. are themselves subject to the reader's active and reflective scrutiny." (McCabe 2008: 102–103)

The question of the authenticity of the *Seventh Letter* has been taken up in a recently published set of seminar lectures by Michael Frede and Myles Burnyeat, each of whom provides arguments against the authenticity of the *Seventh Letter*. While this project concerns primarily how to approach Plato's dialogues, it is important to consider their arguments. The respective arguments posed by Frede and Burnyeat bear similarities. However, I shall present them separately in order to cast each one in a sufficiently strong light so as to give it charitable consideration. Each of their arguments is a historical one and seeks to discredit Plato as the author of the *Seventh Letter*.

Frede's line of thinking is that there are some basic factual errors in the letter that make it such that the author could not have been Plato. More specifically, the author characterizes Dion and Dionysius as philosophers. Yet clearly they are not. This implies that Plato could not have been the letter's author because given his relationship to them he would have known that to characterize them as philosophers is a stretch. In Frede's words about the authenticity of the *Seventh Letter*, "the letter is not by Plato." (Burnyeat and Frede 2015: 3) Now part of Frede's argument against the letter's authenticity is that it is not recognized as such historically. It is essentially a conservative argument to the effect that throughout history scholars for the most part have accepted certain works as comprising the canon of Plato and others do not. Since the *Seventh Letter* is not as strongly accepted as genuine, then it is to be rejected. (Burnyeat and Frede 2015: 5–6) Indeed, the entire lot of letters is in doubt as are most such letters of antiquity, Platonic or otherwise. (Burnyeat and Frede 2015: 6–7) But as such this argument is a vague appeal to authority, despite Frede's citing of a couple of ancient authors who support his claim. Frede goes so far as to assert that "*Ep.* VII is accepted especially if it suits the author for some reason." (Burnyeat and Frede 2015: 7) Indeed, this point is often true of mouthpiece interpreters in their rejection of the authenticity of said letter. So let us set aside vague appeals to authority and accusations of biased and self-serving reasoning in favor of applying logic to the argument that Frede provides in favor of his claim that the *Seventh Letter* is not genuinely Plato's.

As noted, Frede's is a historical argument against the authenticity of the *Seventh Letter*. First, Frede points out that the respective collections of letters attributed to Heraclitus, Democritus, letters ascribed to Socrates in the collection of the letters of Socrates and the Socratics, Archytas, Speusippus, Chion, Crates, Diogenes, Appollonius, etc. are spurious: "So it is because all these collections of letters are spurious that *eo ipso* Plato's letters are suspect, and this all the more so since they would antedate any clearly authentic letters of philosophers by sixty to seventy years. Also, they would constitute one of the earliest collections of letters of which at least some were genuine (Isocrates and Demosthenes)." (Burnyeat and Frede 2015: 11) Now this is a rather conservative reason to reject an entire set of letters as being genuine. If it is taken seriously, then it would seem to suggest that any extant letter is guilty by association rather than judged to be either genuine or not on its own merits, that is, against independent criteria of authenticity. Furthermore, if Frede's reasoning is taken seriously, then it would suggest that no newly discovered collection of letters from antiquity can qualify as being genuine given that none of the extant collections are genuine. To be sure, Frede's evidence of spurious letters counts as some reason for doubting the authenticity of the Platonic collection. But it hardly counts as decisive or even strong evidence against their authenticity. Such factors, combined with the fact of its early date, would not even justify Frede's claim that the *Seventh Letter's* authenticity is "even more suspicious." (Burnyeat and Frede 2015: 23) Moreover, that "they would constitute one of the earliest collections of letters" attributed to ancients is not a sufficiently good reason to find their authenticity spurious. Indeed, one might find it precisely a reason in *favor* of their authenticity! Thus neither of Frede's reasons cited above are in themselves sufficiently good reason to conclude that the *Seventh Letter* is spurious. Not even their cumulative strength is convincing.

Frede considers the question, as few seem to do in philosophy, of the importance of the authenticity of the *Seventh Letter*. He is surely correct to state that "The question is important for antiquity." And he is correct in asserting that "the Letter is important for Plato's attitude towards writing philosophy." (Burnyeat and Frede 2015: 12) But he unwittingly provides considerations that might well lead a reasonable interpreter of Plato's dialogues against the Mouthpiece Interpretation to which Frede and so many other philosophers of Plato's dialogues subscribe. Writes Frede: "We know very little about Plato's life; as D.L. III, 37 points out, Plato says hardly anything about himself in the dialogues (*Phaedo* 59b, *Apol.* 34a, 38b). We know very little about Plato even from external sources." (Burnyeat and Frede 2015: 12) Yet these crucial facts about Plato hardly prohibit Frede from assuming without recognition the Mouthpiece Interpretation through his entire discussion of the authenticity of the *Seventh Letter*.[12]

Additionally, Frede's comments that "the question whether it really can be Plato's view in 354/3 that Syracuse should have been or (perhaps even still) should be turned into a state governed by a philosopher…" depends on "interpretation" are surely correct. (Burnyeat and Frede 2015: 51) This is part of Frede's historical argument against the authenticity of the *Seventh Letter*. However, his interpretation of this matter assumes the Mouthpiece Interpretation of Plato's *Laws*: "We need an explanation why Plato even in writing the Seventh Letter still should be unwilling to consider a second-best constitution, and only countenance the rule of philosophers. I not only do not know of any explanation for this, but also cannot think of any." (Burnyeat and Frede 2015: 52) Moreover, Frede writes: "…the author of the Seventh Letter adopts a certain interpretation of the doctrine of the *Republic* and, given that interpretation, the *Laws* do not make sense; and the use the author does make of the doctrine of the *Laws* seems to run counter to the very point the *Laws* are to make, and seems to invoke a basic misunderstanding of the *Laws*." (Burnyeat and Frede 2015: 56) Yet this "interpretation" by Frede implicitly depends on the idea that Plato expresses his views in the dialogues, more specifically here, in both the *Republic* (wherein, presumably, Plato's ideal political theory is presented) and the *Laws* (wherein, presumably, Plato's non-ideal or "second-best" constitution is presented). This fact is made even more evident by Frede's use of "basic misunderstanding"[13] with reference

---

[12] Note Frede's pointing out about Plato in this very context that "a philosopher himself has to live up to his teaching." (Burnyeat and Frede 2015: 12) Also see Frede's explicit use of locutions such as "Plato's thought." (Burnyeat and Frede 2015: 44)

[13] See also Burnyeat and Frede (2015: 57) where Frede repeats his point that "The author of *Ep.* VII must have basically misunderstood the *Laws*."

to the informational contents of the *Laws*, a locution which assumes that there is a fact about Plato's views on politics and law in these works that can be misunderstood.

But the fact that Frede can point to difficulties in congruence between the informational contents of the *Seventh Letter* and these dialogues based on a Mouthpiece Interpretation of these works hardly shows that Plato is not the author of the former (as well as the latter works). It instead demonstrates that, on a Mouthpiece Interpretation, such hermeneutical problems arise. It is unclear whether such problems of *Seventh Letter* genuineness arise on the Socratic (Anti-Mouthpiece) Interpretation. And this holds true in light of the fact that, as Frede points out, "the author of *Ep*. VII heavily relies on the *Republic*, it also seems clear that he does not overlook the *Laws*." (Burnyeat and Frede 2015: 54) And it also holds true if, as Frede insists, Plato was writings the *Laws* while the *Seventh Letter* was composed.

Moreover, there are specific points made in the *Seventh Letter* that Frede believes are indicative of its not being composed by Plato. The main point of Frede's focus is on the author's reference to Dion as a philosopher. Frede painstakingly attacks the credibility of such a claim. Whether or not one construes "philosopher" in either a strong or weak sense, the category fails to apply to Dion. Therefore, Plato, being a philosopher, would not commit the error of referring to Dion as a philosopher when plainly Dion was not a philosopher in any meaningful sense of the term (Burnyeat and Frede 2015: 61f.):

> …I cannot see how Plato in 354/3 could have thought of Dion as a philosopher who met the qualifications of a philosopher-ruler. There was no sign of theoretical achievement and there were questions about Dion's character. If this is correct, it seems that the letter must have been written at a time when a certain panegyrical tradition concerning Dion already had arisen, which depicted him as a philosopher. (Burnyeat and Frede 2015: 63)

Frede is correct in uncovering a discrepancy in the manner in which the author of the *Seventh Letter* describes Dion, philosophically speaking, and the manner in which history seems to depict Dion on that score. But the language of the *Seventh Letter* with regard to its description of Dion's philosophical abilities might be due to the author's wanting to cast Dion in the best possible light (referring to Dion as having great promise as a philosopher) and that perhaps, the author thought, Dion might be thought of as one who as a political leader has the *potential* to bring a certain degree of justice to a *polis*, without stating that Dion was actually a great philosopher in some strong sense of the term and one who would bring about a just state.

But even if Frede's suspicions concerning the *Seventh Letter's* depiction of Dion as a philosopher are correct,[14] a deeper problem confronts us as interpreters of Plato's works. While Frede refuses to ascribe to Plato a complete lapse in judgment in describing Dion (and Dionysius II, for that matter) in terms of philosophical ability and promise and the entailed moral character therein, one must be ever cautious to avoid an interpretation of Plato that essentially idolifies Plato as one who is not subject to the human frailties to which other philosophers succumb. Many contemporary philosophers have exaggerated the philosophical qualities of their students, former students or even colleagues when writing letters of recommendation for them. In fact, this has been a rampant practice amongst most academics for generations. Why would one think that Plato is not subject to the same temptations that we face? And if Plato is a human being subject to such temptations, he is likely to succumb to them now and then. If so, why would one think that Plato, in depicting Dion and Dionysius II as they are depicted in the *Seventh Letter*, could not have made such errors? Surely such errors are hardly sufficient to impinge Plato's moral character or his brilliance as the author of some of the greatest philosophical work in human history! And if this is reasonable to believe about Plato, then how might the mischaracterization of Dion as a philosopher suffice to discredit Plato as the author of the *Seventh Letter*? He would not be unlike Immanuel Kant, whose philosophical brilliance was not overshadowed by his racist words directed at those from African nations. The history of philosophy is replete with examples of fine philosophers who at some point or another exhibited human frailties, errors, lapses in judgment. On my interpretation of him, Plato was not the first, nor was he the last to do so. Thus Frede's pointing to historical problems with the depiction of Dion's philo-

---

[14] Further reasoning is provided in Burnyeat and Frede (2015: 81–82).

sophical abilities and moral character and Dion's actual philosophical abilities and moral character does nothing much to show that Plato was not the author of the *Seventh Letter*, no more than one's pointing out that in some of his correspondence Kant exhibited racist tendencies demonstrates that Kant was not the author of such letters especially because of Kant's cosmopolitan ideals. That is to say, just as Kant did author such letters and no one to my knowledge questions their genuineness, so might well have Plato authored the *Seventh Letter*, warts and all. Philosophical incisiveness is sometimes accompanied by historical fiction or morally unjustified nonsense.

Furthermore, it does not even follow from the supposition that Frede is absolutely correct in his suspicions of the authenticity of the *Seventh Letter* that it is suspect in its entirety. For it is still an open question as to whether or not the remainder of the letter might be genuine—the parts of it that do not pertain to Dion, Dionysius, and the politics of ancient Syracuse. So even if the entire sections of discussion of these political matters is justifiably suspect as to their authenticity, it does not follow, for example, that the discussion of whether or not Plato ever expressed his own philosophy in writing is in turn suspect. Frede appears to commit an implicit bifurcation fallacy: either the *Seventh Letter* is authentic, or it is not. But there is the distinct possibility that parts of it are authentic, while others are not. Frede does nothing to rule out this distinct possibility.

Burnyeat provides his own reasons for rejecting the authenticity of the *Seventh Letter*, and they differ importantly from Frede's. Burnyeat's argument begins with stylometric considerations, namely, that "bits of the real Plato turn up in reverse order to the original." (Burnyeat and Frede 2015: 130) Of course, this assumes that one knows what constitutes the "real Plato," something that Burnyeat simply takes for granted and for which he never argues (at least, not in this most recent work). So while Burnyeat might be correct in his accusation that the author of the *Seventh Letter* mangles parts of the text of the *Republic* in attempting to "appropriate" it for his own purposes, he begs the question in favor of the Mouthpiece Interpretation in assuming that there is a "real Plato" against which a false Plato might be judged.

Additionally, the fact that certain stylistic differences exist between what are considered to be genuine works of Plato versus those which might not be judged as such is not uncontroversial evidence to the latter's inauthenticity. Why not? Because one would think that one would find similarities of thought between said documents, along with some reversals of phrases from one text to the next, just as we authors sometimes switch the ordering of combined phrases and locutions. Burnyeat's argument would be considerably stronger if it contained actual references from said documents which contained more far-reaching phrases which were not only switched, but contained significant interpretive features such that one might be able to pinpoint such interpretive locutions (additions?) to scribes of a particular philosophical school. For the very fact that it is evident that the author of the *Seventh Letter* has read some or all of Plato's works (whichever they may be, uncontroversially, let us suppose) is insufficient grounds to reject the letter as being genuine. For it might be that Plato wrote the letter in part to expound this or that point therein, or to, as some anti-mouthpiece interpreters would argue, clarify that there is no philosophy of Plato's to be found in the dialogues. And this might hold whether or not how the letter describes Dion or anyone else discussed therein accurately in terms of their philosophical abilities or moral character. Again, contrary to Frede and Burnyeat, it is facile and hyperbolic to reject the entire letter even if one assumes the inaccuracies just noted. And we have seen, as noted above, an early dating of the *Seventh Letter* is a weak reason to be suspicious of its authenticity. And when one considers the fundamental assumption, or presumption, of the Mouthpiece Interpretation which essentially grounds the rejection of the authenticity of the letter, there is inadequate reason to reject it outright, in its entirety.

Burnyeat does offer a hermeneutical argument to reject the genuineness of the *Seventh Letter*, namely, that its author engages in incompetent argumentation and misreads the *Cratylus*. (Burnyeat and Frede 2015: 132) In essence, Burnyeat accuses the author of the *Seventh Letter* of short-changing an argument about words and their meanings from *Cratylus* 439b, and engaging in "a non-sequitur Socrates never commits" and is thus "a philosophical incompetent." But why assume either the incorrigibility of Plato or his inability to engage in short-handed argument? Certainly other famous and excellent philosophers have engaged in errors of reasoning, especially in letters they compose as opposed to articles and books wherein they have more space to refine points of analysis and argument. Why does

Burnyeat seem to implicitly think that an author's aims in composing a letter would be the same as those she has in composing a book or an essay? Would one not reasonably think that a philosopher's letters might in general take for granted certain points of argument? Would we not think it reasonable to expect that the standards of logical rigor might be understandably lower in a letter than they would be for a more substantial work? And would we not think that Plato, being human, would not be expected to have lapses in judgment and even to express them in his letters now and then? As I noted above concerning Kant, even the best philosophers in history make errors in reasoning and judgment, especially when it comes to composing letters. And why would Plato be any different in this respect? Why the implicit idolization of Plato?

Burnyeat writes of the *Seventh Letter's* author: "He might well be surprised at the number of readers, from antiquity to this day, who have taken him to be a philosopher, and even more surprised at those who have taken him to be Plato." (Burnyeat and Frede 2015: 133) Perhaps, on the other hand, Plato himself might be quite indeed surprised after composing at least some of said letter at so many philosophers of the Mouthpiece Interpretation who relentlessly insist that Plato's views *are* found in his dialogues. Alternatively, the letter's author might be surprised to find that there is an all-or-nothing approach to the authenticity of the letter, or that many interpreters such as Frede and Burnyeat refuse to even take sufficiently seriously the Platonic Question that they might dare to critically examine their mouthpiece assumptions in their approach to the matter of the letter's authenticity.

Ironically, Burnyeat accuses Dionysius of suffering "from the worst disease in Plato's book: conceit of knowledge, which is *the* great obstacle to philosophy understood as the quest for wisdom." (Burnyeat and Frede 2015: 162) But why is it not considered a kind of conceit to incessantly assume without adequate argument the Mouthpiece Interpretation? And why would the Mouthpiece Interpretation not be reasonably considered to be *the* great obstacle (or at least one of the greatest obstacles) to the study of Plato's dialogues? There is no question that if Dionysius thinks that he knows "Plato's philosophy," then he is wrong about that because, as the author of the *Seventh Letter* 341c writes: "There is no writing of mine about these matters, nor will there ever be one." Given the context, it is reasonable to construe the referent of "these matters" as "Plato's philosophy." So the letter states that it is wrong to think that Plato ever composed his philosophy for others to read. And if it is wrong to think that Plato ever composed his philosophy for others to read, then it is highly unlikely that there is a reliable manner by which to know his "philosophy."

It is sometimes thought that a famous lecture of Plato's ("On the Good") could reveal his philosophy to those in attendance, and that some of those in attendance might have transcribed or otherwise accurately reported his philosophy as it was articulated in that lecture. But as it turns out, that is a dubious argument in favor of the claim that "Plato's philosophy" can be understood by us.[15]

What besides the weakest of evidence can support the Mouthpiece Interpretation? While it would be premature to infer that mouthpiece interpreters, not unlike Dionysius and some others, "understand nothing of his philosophy. Not a thing" (Burnyeat and Frede 2015: 164), it might be reasonably inferred of mouthpiece interpreters that they are approaching Plato's dialogues with surprising presumptuousness and unexamined assumptions, including the one that the dialogues contain Plato's own philosophy, that is, unless it can be adequately shown that the *Seventh Letter* 340–345 is not genuine. For if it is genuine, then it explicitly supports the Socratic Interpretation, though further work needs to be done in order to establish its authenticity.

Burnyeat's anticipation of this line of reasoning is that "…Plato's next move is to deny that he ever has or ever will write a treatise (σύγγραμμα) on his own philosophy. He is not disowning authorship of his dialogues, but insisting that he would not dream of writing an expository treatise which sets out his ideas in the manner of those who have written books 'On the philosophy of Plato'." (Burnyeat and Frede 2015: 164–165) Of course, this is consistent with the Socratic Anti-Mouthpiece Interpretation: Plato wrote dialogues, not treatises. But the Socratic interpreter sees this as a good reason to not approach the dialogues as if they contained "Plato's philosophy." Instead, they are to be understood as containing brilliant philosophical discussions about some vital topics and problems. Coupled with Burnyeat's own claim about Plato's point that expositions of Plato's philosophy "ought

---

[15] See Appendix I for a discussion of Harold Cherniss' treatment of this point.

not to be written" (Burnyeat and Frede 2015: 165) seems to be sufficient warrant to doubt and reject as wrongheaded any attempt to do otherwise—including the attempt of mouthpiece interpreters to attempt to construe this or that dialogical interlocutor in Plato's dialogues as one who speaks for Plato.

Burnyeat does well to render the philosophical digression in the *Seventh Letter* on whether or not philosophy should or could ever be written down for others to grasp. But he does not do well to address "There is no writing of mine about these matters, nor will there ever be one" in 341c. It is consistent with the Socratic Interpretation of Plato's dialogues, yet in its straightforward reading it poses a particularly strong threat to the Mouthpiece Interpretation.

In conclusion, neither Frede nor Burnyeat have strongly demonstrated the inauthenticity of the entirety of the *Seventh Letter*. In particular, they do not even directly challenge the genuineness of the 341c passage on which I focus in my assessment of their arguments. Furthermore, it is not even clear that either of them provides sufficiently strong arguments against the authenticity of any part of the letter, since Plato might have misjudged the philosophical prowess and moral character of Dion and Dionysius II. What each has accomplished is a rendering dubious of certain passages of the letter. So a wise interpreter of the letter ought not to accept it without question. But neither Frede nor Burnyeat has made it unreasonable to accept the *Seventh Letter* 341c wherein it is claimed that Plato has not nor ever did compose a work communicating his "philosophy." On its face, this implicitly cautions against the Mouthpiece Interpretation of Plato's dialogues, and it supports the Socratic Interpretation.

In light of the respective discussions of the authenticity of the *Seventh Letter* by Frede and Burnyeat and the difficulties with some of their key arguments, we are left with asking mouthpiece interpreters to bear the burden of argument in support of their approach to Plato. Yet they have not done so with an adequate degree of plausibility. Of course, this does not prove the case for the Socratic Interpretation. But it does expose embarrassing features of the dominant contemporary philosophical approach to Plato scholarship. And it paves the way for me to continue to make a case for a plausible alternative to the Mouthpiece Interpretation.

Plato's dialogues are not inscrutable. Of course the contents of the dialogues can be understood. But this is a different matter than what can be legitimately attributed to Plato from the contents of the dialogues. And I quote Socrates in *Meno* 86b–c: "…I would contend at all costs both in word and deed as far as I could that we will be better men, braver and less idle, if we believe that one must search for the things one does not know, rather than if we believe that it is not possible to find out what we do not know and that we must not look for it." This passage captures part of the message of the Socratic Interpretation, namely, that it is one of the main aims of Plato in writing the dialogues to encourage us to never give up on our pursuit of truth and wisdom, for our perseverance will make us better persons.

Thus if the *Seventh Letter* is genuinely Plato's, then there stands significant primary textual evidence against the Mouthpiece Interpretation. But even if it is inauthentic, we see that the Mouthpiece Interpretation has difficulty bearing its burden of argument in support of its attributions to Plato of various and sundry substantive philosophical beliefs, doctrines or theories.

Complex Features of Plato's Writings

Moreover, there is a sense in which most Plato scholars play fast and loose with the use of "dialogues." Works such as the *Timaeus* and the *Apology* are hardly dialogues, but contain speeches. Then there are the thirteen letters. Of course, the *Menexenus* is a funeral oration. Furthermore, the dialogue form in which Plato writes, when he writes dialogues, is multifaceted. As McCabe states:

> … the dialogues come in all sorts of different forms: some are dramatic, others merely formalized discussion (compare the *Phaedo* and the *Statesman*); some are in direct speech, others narrated (compare the *Gorgias* and the *Symposium*); some seem to have a beginning, a middle, and an end, whereas others begin, or end, in the middle of things (compare the *Euthyphro* and the *Philebus*); some have Socrates in the central role, and others are dominated by less engaging, but more authoritative figures (compare the *Theaetetus* and the *Sophist*). (McCabe 2008: 88)

Thus Plato's use of the dialogue form of which I have written is really rather complex. And as McCabe argues, it matters much for the way in which Plato's works ought to be approached:

> ... we cannot make sense of what Plato does if we ignore the effect on the arguments of dramatic context, allusion, characterization—indeed, of all the aspects of the style and drama of the dialogue. This effect is felt both particularly (where the dramatic detail alters radically how we understand individual arguments) and generally (where various strategies render the reader carefully reflective on what is said). I shall conclude that the philosophical content of a dialogue is to be found, at least, in the dialogue as a whole. How Plato writes, therefore, is indissoluble from what he is trying to say. (McCabeb 2008: 89)

Do not these complexities of how Plato composed his dialogues point toward an approach to Plato's dialogues that is closer to the Mouthpiece Interpretation instead of the Socratic Interpretation?[16]

I do not see this line of reasoning as uncongenial to the Socratic Interpretation, but rather as enriching it. The approach to Plato's works which best accounts for the most of Plato's works is, all relevant things considered, the one that ought to be accepted so long as it satisfies the most plausible criterion of philosophical adequacy (whatever that happens to be). Now if it turns out that the Socratic Interpretation is uneasy with the fact that certain speeches might well reflect Plato's views as there is no genuine dialogue the mere form of which might otherwise pose a difficulty for attributions of dialogical contents to Plato, this might mean that the Socratic Interpretation cannot fully account for all of Plato's works with the same level of plausibility. In this way, it might not fully satisfy the desideratum that an approach to Plato's corpus ought to "make sense of the contents of the entirety of Plato's works." (Corlett 2005: 2)[17] However, even in light of this possibility, it would not follow that the Mouthpiece Interpretation is exonerated. Why? Because there are dozens of other works of Plato's which are indeed dialogues, mixed of course with dramatic properties, poetry and the like. And it is precisely these kinds of features which prevent us from accepting the Mouthpiece Interpretation as being a sound approach to Plato insofar as it continuously ascribes

---

[16] I owe this point to David Gallop.

[17] Corlett, *Interpreting Plato's Dialogues*, p. 2. I shall call this the "desideratum of totality."

to Plato various substantive philosophical beliefs, doctrines and theories based on the contents of such dialogues. So even *if* this concern poses a challenge to the Anti-Mouthpiece Interpretation's ability to explain all of the works of Plato, it exposes in even more precise terms how far the Mouthpiece Interpretation falls short in this regard. In this way, the Mouthpiece Interpretation fails to satisfy the desideratum of totality with regard to Plato's works. The Socratic Interpretation satisfies this desideratum greater than does the Mouthpiece Interpretation.

Now mouthpiece interpreters might argue that such non-dialogical works of Plato's might serve as interpretive guides to the ideas of Plato in a similar way that Platonic treatises, if they existed, would. Thus we can begin to decipher Plato's views in light of the contents of these non-dialogical works.[18] But this line of argument assumes that the non-dialogical character of these works is sufficiently similar to a philosophical treatise, which is dubious. A speech by a character is hardly a treatise, and not an unproblematic source by which to unlock the ideas of Plato. This is especially true if Socrates is not the main character presenting the speech, though there is some reason to believe that if Socrates is giving the speech in question that it might serve as some guide to Plato's ideas. But we must be careful to not identify without sufficient reason, for instance, the ideas of Socrates in his speech in the *Apology* with the ideas of Plato. After all, Plato could have been trying to record as best he could the biographical facts of Socrates' trial which may or may not have anything to do with Plato's own substantive philosophical ideas. And to ascribe to Plato various views of Socrates' which are obviously problematic seems to run afoul of the Principle of Charity in Interpretation which states that an author's words, dialogical or otherwise, ought to be construed in such a manner that no blatantly implausible view ought to be attributed to the author unless the textual evidence and context permits no viable alternative. Yet there are so many such views which are placed in the mouths of Socrates and his interlocutors throughout Plato's dialogues. How, then, is it possible to decipher what is reasonable to ascribe to Plato and what is not without violating the Principle of Charity in Interpretation?

---

[18] I owe this point to Gerald Press.

Is Aristotle a Witness to the Substantive Philosophical Beliefs, Doctrines or Theories of Plato?

Additionally, it has been argued that Aristotle, being the most famous of Plato's students and who interprets Plato's works so as to support the Mouthpiece Interpretation, serves as evidence that Plato believes at least some of the substantive philosophical views presented in the dialogues, especially much of what is placed in the mouth of Socrates. Gerson couches the Aristotle-as-a-Witness-to-Plato's-Philosophy Argument as a kind of appeal to authority when he states of the Anti-Mouthpiece Interpretation that "…it does seem odd that if it is true, it has eluded virtually everyone who has written about Plato's views from Aristotle to the present." (Gerson 2002: 227)[19] Of course, the question here is whether or not the appeal is a good one in this case. While Harold Cherniss has done much to discredit this line of

---

[19] Gerson also states of early Platonism that "Since Plato was not the first and therefore not the only champion of Platonism, there was generally held to be nothing in principle untoward in arguing that Plato *meant* what he did not happen to say explicitly." (Gerson 2005: 256) However, Gerson's words betray an assumption that something at least akin to the Mouthpiece Interpretation is correct, or that various secondary sources (and not the primary source of the Corpus Platonicum itself) count as adequate evidence in favor of the claim that Plato had views and that we have good reason to think that based on such secondary sources we can be confident of what they were. But this just begs the point at issue concerning the Platonic Question. On the other hand, Gerson admits that "It hardly needs emphasizing that from the claims that 'Plato believed p' and that 'p implies q', we cannot infer that 'Plato believed q'." (Gerson 2005: 256) The point here seems to be that a secondary source pertinent to Plato ascribing a view to Plato is insufficient reason for us to do the same. In any case, Gerson has apparently not heeded the wisdom proffered about the trustworthiness of Aristotle's testimony of Plato's views in mouthpiece interpreter A. E. Taylor (1963: 10): "…this had the (for us) unfortunate result that we are left to learn Plato's inmost ultimate convictions on the most important questions, the very thing we most want to know, from references in Aristotle, polemic in object, always brief, and often puzzling in the highest degree." Even the most highly regarded of mouthpiece interpreters like Taylor recognize the serious difficulties posed by the appeal to Aristotle as a witness of Plato's views argument for the Mouthpiece Interpretation.

reasoning,[20] and I have noted additional problems with it (Corlett 2005: 28–30), there is yet another difficulty with this approach to Plato. If we assume, rightly, that Aristotle was not the only pupil of Plato's in the Academy, does the fact that Aristotle is the most famous one serve as a sufficiently good reason to think that he adequately understands Plato's views and intentions? The fact that we have inadequate textual evidence of Plato's other students and their views of what might or might not be rightly attributed to Plato raises the question of the incomparability of Aristotle's interpretation of Plato's works with those of other students who were contemporaries of Aristotle's, such as Speusippus and Xenocrates. This weakens considerably the appeal to Aristotle as an adequate source for interpreting Plato, whether or not Aristotle himself was a Mouthpiece Interpreter of Plato's dialogues. The inability to compare and contrast and critically evaluate Aristotle's interpretation of Plato's dialogues with others who studied with Plato does much to further diminish the use of Aristotle as an unproblematic witness to the content of Plato's alleged beliefs as it reasonably questions the testimony of Aristotle as a reliable witness to the content of Plato's supposed beliefs, doctrines, or theories. This is not to deny, however, that Aristotle might be a reliable guide to the dating of this or that dialogue of Plato's, such as in the *Politics* 2.6 where Aristotle states that Plato's *Laws* is later than the *Republic*. But this is hardly evidence that Aristotle knew how to decipher Plato's beliefs, doctrines or theories *from Plato's dialogues*. Nor is it wise to follow a rather limited number of often cryptic remarks by one even brilliant thinker regarding what that thinker attributes to Plato. For just as in contemporary philosophy, it is often the case that in the haste of disagreeing with a particular thinker, one is prone to commit attribution errors for a variety of reasons that pertain to, among other things, problems with the functioning of human cognitive architecture. In other words, often disagreement with an author,

---

[20] Cherniss (1945, 1962). For a discussion of Gerson's replies to Cherniss' objections to Aristotle's testimony concerning "Plato's philosophy," see Appendix I to this book. Also see Shields (2008) for a critique of Aristotle's arguments against Plato's "theory of forms." The fact that many of Aristotle's arguments against Plato's alleged doctrines fail to refute Plato hardly shows that Plato had no beliefs, doctrines or theories of his own. However, it does render dubious the notion that Aristotle ought to be taken as an unquestionable guide to Plato's mind.

coupled with a pre-commitment to a view which is opposed to the view the author in question endorses, can cloud the better judgment of someone who seeks to interpret or best understand that author. Aristotle is not beyond committing this cognitive error. So we must be careful to not attach too much weight to his musings about what Plato "believed." Rather, we must rely on the Platonic corpus itself as our primary evidence.

Gerson admits that when it comes to how to discover the nature of Platonism, "The core evidence is, of course, the Platonic *corpus*." (Gerson 2005: 257, emphasis in original) But this point, while true, must especially be heeded when it comes to matters of the Platonic Question. It is one thing to find unambiguous statements by Plato that would unlock his supposed beliefs, doctrines or theories in his dialogues. But it is quite another matter primarily, not to the primary source evidence of Plato's dialogues for such beliefs, doctrines or theories, but instead to appeal to Aristotle to unlock such views. Such a hermeneutical method would not allow the plain sense of the texts of Plato to speak for themselves. Rather, it would allow the secondary evidence of Aristotle's far from comprehensive and unambiguous attributions to Plato to influence how one approaches Plato's dialogues. One must, then, heed the caution issued by none other than Gerson himself about Platonists regarding "Aristotle's reports of Plato's 'unwritten teachings'" and his "interpretations of the doctrines expressed in the dialogues":

> These were assumed by Platonists to be informed by Aristotle's knowledge of the "unwritten teachings" as well as his intimate contact with Plato over a period of many years. Since they were more concerned with Platonism than with the material contained in the published writings, it was, accordingly, entirely reasonable for them to rely on Aristotle here as it would perhaps not be if their interest were principally historical or scholarly. (Gerson 2005: 258)

Unfortunately, Gerson's advice about Platonists and their appeal to Aristotle to figure out what Plato believed was not heeded by Gerson himself regarding the Platonic Question. Nor is it followed by several other proponents of the Mouthpiece Interpretation. For the Platonic Question just is one that is both philosophical and "historical or scholarly." Setting aside Gerson's implicit and dubious claim that the "historical or scholarly" issue differs from that of the philosophical one in this case, the Platonic Question is truly both. For it is not only about historical accuracy in what ought to be attributed to Plato, but one of Plato's philosophical intentions in composing dialogues. So with regard to the Platonic Question, it does little or no good to rely so heavily on secondary evidence from Aristotle and his contemporaries in order to decipher Plato's meaning in the dialogues. And while it may be true that "Platonists saw no impediment to drinking from the font of Aristotelian wisdom in order to understand Platonism better" (Gerson 2005: 259), one must be careful to not commit the very same error in attempting to attribute to Plato this or that belief, doctrine or theory from the dialogues. Furthermore, while it might be true that there was a degree of harmony between the "philosophy of Aristotle" and the "philosophy of Plato" (Gerson 2005: 271), it is difficult, absent a presumption that the Mouthpiece Interpretation is plausible, to know how to verify such a claim based primarily on the informational contents of Plato's dialogues. So while the appeal to Aristotle's discussions of or references to Plato's alleged views counts as evidence in favor of the Mouthpiece Interpretation, mouthpiece interpreters must provide better evidence for their position if it is to be taken seriously and to gain the assent of reasonable interpreters of Plato. For the appeal to Aristotle is fraught with difficulties.

While many a mouthpiece interpreter has appealed to Aristotle as a witness to Plato's views, when one examines closely the passages to which such interpreters point one finds that Aristotle merely attributes a view to Plato rather than *showing* that such a view is held by Plato *by virtue of what is written in one or more of his dialogues*. Examples here include the assertion that in *Metaphysics* A6 Aristotle names Plato as the originator of the theory of forms. (Beversluis 2006: 101) But a close study of the passage reveals that Aristotle does not *argue* that in this or that *passage from Plato's dialogues* Plato expresses his alleged theory of forms. Rather, it is Aristotle's *belief* that Plato originated the theory. But this is an ambiguous claim. First, it might mean, as mouthpiece interpreters are prone to assume, that Aristotle sees *in Plato's dialogues Plato's expression of his own theory of forms*. Secondly, it might mean that Aristotle sees in the Platonic corpus *what he takes* to be Plato's theory of forms. Thirdly, it might mean that Aristotle is *ascribing* the theory of forms to Plato as its originator, but his reasons for doing so have nothing to do with the informational contents of the Platonic corpus. Perhaps, for instance, Aristotle ascribes the "theory" to Plato based on what he recalls of some conversations he had with his mentor. Yet this evidence, uncorroborated by Aristotle's colleagues in the Academy at the time, is insufficient to ground entire theories to Plato. For as is widely understood, experimental cognitive psychological evidence demonstrates that a single witness to events and expressions within such events is often unreliable, or tainted by interpretive bias. Thus it need not be the case, as has been suggested, that "If Plato did not write dialogues to advance positive doctrine, why did Aristotle say what he did, thereby either betraying monumental ignorance about what Plato was up to or grievously (and presumably intentionally) misleading posterity?" (Beversluis 2006: 101) Given the problematics of witness testimony, it would be harsh and premature to infer that Aristotle intentionally misled others as to the nature of Plato's views. Furthermore, Aristotle need not have been guilty of being monumentally ignorant of Plato's views. Yet it might be "monumentally ignorant" to ascribe various philosophically substantive beliefs, doctrines or theories to Plato based on the problematic testimony of a single witness in this particular case. So it is misleading to claim that it is justified based on this alleged evidence from Aristotle that Plato intentionally expresses his alleged theory of forms in this or that dialogue.[21]

Now it might be argued by the mouthpiece interpreter who appeals to Aristotle as a witness to Plato's alleged views that the fact that Aristotle ascribes a view to Plato counts as a good reason for us to do so. But does this justify the hermeneutical practice of attributing such beliefs to Plato based on what is not in congruence with the plain sense of the informational contents of Plato's dialogues? What principles of interpretation would justify such a practice? Whatever principles would justify this practice would need to accommodate the fact that Plato might indeed hold the view ascribed to him by Aristotle, but that this is quite another matter from what Plato wants his readers to know based on the informational contents of his dialogues. In other words, what if Plato held substantive philosophical belief X? Does it follow that it is good interpretive practice to, if one finds discussion of

---

[21] For further discussion on the ambiguities concerning Aristotle's ascriptions of certain views to Plato, see John J. Mulhern, "Plato's Putative Mouthpiece and Ancient Authorial Practice: A Reply," presented at the Society for Ancient Greek Philosophy, Fordham University, 17 October 2011.

X in Plato's dialogues, to ascribe X to Plato *based on the informational contents of Plato's dialogues*? One must remain cautious about the fact that X might take on or introduce nuances in the dialogue that do not appear in what Plato is alleged to believe by Aristotle, or vice-versa. X might be complicated indeed, and raise more questions than give answers to a philosophical problem. And it is far from obvious that any of Plato's dialogues provides the sort of nuances that would capture his considered judgments on X, whether X is his alleged view of philosophically substantive matters such as knowledge, art, language, justice, etc.. And even if Aristotle attributes to Plato a theory of X, we find no justification for that in Aristotle as whatever Aristotle ascribes to Plato falls well short of being a *theory* of anything, but mere doxastic ascriptions to Plato instead on a very limited array of philosophical topics compared to the vast array of them discussed throughout Plato's dialogues. So while Aristotle counts as a witness to Plato's views, it is unwise to think that his testimony ought to count for more than a problematic one. For mouthpiece interpreters to repeatedly and in certain ways misleadingly appeal to Aristotle as a (presumably important and strong) witness to Plato's views is itself misleading at best, and problematic in a multitude of ways. It is problematic enough to implicitly or otherwise make the inference from, for instance, "Socrates says…" to "Plato says…", as Mulhern argues. (Mulhern 1971) But it is even more problematic to implicitly or otherwise infer from "Aristotle says Plato says …" to "Plato says…"[22] We see, then, that the "Plato says" fallacy can be committed in various ways: directly as well as indirectly.

A variety of scholars have stated the Mouthpiece Interpretation (especially in its dogmatic form) in terms of Socrates rather than Plato (see the next chapter for a fuller discussion of this matter). Instead of claiming that Plato expresses his own theories, doctrines or beliefs by way of what Plato's Socrates says in the dialogues, they claim that what Plato puts in the mouth of Socrates amounts to *Socrates'* theories, doctrines, or beliefs. One recent statement of this view is found in Christopher Rowe:

---

[22] For further discussion of the Aristotle-as-a-Witness-to-Plato's-Philosophy hypothesis, see Appendix I to this book.

> It must be said at once that the balance of probability seems to lie with the "dogmatic," or "doctrinal," sort of interpretation rather than with its "skeptical" counterpart. There are just too many occasions in the dialogues when even Socrates not only appears to commit himself to positive ideas (to the extent that he commits himself to anything), but offers no reason for rejecting them:... (Rowe 2006: 14)[23]

But like the "Plato says" approach to Plato's works, what might be termed Rowe's "Socrates theorizes or believes" perspective suffers from a malady of difficulties. First, to state that "there are just too many occasions in the dialogues when even Socrates not only appears to commit himself to positive ideas…" without explicit supporting evidence hardly serves as a good argument in favor of the assertion that Socrates believes the words placed in his mouth by Plato, but rather begs the question in favor of the view that this is the case. Precisely how is it the case that Socrates "appears to commit himself to positive ideas"? And what are the textual clues that would indicate when he does this and when he does not? Rowe provides no answers to these crucial questions. Instead, he offers the mere claims that Socrates' words amount to his theories, dogmas, or beliefs. Secondly, Rowe's assertion that Socrates "offers no reason for rejecting" his putatively "positive ideas" amounts to a blatant fallacy of *ignoratio elenchi*. That Socrates fails to offer reasons to reject a "positive" theory, doctrine or belief that Rowe and many others impute to him does not imply or entail that Socrates accepts X either as a theory, dogma or belief. Socrates could instead be putting forth X in order to urge interlocutors (and Plato, to urge readers) to think more deeply and philosophically about X, which is precisely what my Socratic Interpretation states that Plato is doing.

But this notion that Socrates believes the words placed in his mouth by Plato might be restated in a more nuanced way:

> What Socrates is doing in these [aporetic, early] dialogues is arguing *ad hominem* in the precise sense: arguing only from the claims made by the interlocutor himself rather than claims of his own, thus showing the interlocutor that he has problems just from holding his own position, independently of Socrates' own views. (Annas 2006: 33)

---

[23] Another view that attributes to Socrates theories and doctrines is found in Reshotko (2006).

While this position on how to interpret Socrates is a bit more complex than some others, it too suffers from difficulties. First, it fails to explain what makes a pericope of Plato's works "doctrinal" as opposed to "*ad hominem*." Lacking a good explanation of the difference between them and what exactly makes a passage doctrinal and not *ad hominem* begs the question in favor of the dogmatic interpretation of Plato's works as they regard Socrates' alleged theories, doctrines, or beliefs. Merely asserting that there is a difference between Socrates' speaking for the sake of argument versus his advancing his own theories, doctrines, or beliefs is not the same as providing sound argumentation for there being such a distinction, or explaining how one is to discern such passages from one another. Moreover, it also does not demonstrate how we are to come to understand which of Socrates' words are "his own," that is, when and where he speaks in his own person and when and where he does not.

Thus the attempt to apply the Mouthpiece Interpretation to Socrates fails for similar reasons that it fails in the case of attributing Socrates' words to Plato.[24] And we are left with the fact that there has been not one sound argument provided in favor of the Mouthpiece Interpretation or its sister approach to Plato/Socrates. Perhaps certain Plato scholars will admit that it is time to put to rest an approach that has run its course as not even the brightest minds who have tried have been able to provide unproblematic arguments to support this dominant approach to Plato.

The Origin and Development of the Platonic Corpus and the Mouthpiece Interpretation

Until now, I have argued that the very dialogue form in which Plato chose to write most of his works prohibits with adequate confidence an attribution of substantive philosophical views therein to Plato. But, as if the previous reasoning were insufficient to undermine the plausibility of the Mouthpiece Interpretation, there is yet another reason to see the Mouthpiece Interpretation as highly dubious. It is not just that

---

[24] This attribution of various beliefs, doctrines or theories to Socrates is discussed in Chapter 4 of this book.

mouthpiece interpreters have failed on several attempts to justify their approach. It is not just that they have failed to undermine (or even succeeded in understanding and stating accurately) the Socratic Interpretation. Instead, it is that objective evidence concerning the very origin and development of the Platonic corpus itself speaks against the Mouthpiece Interpretation.

While the Socratic Interpretation openly assumes that the Thrasyllean collection of what Plato wrote (not necessarily that view of the chronology of Plato's works) is indeed genuinely Plato's, whether directly from Plato himself or indirectly from scribes and/or his philosophical disciples some years after Plato's death, the Mouthpiece Interpretation seems implicitly and unwittingly committed to the idea that Plato actually composed at least a good part of the Thrasyllean collection or that who(m)ever did compose the corpus centuries after his death somehow knew Plato's philosophically substantive beliefs, doctrines and theories and copied them accurately into the dialogues. Otherwise, how could a mouthpiece interpreter seriously argue that "Plato says…" or "Plato believes…" etc.? Recall that it is the Socratic interpreter who stands firm on the commitment to not commit the "Plato says" fallacy, and is instead committed to the idea that we ought to render exegeses of Plato's works as something akin to "In the *Republic*, Socrates states…" or the like, avoiding the "Plato says" fallacy altogether. Yet the various difficulties arising in the study of how the Platonic corpus came to be poses problems for the Mouthpiece Interpretation that it does not pose for the Socratic Interpretation. For while both approaches can assume the genuineness or at least the reliability of much of the informational contents of the Thrasyllean collection (Socratic interpreters for the sake of discussion, and many mouthpiece interpreters perhaps making the assumption *simplicitor*), the Mouthpiece Interpretation must go beyond this rather modest assumption and further hope that it really is the case that a good number of what we assume to be Plato's works really belong to Plato, directly or indirectly. Furthermore, the mouthpiece interpreter relies implicitly on the idea that the Platonic corpus is complete. For if it is not, then every single attribution to Plato with the confidence that so many mouthpiece interpreters make to Plato is indeed in question because it might be undone by the discovery that what we think is Plato's is not genuine, or by further archeological discoveries of additions to the extant corpus that might disconfirm, in one way or another, what has been attributed to Plato by mouthpiece interpreters.

In other words, if it turns out that few or none of the works in the Thrasyllean collection are genuine or even reliable reproductions of Plato's original works, then nothing is suffered (except disappointment that the assumption of Plato's authorship was mistaken) by Socratic interpreters. For them nothing regarding the Platonic Question hinges on whether or not Plato wrote the dialogues or whether or not their contents are attributable to Plato. But for the mouthpiece interpreter, hermeneutical disaster ensues if it turns out that the corpus in question is not genuinely Plato's. For on what grounds would it then be justified to attribute anything to Plato from the contents of the said collection? Yet the genuineness and reliability of what we take to be Plato's works is hardly uncontroversial or solid. For it was several centuries subsequent to Plato's death that the corpus of what we believe are his writings were collected and redacted. Irwin suggests that "After he had sold copies of the dialogues to booksellers, Plato seems to have continued working on them." (Irwin 2008: 66) But if this is true, then what is the likelihood that we can with confidence attribute without careful qualification any of the contents of the extant dialogues to Plato as Irwin and so many other mouthpiece interpreters are bent on doing? Might there not have been significant changes to the "original" Plato manuscripts during these several centuries, as occurred with early Christian writings?[25] If not, why not? And might such revisions be sufficient to render highly dubious any attribution of any of the contents of the Platonic corpus to Plato?

Furthermore, Irwin points out that Plato was said to have constantly revised his dialogues and that "…someone had access to his drafts, notes, and unpublished papers." (Irwin 2008: 66–67) Might these factors also contribute to the lack of confidence mouthpiece interpreters ought to possess when they ascribe this or that theory, doctrine or belief found in the dialogues to Plato, especially given the centuries of revisions occurring between Plato's writing them and what we actually possess thereof? This matter is compounded by the fact that we

---

[25] Among the several excellent works on the origin and development of the documents of the Christian scriptures, see Goodspeed (1916), Grant (1933), Grant (1977), Koester (1990), and Streeter (1924).

possess no credible evidence that Aristotle, the mouthpiece interpreters' seemingly favorite ancient authority on Plato's alleged ideas, ever asked Plato about his views. (Irwin 2008: 67)

Moreover, "The oldest sources for the text of Plato are papyri written in the second and third centuries AD. Unfortunately, these contain only fragments of text.. .. Our oldest surviving manuscript ... was copied by John the Calligrapher, who finished his work. .. in 895. .." (Irwin 2008: 71) Insofar as authenticity is concerned, the works of Plato are in a significantly more problematic position than, say, the early Christian scriptures. For unlike the latter wherein the earliest manuscripts and fragments date from within the first century CE, "our earliest manuscripts [of the Platonic corpus] come from about 1250 years after the lifetime of Plato," thus "we cannot reasonably suppose that they contain all and only the very words that Plato wrote. Copyists make mistakes: later copyists multiply mistakes because of ignorance, inattention or illegible handwriting. Such mistakes were easy with Greek manuscripts.. .. The surviving manuscripts of Plato display variations that show the effects of. .. processes of textual corruption." (Irwin 2008: 72) Nonetheless, "The text of Plato is generally sound." (Irwin 2008: 74) Even so, such textual matters pose significant problems for mouthpiece interpreters who more often than not state with confidence that "Plato says…" or "Plato thinks…" or "Plato believes…" as if the textual problems just mentioned do not exist.

Not only is the origin of the Platonic corpus in a worse state than, say, the origin of the Christian scriptures, but "We do not know the form in which the dialogues were 'published'." (Irwin 2008: 75) Were they originally intended, as some believe, for public dramatic performances? Irwin notes that

> We do not know how many dialogues Plato intended to publish in the form in which we have them. He left the *Laws* unfinished at his death; we do not know whether he was also engaged in revising other dialogues that he had previously published or had performed. These possibilities remind us of our ignorance about the initial circulation or publication of the dialogues. (Irwin 2008: 75)

What Irwin does not remind us of is also the level of ignorance we have in terms of what we can attribute to Plato from the dialogues in light of such factors just mentioned. For if it turns out that Irwin is correct in what he noted above, then on what grounds is it justified to ascribe this or that belief, doctrine or theory to Plato from the Platonic corpus we now possess?

A mouthpiece interpreter might answer by pointing to the facts that it is reasonable to regard the *Clitophon* as an alternative introduction to the *Republic*, the *Minos* as an alternative introduction to the *Laws*, that there was an alternative prologue to the *Theaetetus* in circulation early on, etc., suggesting, according to some, that Plato produced second editions of some of his dialogues. (Irwin 2008: 75–76) On the other hand, writes Irwin,

> Plato may have taken a long time to compose the *Republic* and the *Laws*, and he may have changed his mind in the course of composing them; perhaps he even published parts of them before the whole works were completed. None of this implies that he went back over an earlier draft and composed a second edition. Even if he was aware of inconsistencies or changes of direction in a published work, he may have lacked the time or enthusiasm to revise them substantially. (Irwin 2008: 76)

In either case, I would add, it is the Socratic Interpretation, more than the Mouthpiece Interpretation, that is significantly more accommodating of such factors concerning the Platonic corpus. For the Socratic Interpretation does not ascribe to Plato any substantive philosophical view in the dialogues, while the Mouthpiece Interpretation does. Yet the origin and genuineness of the Platonic corpus itself is questionable, making any attributions to Plato of their contents problematic. Without careful clarification, then, clarification that is typically absent from the writings of most mouthpiece interpreters, it is far from adequately justified to ascribe this or that substantive philosophical belief, doctrine or theory to Plato from the words embedded in his dialogues. Additionally, "It is probably a hopeless task. .. to look for different layers of composition, or later revisions, alternative versions, in a single dialogue.. .. given our ignorance about how they were composed and circulated. We do not know when Plato began to write philosophical dialogues,. .." (Irwin 2008: 76) Yet all of these and the above factors about the origin of the Platonic corpus prohibit our reasonably attributing as mouthpiece interpreters do seemingly all manner of substantive views to Plato.

In the case of Irwin, an exemplar of the Mouthpiece Interpretation, it becomes a bit puzzling just why, in light of his previous assertions about how to approach Plato (Corlett 2005: 28–31), and in light of his grasp of the array of complexities surrounding the origin and development of the Platonic corpus, and in light of his statement that "Since Plato wrote dialogues, he does not address his reader directly, as an author of a philosophical treatise would" (Irwin 2008: 84),[26] he (or any other reasonable interpreter of Plato) would cling to the mouthpiece approach. Perhaps a clue is that Irwin still believes that since Aristotle cites (in criticizing Plato) what Irwin believes to be Plato's views, Aristotle is "probably confident that they are Plato's views." (Irwin 2008: 84) And, Irwin reasons, "since we have no reason to believe that anyone accused Aristotle" of misunderstanding Plato's dialogical works, Aristotle serves as evidence of Plato's views. (Irwin 2008: 84) But this argument from silence cannot serve as either strong or adequate justification for the Mouthpiece Interpretation. Fallacies do not count as plausible argumentation.

I have already addressed the Aristotle-as-a-Witness-to-Plato's-Views Argument embraced in one way or another by Irwin and so many other mouthpiece interpreters.[27] Suffice it to point out here that Irwin engages in a kind of *ignoratio elenchi* style of argumentation. The most that can be said of Irwin's reasoning in favor of his Aristotle-as-a-Witness-to-Plato's-Views Argument is that it is weak. For it effectively states that what Aristotle writes of Plato's alleged views is plausible until contrary evidence can be adduced. But why is not Irwin troubled by the fact that "Plato writes dialogues, he does not address his readers [including Aristotle!] directly, as the author of a philosophical treatise would"? And why is not Irwin equally troubled by the facts of the origin and development of the Platonic corpus enough to *not* attach so much weight to the viability of the Aristotle-as-a-Witness-to-Plato's-Views Argument? Is this argument the best evidence for the Mouthpiece Interpretation? If so, then it has been exposed for what it is, especially in light of the above considerations that would cause a more cautious interpreter of Plato to become more scrupulous than mouthpiece interpreters appear to be in what they ascribe to Plato. And this is especially true in light of the multifarious testimony of antiquity, as Irwin rightly, though concisely, describes:

---

[26] Recall that such a statement is part of the very basis of the Socratic (Anti-Mouthpiece) Interpretation of Plato.

[27] See above, and also see Corlett (2005: 30–31). See also Appendix I to this book.

> The Skeptical Academy rejected the doctrinal [mouthpiece] interpretation of Plato's dialogues and understood the dialogues as critical exercises, examining the arguments for and against each side in order to leave the reader in a puzzled condition (*aporia*). The point of these exercises is to induce suspension of judgment about dogmatic claims. According to the Skeptical Academy, the dialogues were primarily 'peirastic' ('testing') rather than dogmatic. (Irwin 2008: 84–85)

Why would not an entire Platonic tradition count at least as much for Irwin as the testimony of a single witness, Aristotle? It is because, Irwin states,

> ... the Skeptical interpretation was an innovation that tried to enlist Plato in a Skeptical project. We have no evidence that it goes back to Plato's contemporaries. The later Academy rejected it and returned to a doctrinal interpretation of the dialogues. We may therefore claim the support of most ancient readers for a doctrinal interpretation, even though readers differed among themselves about what doctrines should be ascribed to Plato. (Irwin 2008: 85)

So "even though readers differed among themselves about what doctrines should be ascribed to Plato," and even though Plato wrote dialogues and does not address his readers directly as an author of a philosophical treatise would, and in light of the testimony of the complex difficulties with the origin and development of the Platonic corpus itself, Irwin finds it more reasonable to remain an adherent of the Mouthpiece Interpretation because Aristotle was a mouthpiece interpreter and the Socratic Interpretation (or something akin to it) was rejected *by mouthpiece interpreters* of the later Academy. And this seems to lead him to claim that if we find a reasonably coherent philosophical outlook and a reasonably intelligible line of philosophical development in Plato's Socrates, "we have some grounds for claiming to have found Plato's views." (Irwin 2008: 85)

While this cautious statement (inclusive of the locution, "some grounds") is true, it is hardly sufficient to ground the Mouthpiece Interpretation. First, it fails to counter-balance Plato's use of the dialogue form throughout almost all of his writings, a form which, as I have argued, makes it extremely difficult from which to extract Plato's own views. This is especially the case given that, as far as I know, there exists no mouthpiece theory of Platonic interpretation which would provide and justify supportive principles by which Plato's works ought to be interpreted. And while it is not logically impossible that Plato chose the dialogue form to communicate his views to readers as mouthpiece interpreters want to suggest, it is more likely that Plato would have written treatises rather than dialogues to convey his views, as the Socratic Interpretation holds. Secondly, that one can, through rational reconstruction, sift through Plato's corpus and extract a "reasonably coherent philosophical outlook and a reasonably intelligible line of philosophical development" hardly justifies ascribing it to Plato. The *Theaetetus* serves as one example of where *aporia* would suggest, if anything, an interpretation ascribing to Plato the idea that justified true belief is insufficient for human knowledge. Yet within the *Theaetetus* there just is a somewhat generally coherent philosophical analysis of the nature of human knowledge (one that forms the basis of the traditional justified true belief theory of human propositional knowledge), one which develops throughout much of the dialogue until it is finally refuted. Based on Irwin's criteria, then, we would have "some grounds" for attributing to Plato the justified true belief theory of knowledge. Yet, *if* anything, we would be wiser to ascribe to *Socrates*—not to Plato—the *rejection* of such an analysis. Thirdly, moreover, Irwin's reasoning begs the Platonic Question in assuming that what Socrates states in Plato's dialogues is what Plato (might) believe.

The Platonic Question and the Burden of Argument

While it is true that "merely to have pointed out that an interpretation is based on assumptions is not sufficient to discredit it—unless those assumptions are so patently absurd or otherwise indefensible that merely to have brought them to light is to have provided a sufficient reason for abandoning them" (Beversluis 2006: 91), this consideration does not apply to the Mouthpiece Interpretation. For each and every piece of evidence adduced in favor of it has been demonstrated to be flawed, and each and every objection to the Socratic Interpretation (or objections that might be raised to it) has been either defeated or neutralized. And this is true even though the assumptions underlying the Mouthpiece Interpretation might be stated to be internally coherent. It is argued that "…what is needed is textual evidence and philosophical argumentation which successfully challenge those assumptions and constitute *grounds* for abandoning them." (Beversluis 2006: 92) However, I have provided precisely the textual evidence which places the Mouthpiece Interpretation in the unenviable position of having to do more than repeat its assumptions and provide straw man arguments against what many of its adherents think is the Anti-Mouthpiece Interpretation, especially the most extreme versions of it. First, there is the primary textual evidence of the dialogues themselves which constitute the majority of the Corpus Platonicum. Secondly, there is the evidence from the *Seventh Letter* the mere denial of authenticity of which by many mouthpiece interpreters hardly serves as strong evidence for its not being authentically Plato's. What further primary textual evidence is needed besides the very dialogues themselves which, I assume, Plato wrote that would convince the reasonable person to see that—lacking a theory of textual interpretation replete with plausible principles of interpretation grounding the Mouthpiece Interpretation—it is highly problematic to ascribe dialogical contents to Plato lacking either a statement of his views *to be found therein* or uncontroversial textual clues which do not beg the Platonic Question in favor of the Mouthpiece Interpretation or against the Anti-Mouthpiece Interpretation? And have I not provided sufficient philosophical argumentation which exposes the fallacious argument provided for the Mouthpiece Interpretation and against any plausible Anti-Mouthpiece Interpretation such as the Socratic Interpretation? While it is true that "there is nothing suspect about approaching the Platonic corpus with assumptions" (Beversluis 2006: 92), what matters here is the overall plausibility of those assumptions and a ruling out, without question-begging arguments, of alternative ways of approaching Plato's dialogues.

It is also true that "from the fact that Plato never explicitly and unambiguously *says* that Socrates is his mouthpiece, it does not follow that Socrates is *not* his mouthpiece." (Beversluis 2006: 92) However, this constitutes a straightforward argument from silence if it is intended to support the Mouthpiece Interpretation, and as such, must be rejected as logically fallacious. Furthermore, since the Mouthpiece Interpretation makes several claims about how to approach Plato's dialogues beyond what the more minimalist Anti-Mouthpiece Interpretation does, it is the burden of the Mouthpiece Interpretation to support the claim that Socrates or some other character or another in Plato's dialogues is Plato's mouthpiece. And to infer that it is not logically ruled out that Socrates is Plato's mouthpiece is hardly a strong reason to accept that Plato's Socrates speaks for Plato in any philosophically substantive manner. Again, plausible hermeneutical principles must be adduced to justify such a position. Yet no mouthpiece interpreter has ever, to my knowledge, even attempted to state and defend such principles. But unless and until such principles are forthcoming, it is unreasonable (though perhaps not irrational in a limited sense) to accept the Mouthpiece Interpretation. Thus it is problematic to state that "The fact that Plato wrote dialogues and never designates Socrates as his mouthpiece should alert us to the dangers of making straightforward inferences from *what Socrates believes to what Plato believes* as a matter of course, but it need not render us mute for fear of committing some alleged 'fallacy of transparency'." (Beversluis 2006: 97)

Nor is it appropriate to attempt to skirt a reasonable expectation by Socratic interpreters that the author of a dialogue provide an explicit statement as to which character, if any, speaks for the author. Yet this is precisely what we read by some of the staunchest defenders of the Mouthpiece Interpretation:

> However, to demand that Plato issue a statement of that kind, and thereby provide us with the airtight assurance required, we must anachronistically saddle him with the disposition and vocabulary of a contemporary legal bureaucrat writing in such a way as to satisfy the requirements of that premise just in case he intended the Socrates of the dialogues to be understood as speaking in the authorial mode. (Beversluis 2006: 93)

However, in reply to this attempt to evade a reasonable standard of textual interpretation of dialogical writings, especially with regard to ancient writings, it must be pointed out that a standard does not become unreasonable because it is upheld by contemporaries, or that it is a reasonably high standard. What would make it an unreasonable standard of Plato's authorship is if it were impossible to verify or falsify. But in this case it is both verifiable and falsifiable to satisfy such a standard, namely, by the discovery of genuine texts from Plato, whether autographed by him or otherwise reliably transcribed from autographs of Plato, to the effect that this or that character in the dialogues expresses Plato's philosophically substantive beliefs, doctrines or theories. This straightforwardly rebuts the idea that "…the claim that the Platonic corpus does not contain positive doctrine is compatible with *whatever* Plato says (or does not say) and with *whatever* we find (or do not find) in the dialogues. In short, it is textually unfalsifiable." (Beversluis 2006: 95–96) So recognizing that the standard of evidence in this case is high is not the same as showing that it is unreasonably such. Nor is it the same as demonstrating that the said standard is in some way or another inappropriate. *Prima facie*, there is nothing about Plato to the extent that we know him that would prohibit his ability to have provided such evidence. If the *Seventh Letter* is genuine, then there would precisely exist such evidence from Plato himself! So it is not a stretch to think that Plato could have provided such a statement had he desired to do so. As such, the above quoted words seem to serve as an attempt by mouthpiece interpreters to obfuscate the issue and perhaps to even unwarrantedly attempt to shift the burden of proof to Anti-Mouthpiece Interpreters.

Indeed, the burden of proof of mouthpiece interpreters does not shift because some mouthpiece adherents desire it to shift. Each approach to Plato's works must bear its own burden of proof. This will involve the refutation of opposing approaches, constituting negative justification. But it must also, in order to avoid straightforward logical fallacies, provide positive and unrefuted argumentation in favor of its own position. In light of this, the following statement stands as especially logically and epistemically problematic:

> Since no convincing philosophical arguments or compelling textual evidence have been adduced for abandoning dogmatic [mouthpiece] readings of the Platonic dialogues, I conclude that we are justified in continuing to read them as advancing [Plato's] positive doctrine and that recent claims to the effect that non-dogmatist approaches are hermeneutically more defensible and truer to Plato's authorial intentions are unfounded. (Beversluis 2006: 110)

This passage essentially denies the burden of proof that the Mouthpiece Interpretation must bear in order to establish itself as a reasonable approach to Plato's dialogues. Logically and epistemically speaking, even if it were the case, contrary to the argumentation and primary textual evidence adduced herein, that there is inadequate grounding for any version of the Anti-Mouthpiece Interpretation (even for the Socratic Interpretation defended herein), it hardly follows that the Mouthpiece Interpretation is more than weakly justified indeed. And such a lack of epistemic justificatory strength is not adequate to ground the Mouthpiece Interpretation especially when so much is at stake concerning the history of philosophy.

Again, as noted earlier, that Socrates is not just one character among others in Plato's dialogues does nothing to show that he expresses Plato's philosophically substantive beliefs, doctrines or theories. For as one mouthpiece interpreter states of Plato's Socrates: "It is he who determines the topics to be investigated, the methodology to be employed, and the assumptions to be made." (Beversluis 2006: 93) But while all of this might be true,[28] it hardly follows that Socrates "speaks" for Plato, except in these sorts of ways. Yet these do not amount to the far more philosophically substantive beliefs, doctrines or theories that mouthpiece interpreters typically attribute to Plato, as noted earlier. It is one thing to ascribe to Plato a respect for reason and philosophical analysis and an interest *in* the concepts of justice, knowledge, art, education, etc.. It is quite another to attribute to him far more philosophically substantive beliefs, doctrines or theories *of* justice, knowledge, art, education, etc..

While the Socratic Interpretation does not hold that it is logically impossible to find Plato's substantive philosophical views in the Platonic corpus, it insists that without plausible and non-question-begging principles of interpretation to support some version of the Mouthpiece Interpretation, it would appear to be by good fortune rather than by either the intent of Plato or by plausible hermeneutical method that Plato's philosophically substantive beliefs, doctrines or theories would be extracted from the Corpus Platonicum. And while it is plausible to suggest that "Plato's authorial inaccessibility does not follow from the fact that he wrote dialogues" (Beversluis 2006: 94), that he composed dialogues stands as a *prima facie* reason against approaching the dialogues in the manner that mouthpiece interpreters do. So it is the burden, again, of mouthpiece interpreters, given that they take Plato's corpus seriously, to provide unproblematic reasons

---

[28] More precisely, it is the author of the dialogues who "...determines the topics to be investigated, the methodology to be employed, and the assumptions to be made..." So strictly speaking, the quoted claim is false, or at least misleading. It is particularly ironic that a defender of the Mouthpiece Interpretation would make such an erroneous claim since on its own view it is Socrates who "speaks" for Plato.

for their approach, especially in light of the dialogue form in which Plato wrote most of his works.

Generally, primary textual evidence overrides secondary evidence in such cases, but the dialogue form—lacking some plausible theory of interpretation to the contrary—does not appear to lend itself to an unproblematic manner by which to identify Plato's philosophically substantive beliefs, doctrines or theories. And the secondary evidence of Aristotle's testimony has been misused by plenty a mouthpiece interpreter to support the ascription of this or that view to Plato, as noted above. What remains in support of the Mouthpiece Interpretation is not unproblematic, making it reasonable to not accept it unless and until the acceptable level and kind of evidence needed to gain our assent to the Mouthpiece Interpretation is adduced. We must, then, refuse to accept the Mouthpiece Interpretation in that it lacks sufficient rational and textual evidence to ground it as opposed to the competing hypothesis of how to approach Plato: the Socratic Interpretation, which takes the dialogues at their face value and in terms of a plain reading of them.

Once again, my Socratic Interpretation does not reject as logically impossible the finding of Plato's philosophically substantive beliefs, doctrines or theories in the dialogues. Rather, it is a refusal to accept as epistemically justified in an adequate sense the attribution of such beliefs, doctrines or theories to Plato unless and until far superior arguments are brought to bear in support of the Mouthpiece Interpretation. For practical purposes, this may take on the form of a staunch, but tentative, rejection of the Mouthpiece Interpretation, though not absolutely in light of the possibility of such evidence being adduced at some future date.

Thus it is misleading to suggest, as some mouthpiece interpreters do, that mouthpiece interpreters and anti-mouthpiece interpreters come to the Platonic Question with assumptions and that it is a matter of which assumptions "…enable us to arrive at the most coherent and plausible account of the dialogues." (Beversluis 2006: 96) For this attempts to evade the precise burden of argument which is faced alike by the Mouthpiece Interpretation and the Anti-Mouthpiece Interpretation. For as I pointed out above and in *Interpreting Plato's Dialogues*, both the Mouthpiece Interpretation and the Socratic Interpretation share several non-substantive beliefs about Plato and his writings: that Plato is the author of the Thrasyllean collection, that they are mostly dialogues, that there are better and worst ways to interpret them, etc.. But what mouthpiece interpreters believe and what their detractors do not is the notion that, for instance, this or that philosophically substantive belief, doctrine or theory found in the dialogues of Plato is Plato's own. And it need not be the case that such detractors reject such a claim as being impossible to justify. Rather, Socratic interpreters such as myself refrain from accepting such a claim unless and until adequate evidence is adduced to justify our acceptance of it. Or, Socratic interpreters deny, based on the reasons articulated above, that the evidence and arguments for the Mouthpiece Interpretation are currently sufficiently justified to accept. This being the case, it is incorrect to suggest that each position makes assumptions as if each made opposite assumptions relative to the other and that it is necessary to figure out which position held the most plausible approach to Plato's dialogues. Rather, it is that each position shares a number of basic beliefs about the Platonic corpus. But the Mouthpiece Interpretation also makes philosophically substantive attributions to Plato from the informational contents of what Plato wrote, and *that* requires adequate justification in order for reasonable persons to accept. For claims are not innocent until proven guilty, as Thomas Reid believed of certain perceptual beliefs. (Lehrer 2000: 71, 73) But non-perceptual claims are acceptable, rather, when they gain a sufficient degree of acceptability, epistemically speaking. And this general point about epistemic justification applies to the Platonic Question as well as to other areas of philosophical investigation.

Furthermore, "…that Plato did not want to be taken as an authority advancing knowledge-claims needs to be established independently. It does not follow from the mere presence of the 'formal features' in the dialogues." (Beversluis 2006: 105) While this is true, the indisputable fact accepted by both mouthpiece and anti-mouthpiece interpreters alike is that Plato composed most of his works in dialogue form, and this fundamental feature of Plato's works places the burden of proof on anyone who supposes that: (a) Plato intends his dialogues to convey his philosophically substantive beliefs, doctrines or theories; and (b) It is justified to attribute this or that substantive belief, doctrine or theory found therein to Plato. So while the fact that Plato wrote dialogues does not absolutely prohibit such ascriptions to Plato, it makes it difficult for the reasonable interpreter to attribute such ideas to Plato absent a plausible theory of dialogical interpretation which would warrant such attributions to Plato. And this holds true despite "…the fact that the dialogues depict fictitious conversations which take place in fictitious contexts," for it would "not follow that they do not advance positive doctrine" in such instances. (Beversluis 2006: 105)

All in all, many a mouthpiece interpreter has sought to discredit the Anti-Mouthpiece Interpretation by either addressing the most extreme versions of it or by addressing straw man versions of the position. We saw an example of the straw man fallacy in this regard with the writings of Gerson on the topic. But another such example is found in the implied bifurcation regarding the alleged choices with which the Anti-Mouthpiece Interpretation leaves us: either accept the problems with the Mouthpiece Interpretation, or accept that according to the Anti-Mouthpiece Interpretation, "everything is iffy" (Beversluis 2006: 107)[29] when it comes to trying to decipher what Plato wants us to learn or take from the dialogues. But that some anti-mouthpiece interpreters might hold such a position of absolute iffy-ness in Plato's writings[30] is no excuse for ignoring the fact that the Socratic Interpretation as I have articulated it both here and elsewhere holds no such position. Again, Plato obviously commits himself to the values of philosophical argumentation and analysis, and perhaps related methodological considerations. But what the Mouthpiece Interpretation needs to demonstrate is its constant and apparent need to ascribe to Plato a wide array of substantive philosophical beliefs, doctrines or theories such as a theory of forms, a theory of art, a theory of knowledge, etc.. As pointed out earlier, this is the main dispute between the mouthpiece and anti-mouthpiece positions on the Platonic Question. One must not be led astray to lose sight of it.

---

[29] Or, that Plato remained "formally uncommitted" to everything expressed in the dialogues. (Beversluis 2006: 106)

[30] It would seem to me that such a view is self-contradictory. For if everything is iffy in Plato's writings, why would not the view of everything being iffy itself be iffy? Again, this appears to be another attempt by a mouthpiece interpreter to discredit an extreme version of the Anti-Mouthpiece Interpretation by way of refuting a straw man position posing as a view implied by the Anti-Mouthpiece Interpretation.

Are There Not Some Philosophically Substantive Beliefs Which Are Attributable to Plato?

Furthermore, it might be argued that there are several ideas that recur in the dialogues so often that it is hard to believe Plato did not believe them. It is difficult not to imagine that Plato wished his audience to accept certain general principles and beliefs.[31] In reply to this concern, it is important to note that a consequential feature of my refutation of the Mouthpiece Interpretation is that it fails to explain how we might know which views are Plato's and which are not. And this objection seems to fall prey to the same concern. Once again, the Socratic Interpretation does not argue that Plato had no philosophy, or that he had no beliefs. What it holds is that the Mouthpiece Interpretation's attributing from the contents of the dialogues to him philosophically substantive beliefs, theories or dogmas is inadequately founded. For the fact that an idea appears (even several times) in one or more of Plato's dialogues does not justify our ascribing it to him.

Relatedly, it has been suggested that there are some beliefs beyond mere philosophically methodological ones (i.e., philosophically substantive ones) to which Plato obviously subscribes in the dialogues: that the unexamined life is not worth living, that one ought never to requite evil with evil, that nobody does wrong voluntarily and that all wrongdoing is the result of ignorance, that the soul is more important than the body, and that the care of the soul is our most important task, that it is better to suffer injustice than to commit it, etc..[32] But even though I imply that the first of these sayings represents a way of life that Plato is exemplifying through Socrates to his readers (rather than a philosophically substantive belief),[33] there are problems with the ascription of such sayings *qua* beliefs, doctrines or theories (as attractive as some are) to Plato. First, it begs the Platonic Question to insist that these are attributable to Plato in that they are most obviously sayings of Plato's character *Socrates*. And it does no good to infer that an attractive or oft-repeated slogan in the dialogues from the hero of the

---

[31] I owe this point to Gerald Press.
[32] The full list of ten such claims allegedly ascribable to Plato is found in Beversluis (2006: 99).
[33] Corlett (2005: 44).

dialogues belongs to Plato in the sense that Plato sincerely assents to it. One must argue plausibly for such an attribution in order that one not end up committing a fundamental attribution error regarding Plato, as argued earlier. Secondly, why *not* think that Plato wants readers of his dialogues to consider the plausibility of such sayings rather than infer that Plato necessarily believes them? Some may strike us as being more *prima facie* plausible than others. For instance, while it is *prima facie* plausible to think that the unexamined life is not worth living, one might also think that contending with the ignorance and vice that abounds in the world might leave the life examiner rather frustrated indeed. And while some might think that one ought never to return evil for evil, this surely violates principles of desert, responsibility and proportionality in punishment theory. So to accept such a statement on its face is a bit naïve. And surely the claim that nobody commits a wrongdoing voluntarily is problematic. So there is at least some reason to doubt the plausibility of these and perhaps the other claims on the list, making one wonder whether or not Plato places them in the mouth of Socrates or certain other interlocutors in his dialogues as a way to raise critical discussion about them instead of somehow communicating to readers his own philosophically substantive beliefs, doctrines or theories. That they are dubious in some meaningful sense raises the question as to whether or not it is a violation of the Principle of Charity in Interpretation to ascribe them to Plato, or even to Socrates for that matter. So it is far from obvious that such views, no matter how palatable to many, are legitimately attributable to Plato for the above reasons.

It is also problematic to think that my allowing for Plato's likely commitment to methodological matters such as philosophical argumentation and analysis count against the plausibility of the Socratic Interpretation in that it is arbitrary for the Socratic Interpretation to then insist that philosophically substantive beliefs, doctrines or theories are not justifiably attributable to Plato. Why is it justified to attribute the basic method of philosophical argument and analysis to Plato, but not much else? The reason for this is grounded in a basic notion of epistemic justification. If it is true that non-perceptual beliefs are not "innocent until proven guilty," then it is not epistemically justified to accept them absent adequate reasons. Once again, if mouthpiece and Socratic interpreters concur with one another on, say, the matter that

Plato might well be committed to the basics of philosophical argumentation and analysis as they are found throughout most of Plato's works, then it remains the burden of whomever thinks there is something beyond that that is rightly attributable to Plato to prove as much. Recall that my intended interlocutors in this discussion are not those who might be strongly skeptical concerning the Platonic Question, but rather mouthpiece interpreters who already share the belief that if anything in the dialogues is plausibly attributable to Plato, then the basics of philosophical method are. But, as stated earlier, the disputation between mouthpiece interpreters and anti-mouthpiece interpreters of Plato's works is whether or not it is justified to ascribe to Plato various other (substantive) beliefs, doctrines or theories found in the texts. In light of this fact, then, it does not pose a problem for the Socratic Interpretation *in addressing the Mouthpiece Interpretation* to insist on adequate argumentative support for the several attributions they make to Plato far beyond the modest ones I suppose.[34]

Thus the Socratic Interpretation holds that *if* anything in the Corpus Platonicum is legitimately attributable to Plato, then it would include the basics of philosophical method. Beyond that, there are varying degrees of problems facing other attributions to Plato insofar as beliefs, doctrines or theories are concerned. The burden of argument lies with those who seek to ascribe more to Plato than those who might seek to attribute less to him, especially when both parties to the discussion concur on what the party seeking to attribute less to Plato might ascribe to him. This is the gist of my devoting a section of *Interpreting Plato's Dialogues* to the Socratic "method." (Corlett 2005: 44–57)

Thus it is false to assert that "…no convincing philosophical arguments or compelling textual evidence have been adduced for abandoning dogmatist readings of the Platonic dialogues," and it is false to "… conclude that we are justified in continuing to read them as advancing positive doctrine and that recent claims to the effect that non-dogmatist approaches are hermeneutically more defensible and

---

[34] As I state in Corlett (2005: 57): "…the burden of argument is on the mouthpiece interpreters to support their claim that the *dialogues* express, unambiguously, Plato's theories, doctrines, and/or beliefs." Of course, as in several other related contexts, I mean philosophically substantive theories, doctrines or beliefs beyond methodological ones.

truer to Plato's authorial intentions are unfounded." (Beversluis 2006: 110) The first of these claims is false given the plausibility of the preceding lengthy argumentation rebutting considerations in favor of the Mouthpiece Interpretation and against the Anti-Mouthpiece Interpretation. The second claim is dubious in that it does not follow that the Mouthpiece Interpretation serves as the default position on the Platonic Question even if it were true, contrary to fact, that the arguments in favor of the Anti-Mouthpiece Interpretation were unsound. Moreover, all that has been shown to date with regard to the Anti-Mouthpiece Interpretation is that some of the reasoning attempting to ground some "extreme" versions of the Anti-Mouthpiece Interpretation is problematic. But this hardly demonstrates that the Socratic Interpretation, the more plausible and more moderate version of the Anti-Mouthpiece Interpretation, is implausible. So in possibly rendering problematic some versions of the Anti-Mouthpiece Interpretation, it has not been shown that the other versions of the Anti-Mouthpiece Interpretation, such as the Socratic Interpretation, are implausible. Nor does any of this satisfy the burden of proof which the Mouthpiece interpretation bears on its own.

Do Elements of Style Within the Dialogues of Plato Provide Clues to Plato's Beliefs, Doctrines, or Theories?

There are recent attempts by David J. Murphy (2011) and Jay B. Kennedy (2010), respectively, to provide, I take it, apparently philologically novel grounds for the Mouthpiece Interpretation of Plato's works. In the case of Murphy, one might agree with his claim that "the assumption that the dialogue form excludes the author's views is neither empirical nor analytic" may itself be true with regard to Plato and his works and views. However, this in turn hardly justifies the ascription of this or that philosophically substantive belief, doctrine or theory to Plato based on the mere *style* in which Plato writes. And this is true no matter how congruent Plato's style is with some of his contemporaries and some of those subsequent to him who interpreted his body of work! And this holds even if one assumes, as I do, a somewhat coherentist epistemological framework,[35] including principles of interpretive charity, what counts as what kind of evidence (internal or external), etc.. Even if one makes all of these assumptions and further accepts Murphy's evidence of Plato's style, such evidence fails to support the Mouthpiece Interpretation exclusively. For as a Socratic interpreter I can and do accept such evidence, but am not forced by logic to accept the Mouthpiece Interpretation in that such evidence does nothing to rule out the Socratic interpretation of Plato's works. Indeed, Murphy's evidence of Plato's style seems to provide even more reason to adopt the Socratic Interpretation as it more deeply grounds the notion that Plato's dialogical style prohibits readers from deciphering Plato's mind.

Furthermore, Murphy's claim that no one in the fourth century denied that fictional characters can convey their author's views is weak secondary textual support for the claim that the same is true of Plato and his works. That such characters *can* convey their author's views is not the same as providing strong evidence that they *do* reflect their author's views. No one of whom I am aware denies that this or that character in a Platonic dialogue *might* represent Plato's own views. The more interesting claim about the Platonic Question is whether or not they *in fact* do so. And it is this latter point that remains inadequately supported by Murphy's approach to Plato's dialogues.

The same line of reasoning applies, *mutatis mutandus*, to the thesis of Kennedy. His structural argument from the evidence derived from stichometry found in both various authoritative Platonic dialogues and even some spurious dialogues of Plato, while interesting, fails to address what is foundational to the Platonic Question. For it fails to explain how such evidence grounds the Mouthpiece Interpretation's attributions of this or that substantive belief, doctrine or theory to Plato. And this holds even if it were true that this or that ancient Greek poet, for instance, employed the same musical or poetic cadence or overall style found in Plato's works and yet used that style to, one might insist, communicate to readers his own views. For as long as those writers employed the dialogue form as did Plato, the same general arguments that ground the Socratic Interpretation of Plato's dia-

---

[35] More specifically, I adopt something of a coherentist-reliabilist naturalistic epistemic framework in Corlett (1996: Chapters 5–6).

logues would serve as considerable reason to reject any Mouthpiece Interpretation of those other authors. And if one were to insist that the cases in question are significantly dissimilar to one another, then the analogical argument to attempt to ground the Mouthpiece Interpretation of Plato's dialogues on stichometrical evidence is dubious.

My reasoning here is consistent with Debra Nails' point that even if we accept the evidence of structural style of Plato's works as being similar to other works of his day, this is inadequate, textual as it is, to ground the Mouthpiece Interpretation of Plato's dialogues. (Nails 2011) But I would add that this holds regardless of whether it might be shown that Plato's style is perfectly and comprehensively congruent with those of his day.

Again, my reasoning in rejecting the Mouthpiece Interpretation is hardly unfalsifiable. For as with the *Seventh Letter*,[36] it is in principle possible to adduce textual evidence to refute the Socratic Interpretation, as further archeological evidence might uncover a work of Plato's wherein he unproblematically assents to this or that philosophically substantive statement made in his corpus of writings. It is rather that evidence of textual style alone will fail to accomplish this task in light of the fact that Plato's very dialogical style obscures from us his substantive philosophical commitments. Instead, what it will tend to do is to further deepen the philosophical ground on which the Socratic Interpretation rests. Given that it is the dialogical style that Plato

---

[36] For the sake of argument, I grant the questionable status of the *Seventh Letter*, though one ought to consider some of the refutations of the poor arguments from stylometry that are said to disprove the authenticity of the said letter [See, for example, Levinson, et al. (1968); for a critique of this approach, see Deane (1973). For an argument based on the informational contents of the letter that is meant to support its authenticity, see Lewis (2000)]. Of course, it is one thing to challenge the authenticity of the *Seventh Letter*, yet it is quite another to ask whether or not it might be a *reliable* indicator of Plato's mindset nonetheless. [See Guthrie (1975: 8)] So even if it turns out that the *Seventh Letter* is not authentically Plato's but instead written by some of his disciples around the time of Plato's death, then it still might well serve as a secondary confirmation of the Socratic Interpretation, or at least some version of the Anti-Mouthpiece Interpretation, in that of its stark denial that Plato put any of his substantive ideas in writing: *Seventh Letter* 341c, 344c. Perhaps some evidence in favor of its authenticity is both the implausibility of reasons in favor of the Mouthpiece Interpretation, on the one hand, and the plausibility of reasons grounding the Socratic Interpretation, on the other.

adopts that grounds the Socratic Interpretation, the attempt to anchor the Mouthpiece Interpretation in stylistic considerations falls straightaway into the trap awaiting mouthpiece interpreters unless the Mouthpiece Interpretation can be well-established in plausible principles of textual interpretation that would otherwise and uniquely support the Mouthpiece Interpretation in a non-question-begging manner. Yet it is difficult to think of precisely what such principles of interpretation might be. But it is the devising and defending of such principles that is the burden of mouthpiece interpreters given their commitment to attributing this or that philosophically substantive belief, doctrine or theory to Plato.

While it is true that the plausibility of the Anti-Mouthpiece Interpretation, whatever its form, does not follow straightaway from the implausibility of the Mouthpiece Interpretation, it is false of Gerson to assert that "I believe that in the large issue of how to read the Platonic dialogues, the only satisfying refutation of one position is to be found in the cogency of its contrary." (Gerson 2002: 218) For this attempt at a logical sleight of hand ignores the facts that, first, each position bears its own burden of proof in philosophical argumentation regardless of the arguments against or in support of its contrary view, and second, Gerson's assertion notwithstanding, the Mouthpiece Interpretation enjoys no reasonable support insofar as there are seemingly no unproblematic reasons to be offered in its favor. So even if it were true that no Anti-Mouthpiece Interpretational stance enjoyed rational support based, say, on the corpus of Plato's writings, it would not follow that it is reasonable or epistemically justified to adopt the Mouthpiece Interpretation. Thus Gerson's statement is to be rejected.

In the end, arguments from Plato's style, whether stichometric or otherwise, must take account of whatever else is true of Plato's style, including the fact that nowhere does Plato clearly and unproblematically speak in his own name. Of course, this is the very essence of Plato's dialogues insofar as style is concerned. And details of stichometry of whatever kind hardly discount this fact. In fact, they appear to be currently irrelevant to the Platonic Question in that we do not possess autographed copies of Plato's writings. Indeed, as I just indicated, they tend to further support the Socratic Interpretation rather than the Mouthpiece Interpretation. In short, the idea that some aspect of Plato's style somehow reveals his substantive philosophical beliefs, doctrines or theories to his readers seems to already assume the Mouthpiece Interpretation to begin with, further stiffening the already reasonable suspicions of anti-Mouthpiece interpreters that the Mouthpiece Interpretation eventually rests on an unfortunate and viciously question-begging method of approaching Plato's dialogues, namely, that certain words found in Plato's writings are indicative of his own ideas in the sense that Plato believes (sincerely assents to) them.

I take it that the locution "privileged interlocutors" (Murphy 2011) is intended by Murphy to indicate that such interlocutors in Plato's dialogues are privileged in the sense that they have the authority of speaking for Plato on this or that issue. That this is question-begging in an unacceptable way is especially true if my articulations of various themes found in Plato's dialogues can be set forth coherently absent the reliance on any version of the Mouthpiece Interpretation, including this notion of privileged interlocutors in Plato's works.

Nor does the fact that Isocrates and some others take statements in Plato's dialogues as arguments, except in the obvious sense in which those authors ascribed such views to Plato, justify the Mouthpiece Interpretation. But the point of my investigation of the Platonic Question is to establish through solid argumentation just how trustworthy such secondary sources are in interpreting Plato's dialogues. Noting their take on Plato's dialogical characters does not serve as an adequate argument for the Mouthpiece answer to the Platonic Question itself absent more impressive textual evidence from Plato himself. Murphy admits as much. (Murphy 2011) However, we still lack a literary theory replete with hermeneutical principles that would justify attributions of a character's statement in Plato's dialogues to Plato more than secondary source evidence can hope to justify. One reason why this is the case is because of the plausibility of Paul Grice's theory of meaning according to which authorial or speaker's intent (in this case, Plato's) is essential in discerning linguistic meaning. (Grice 1971) But insofar as we lack a credible means by which to understand Plato's meaning except for the naïve and question-begging assumption employed by many devotees of the Mouthpiece Interpretation, we are left at this point of time with no unproblematic evidence of Plato's intended meaning without which the ascription of any character's words in Plato's dialogues constitutes a fundamental attribution error.[37]

Those who seek to attribute a substantive claim to this or that speaker or author bear the burden of argument in demonstrating that such an attribution is reasonable, all relevant things considered. In the case of the Platonic Question, neither Murphy nor Kennedy has adduced sufficient evidence to ground the Mouthpiece Interpretation concerning Plato's corpus of writings. And it is unreasonable to accept the Mouthpiece Interpretation unless and until plausible evidence is provided on its behalf.

As noted above, it might be argued that the Socratic Interpretation is self-contradictory in that it argues that Plato's dialogical style prevents readers from deciphering his beliefs, doctrines or theories, yet it simultaneously claims Plato's commitment to the basics of logical argumentation and philosophical analysis. In further reply to this criticism, however, it must be pointed out that the texts of Plato, though dialogical, make clear a commitment to logical argumentation and philosophical analysis in virtually every one of his dialogues with the exception, for instance, of the creation myth in the *Timaeus* and certain sections of the *Laws*, the *Crito* and elsewhere wherein lengthy speeches are found.[38] The fact is that no one of whom I am aware would deny that philosophical argumentation and analysis are prevalent throughout Plato's works, so much so that perhaps only an extreme skeptic would deny Plato's commitment to them at least in some general sense as I suppose. And while it is possible that Plato's general point in his writings is to demonstrate the futility of philosophical reasoning, even that thesis requires, it appears, a commitment on Plato's behalf to the utility of philosophical reasoning in order to prove its ultimate futility! Thus even an extreme skeptical position on Plato's motive for composing the dialogues requires a commitment to the utility of philosophical argumentation and analysis. So it seems safe to conclude that it is unproblematic to attribute to Plato at least a commitment to basic analytical philosophical

---

[37] For psychological discussions of attribution theory, see Fiske and Taylor (1991: Chapters 2–4).

[38] Even in such speeches, however, we often find the employment of the basics of philosophical argument and analysis.

method.[39] I assume that this minimal philosophical attribution to the author of the corpus in question is reasonable.

The Socratic Interpretation, I shall argue, remains intact, withstanding the various concerns raised about it. However, the same cannot be said of the Mouthpiece Interpretation. Regardless of which permutation it might assume, the Mouthpiece Interpretation faces what appear to be insurmountable problems. It seems to either require of evidence an unacceptable degree of question-begging, or it fails to adduce primary textual evidence that can be coherently and otherwise plausibly interpreted to support only the Mouthpiece Interpretation. Since everyone but perhaps the extreme skeptic concurs that the fundamentals of philosophical argument and analysis are exemplified throughout most of Plato's works, it remains the burden of mouthpiece interpreters to provide substantially better evidence for the acceptance of their view that Plato actually communicates his own more substantive beliefs, doctrines or theories in his dialogues. For the Socratic Interpretation does not deny that Plato was a philosopher who employed philosophical method in his brilliant works. Nor does it disagree with the evidence of the *Seventh Letter* 345b wherein the author, perhaps Plato, refers to "my teachings," indicating (if Plato is indeed its author) that Plato had teachings. However, even here it is unclear whether or not such teachings amount to substantive beliefs, doctrines or theories above and beyond the methodological ones mentioned above. Yet if we accept the authenticity of the *Seventh Letter*, then we must also recall that it is precisely that source that clearly states that Plato does *not* express his own views in his dialogues. For we must remember that of important philosophical investigations and truths, the author of the *Seventh Letter* 340c writes: "There is no writing of mine about these matters, nor will there ever be one." Once again, that Plato had views does not entitle readers to ascribe to Plato anything in what we consider to be Plato's writings. Nor does it justify our reading into such writings what we think, via Aristotle or another, constitute Plato's views.

What the Socratic Interpretation refuses to accept pending plausible argument to the contrary is the insistence of the Mouthpiece Interpretation on the idea that Plato holds more philosophically sub-

---

[39] More shall be argued about this matter below.

stantive beliefs, doctrines or theories that he seeks to convey to his readers. The Socratic Interpretation and the Mouthpiece Interpretation agree on Plato's commitment to the basics of philosophical method. However, regarding more philosophically substantive beliefs, doctrines or theories putatively held by Plato, that burden of argument belongs to mouthpiece interpreters alone. It is not, contrary to what some mouthpiece interpreters insist, the burden of the anti-mouthpiece interpreters to prove what has yet to be proven, namely, that Plato's beliefs, doctrines or theories can be found in Plato's dialogues. That would amount to requiring such interpreters of Plato's dialogues proof of what such interpreters have inadequate reason to confirm!

It is one thing to be an aporetic philosopher like Plato in the sense of his investigating many a problem without final results. But it is quite another thing to be one who is said to expound one's own beliefs, doctrines or theories mostly in the guise of dialogues. That is a central tenet of the Mouthpiece Interpretation that has yet to withstand philosophical scrutiny insofar as it refers to Plato as being exactly *that* kind of thinker.

Murphy states that his "reasons for believing that Plato expresses his views through characters' words include: the argumentative structure of the dialogues; recurrence of and harmony among a set of conclusions expressed in universal—thus, context-independent—terms (e.g. it is better to suffer injustice than to commit it, the just person is happier than the unjust, etc.); dominance of leading interlocutors' arguments and claims, and indeed, heroic role of Socrates;..." But the argumentative structure of the dialogues also supports the Socratic Interpretation's insistence that the main purpose of Plato's composing dialogues was to engage readers in the process of philosophical dialectic as an example of the best way to attempt to discover wisdom. Moreover, that there are some claims that appear context-independently sound is insufficient reason to think that Plato did not want his readers to test them thoroughly, as they might not be as sound as they appear upon deeper inspection. Thus this evidence can be used to support the Socratic Interpretation also. Furthermore, that some characters appear to make dominant claims throughout Plato's dialogues is also evidence for the Socratic Interpretation's claim that philosophical dialectic involves wisdom-seeking critical reason wherein some views are shown to be unsound, and why. But this at best points to some negative views of Plato, for example, that in the *Theaetetus* he might, as does Socrates, hold that justified true belief is insufficient for knowledge. But this says nothing positive and substantial about what Plato took knowledge to be, contrary to Christopher Bobonich's claims that Plato had an epistemology, among other theories. (Bobonich 2008) That Socrates is the clear hero of most of the dialogues supports the Socratic Interpretation's idea that it is Socrates and his method of dialectic that most influences Plato's philosophical method, as exhibited in Plato's choice of the dialogue form itself. Thus it is unclear that Murphy's reasons for the Mouthpiece Interpretation are adequate as they can either be used to support the Socratic Interpretation, or they are problematic in the ways that I suggested earlier.

My general point of argument here is not that the Socratic Interpretation has answered all there is to answer about problems related to the Platonic Question. It is, rather, that in light of the implausibility of the Mouthpiece Interpretation and in light of the lack of telling objections to the Socratic Interpretation, it is more reasonable to accept the Socratic Interpretation as the least problematic of all competing approaches to Plato's works.[40] Just as in legal interpretation there is an all relevant things considered best interpretation of law, there is an all relevant things considered best approach to Plato's works. Given the arguments provided thus far by a host of leading contemporary philosophers of Plato, it is evident that there is better reason to accept the Socratic Interpretation over the Mouthpiece Interpretation and that one is epistemically more justified in accepting the Socratic Interpretation than the Mouthpiece Interpretation. This is the conclusion reached in *Interpreting Plato's Dialogues* subsequent to the examination of a host of arguments provided in favor of the Mouthpiece Interpretation and against certain versions of the Anti-Mouthpiece Interpretation, and it is the same conclusion reached herein based not only on the results of that previous critical examination of those arguments, but on the basis of this examination of different and newer arguments raised in favor of the Mouthpiece Interpretation and against certain versions of the Anti-Mouthpiece Interpretation. Again, it is not logically impossible for one to extract Plato's philo-

---

[40] For replies to a host of other concerns with the Socratic Interpretation, or views roughly akin to it, see Corlett (2005: 57–65).

sophically substantive beliefs, doctrines or theories from his dialogues. But based on the arguments considered in favor of such a task, and against some competing approaches to Plato's writings, the Mouthpiece Interpretation does not seem promising. There is seemingly no unproblematic argument in its favor, and no piece of uncontroversial and plausible evidence that counts exclusively in its favor. Thus there is good reason to not accept the Mouthpiece Interpretation as an adequately epistemically justified approach to Plato's dialogues.

In conclusion, I have argued that in light of the implausibility of the Mouthpiece Interpretation, and given that the Socratic Interpretation evades each of the objections raised to it, the Socratic Interpretation is significantly more plausible than the Mouthpiece Interpretation. I have warded-off various criticisms of the Socratic Interpretation. But it is important to point out that attempting to refute the Socratic Interpretation will do little or nothing to rescue the Mouthpiece Interpretation from the numerous difficulties it faces. In light of the problematic arguments given in favor of the Mouthpiece Interpretation, and given the poor arguments provided against the Anti-Mouthpiece Interpretation, the Socratic Anti-Mouthpiece Interpretation remains as a plausible contender for our serious consideration regarding the best answer to the Platonic Question. If this is true, then it is inadequately justified to attribute to Plato any philosophically substantive beliefs, doctrines or theories found in his dialogues.

In the following chapter, I shall consider whether or not it is justified to attribute the alleged philosophy of Plato's Socrates to either the historical Socrates, or even to Plato's Socrates. In subsequent chapters, I shall explicate what Socrates and some others state about justice concepts in order to provide further positive evidence in favor of the Socratic Interpretation in terms of how a Socratic interpreter might approach Plato's dialogues.

References

Annas, Julia. 1981. *An introduction to Plato's Republic*. Oxford: Oxford University Press.
———. 2006. Ethics and argument in Plato's Socrates. In *The virtuous life in Greek ethics*, ed. B. Reis, 32–46. Cambridge: Cambridge University Press.

Beversluis, John. 2006. A defence of dogmatism in the interpretation of Plato. In *Oxford Studies in Ancient Philosophy*, ed. David Sedley, vol. 31, 85–112. Oxford: Oxford University Press.

Bobonich, Christopher. 2008. Plato's politics. In *The Oxford handbook of Plato*, ed. Gail Fine, 311–335. Oxford: Oxford University Press.

Burnyeat, Myles, and Michael Frede. 2015. *The pseudo-Platonic Seventh Letter*, ed. Dominic Scott. Oxford: Oxford University Press.

Cherniss, Harold. 1945. *The riddle of the early academy*. Berkeley: University of California Press.

———. 1962. *Aristotle's criticism of Plato and the academy*. New York: Russell & Russell.

Corlett, J. Angelo. 1996. *Analyzing social knowledge*. Totowa: Rowman & Littlefield Publishers.

———. 2005. *Interpreting Plato's dialogues*. Las Vegas: Parmenides Publishing.

Deane, P. 1973. Stylometrics do not exclude the *Seventh Letter*. *Mind* 82: 113–117.

Fiske, Susan T., and Shelley E. Taylor. 1991. *Social cognition*. 2nd ed. New York: McGraw-Hill.

Gerson, Lloyd. 2000. Plato *Absconditus*. In *Who speaks for Plato?* ed. Gerald Press, 201–210. Lanham: Rowman & Littlefield Publishers.

———. 2002. *Elenchos*, Protreptic, and Platonic philosophizing. In *Does Socrates have a method?* ed. G.A. Scott, 217–231. University Park: Pennsylvania State University Press.

———. 2005. What is Platonism? *Journal of the History of Philosophy* 43: 253–276.

Goodspeed, E.J. 1916. *The story of the new testament*. Chicago: University of Chicago Press.

Grant, F.C. 1933. *The growth of the gospels*. New York: Abingdon Press.

Grant, M. 1977. *Jesus: An historian's review of the gospels*. New York: Charles Scribner's Sons.

Grice, Paul. 1971. Meaning. In *Philosophy of language*, ed. Jay Rosenberg and Charles Travis, 436–444. Englewood Cliffs: Prentice-Hall.

Guthrie, W.K.C. 1975. *A history of Greek philosophy: Plato: The man and his dialogues*. Cambridge: Cambridge University Press.

Irwin, Terence. 1995. *Plato's ethics*. Oxford: Oxford University Press.

———. 2008. The Platonic corpus. In *The Oxford handbook of Plato*, ed. Gail Fine, 63–87. Oxford: Oxford University Press.

Kennedy, J.B. 2010. Plato's forms, Pythagorean mathematics, and Stichometry. *Aperion* 43: 1–30.

Koester, Helmut. 1990. *Ancient Christian gospels: Their history and development*. London: SCM Press.

Lehrer, Keith. 2000. *Theory of knowledge*. 2nd ed. Boulder: Westview Press.

Levinson, M., A.Q. Morton, and A.D. Winspear. 1968. The Seventh Letter of Plato. *Mind* 77: 309–325.

References

Lewis, V.B. 2000. The rhetoric of philosophical politics in Plato's *Seventh Letter*. *Philosophy & Rhetoric* 33: 23–38.

McCabe, M.M. 2008. "Plato's ways of writing," In *The Oxford handbook of Plato*, ed. Gail Fine, 88–113. Oxford: Oxford University Press.

Mulhern, John J. 1971. Two interpretive fallacies. *Systematics* 9: 168–172.

———. 2011. Plato's putative mouthpiece and ancient authorial practice: A reply. Presented at the Society for Ancient Greek Philosophy, Fordham University, 17 October 2011.

Murphy, David. 2011. 'A certain Socrates swinging around there and claiming…' Characters' Utterances and authors' views in Plato's practice. Presented at the Society for Ancient Greek Philosophy, Fordham University, 22 October 2011.

Nails, Debra. 1995. *Agora, academy, and the conduct of philosophy*. Dordrecht: Kluwer Academic Publishers.

———. 2011. The structures of Plato's dialogues. Presented at the Society for Ancient Greek Philosophy, Fordham University, 22 October 2011.

Press, Gerald, ed. 2000. *Who speaks for Plato?* Lanham: Rowman & Littlefield Publishers.

Reshotko, N. 2006. *Socratic virtue*. Cambridge: Cambridge University Press.

Rowe, Christopher. 2006. Interpreting Plato. In *A companion to Plato*, ed. Hugh Benson, 13–24. London: Blackwell Publishing.

Shields, Christopher. 2008. Plato and Aristotle in the academy. In *The Oxford handbook of Plato*, ed. Gail Fine, 504–525. Oxford: Oxford University Press.

Streeter, B.H. 1924. *The four gospels: A study of origins*. London: MacMillan and Company Limited.

Taylor, A.E. 1963. *Plato: The man and his work*. London: Methuen & Co., LTD.

Chapter 4
In Defense of Socratic Studies

Having in the previous chapters provided a discussion of the Platonic Question, and having rendered problematic the claim that it is plausible to accept the Mouthpiece Interpretation according to which it is reasonable to attribute certain philosophically substantive beliefs, doctrines or theories to Plato, it is important to discuss a related problem in Socratic and Plato studies. "The Socratic Question," as I refer to it, asks whether or not it is justified to attribute to either the historical Socrates or the character Socrates (Plato's Socrates) any proposition of philosophical substance found in Plato's dialogues. The Socratic Question encompasses what has come to be known as the Socratic Problem, which is the difficulty in discovering which, if any, account of Socrates is historically accurate, or most accurate. Here the leading candidates are accounts of Socrates found in Aristophanes, Plato, and Xenophon.[1]

There are many possible positions that might be taken on the Socratic Question. One is that it is justified to attribute to the historical Socrates every proposition or phrase that Plato puts in Socrates' mouth in the dialogues. This might be called the "Maximal Literalist Interpretation." Secondly, one might hold that it is justified to ascribe to the historical Socrates many propositions or phrases that Plato places in his mouth throughout the dialogues. I shall refer to this as the "Moderate Literalist Interpretation." The "Minimalist Literalist Interpretation," by contrast, holds that it is justified to attribute to the

---

[1] On the Socratic Problem, see Guthrie (1969: 6); Nails (1995: Chapter 2).

© Springer International Publishing AG, part of Springer Nature 2018
J. A. Corlett, *Interpreting Plato Socratically*,
https://doi.org/10.1007/978-3-319-77320-9_4

historical Socrates relatively few such assertions and phrases. The difficulty with each of these views is that Plato's selection of the dialogue form itself tends to make it problematic to discern which, if any, such claims and phrases can be attributed to the historical Socrates with any reasonable degree of confidence. Perhaps this is why it is unusual to find a scholar who takes a literalist line on this matter, except for those who make the assumption that one or another of these positions is plausible. But to argue in favor of one of these approaches is to find oneself facing a paucity of textual evidence to support one's view.

Instead, many scholars tend to adopt what might be called a "Non-Literalist Interpretation" of the Socratic Question, arguing that whatever might be attributable to anyone from the informational contents of the Platonic corpus is ascribable to the character Socrates, not to the historical Socrates. And this position might take on maximal, moderate, and minimalist permutations. The "Maximal Non-Literal Interpretation" states that all of what Plato puts in the mouth of Socrates is attributable to the character Socrates, while the "Moderate Non-Literalist Interpretation" holds that many propositions Plato's places in Socrates' mouth belong to the character Socrates, while the "Minimalist Non-Literalist Interpretation" claims that few of the words that Plato puts in Socrates mouth belong to the character Socrates.

While it is obvious why someone might hold one or the other of the non-literalist interpretations regarding the Socratic Question, it is unclear why one might choose to deny both the literalist and non-literalist stances. One reason why one might be reluctant to accept even a non-literalist interpretation as described is that, consonant with *Charmides* 161c, it does not matter for Plato's purposes in composing the dialogues whether or not anyone in particular believes this or that claim found therein. A proponent of an Anti-Mouthpiece Interpretation described in the previous chapters might take precisely such a stand, though she might instead hold, congruent with the Socratic Interpretation of the Platonic Question as described in the previous chapter, to the Minimalist Non-Literalist Interpretation in that there seems to be a straightforward employment of basic philosophical method by the character Socrates, and apparently even by Plato when he writes the dialogues. The values of philosophical argumentation and analysis are transparent throughout Plato's dialogues. In fact, one might even argue that they are their main features, e.g., what is "on display" for readers. In any case, it behooves one who is serious about arriving at a plausible answer to the Platonic Question to also consider the Socratic Question, especially if it turns out that the Mouthpiece Interpretation is a poor answer indeed to the former. So if the words put in Socrates' mouth by Plato are not plausibly attributable to Plato, then are they plausibly ascribable to Socrates? And if it is problematic due to lack of sufficient textual evidence to attribute the words of Plato's Socrates to the historical Socrates, is it even justified to ascribe them to the character Socrates?

Thomas C. Brickhouse and Nicholas D. Smith argue in defense of what they refer to as "Socratic studies," a way of approaching Plato's dialogues such that an interpretation of "Socratic philosophy" or "the philosophy of Socrates" is articulated and examined. In part, theirs is a response to Charles Kahn, who they report as arguing that scholars should give up discussion of "Socratic philosophy" altogether. (Brickhouse and Smith 2010: 11) Brickhouse and Smith seek to undermine this claim. I will argue that, Kahn's proclamation aside, Brickhouse and Smith do not fully succeed in defending their version of "Socratic studies." In explaining why this is so, I shall set forth a more moderate stance on Socratic studies, one that does not fall prey to the concerns facing the position of Brickhouse and Smith.

The Case for "Socratic Studies"

Brickhouse and Smith "propose to offer a new interpretation of a central aspect of the philosophy of Socrates. This project, plainly, presumes that there is something to which 'the philosophy of Socrates' refers." (Brickhouse and Smith 2010: 11) They clarify that they use "the philosophy of Socrates" and "Socratic philosophy" synonymously, and that by these locutions they do not mean to ascribe beliefs of views found in Plato's dialogues to the historical Socrates, but to the character Socrates in some of Plato's works. (Brickhouse and Smith 2010: 16–17) While I concur with the basics of their view here, I shall raise concerns about how they arrive at their position. I believe that the reasons they offer in favor of the field of Socratic studies are fraught with difficulties.

Brickhouse and Smith defend their version of Socratic studies in part by defending what they call the "identity principle" and the "relevant dialogues assumption." The identity principle states that "Socrates is the same character, with essentially the same philosophical views, in each of a certain group of dialogues by Plato." (Brickhouse and Smith 2010: 13) They clarify their position by affirming what they refer to as the "Philosophical Identity Thesis," namely, that "'the philosophy of Socrates' or 'Socratic philosophy' is identical to the philosophy given to Socrates [the character] in the relevant group of Platonic dialogues." (Brickhouse and Smith 2010: 17) They are careful to distinguish their view from the "Journalistic Historical Identity Thesis" which states that, "in the relevant group of dialogues, in every detail of word, deed, and description, Plato has attempted to present a precisely accurate portrait of the historical Socrates." (Brickhouse and Smith 2010: 14) However, there are problems facing the Philosophical Identity Thesis.

As articulated by Brickhouse and Smith, the identity principle is agreeable. But some of the reasons provided in favor of the Philosophical Identity Thesis that is intended to clarify or support the identity principle are problematic. While it is incorrect, strictly speaking, to construe the locutions "the philosophy of Socrates" and "Socratic philosophy" similarly, this is not a major problem for Brickhouse and Smith given their clarification that it is not the historical Socrates to whom they ascribe any beliefs or views.[2]

In response to the Brickhouse and Smith defense of Socratic studies, it might be argued that it is not that nothing in Plato's dialogues

---

[2] The philosophy of Socrates is not the same as a Socratic philosophy. For while a Socratic philosophy is inclusive of Socrates' philosophy (whatever that is), Socrates' philosophy need not include each of the features of a Socratic philosophy. For the latter only endorses enough of what Socrates believes (whatever that is) to be rightly classified as "Socrat*ic*," where "Socratic" refers to that claim or view that at least approximately reflects the content of what Socrates communicates in the Platonic corpus. So, strictly speaking, it amounts to an equivocation by Brickhouse and Smith to use "the philosophy of Socrates" and "Socratic philosophy" synonymously. The latter seems to be a more general category that can include but also go beyond whatever Plato's character Socrates believes.

can be understood, or that nothing in his dialogues that is placed in the mouth of Socrates is able to be understood. Rather, it is that the dialogue form itself prohibits readers from discerning what of philosophical substance can be ascribed to Plato's Socrates (the character) with any meaningful degree of confidence, with the exception of a certain method of reasoning, along with certain arguments and analyses. The fundamentally *aporetic* nature of Plato's dialogues, to one degree or another of the "relevant ones," speaks against their attempt to decipher to what of philosophical substance Socrates assents, making it overly difficult to construct anything but a loosely Socratic *philosophy* of this or that. This is not to say that Plato's Socrates cannot be said to, say, believe in the importance of reasoning and other such basic ideas. Rather, it is that it is unjustified to ascribe to the character Socrates philosophically substantive beliefs, doctrines, or theories such as a theory of forms, a theory of art, a theory of language, etc.. Even considering the fact that Brickhouse and Smith have delimited their position to one of ascribing certain beliefs or views to the character Socrates, the dialogue form itself does not justify the attribution of such beliefs or views even to Socrates' character therein. This is true despite aspects of conversational implicature in some of Plato's dialogues. In the end, what we can be confident about is the attribution to the character Socrates the *philosophical examination of certain issues and his commitment to basic philosophical method of argument and analysis*. But these are not the same things as ascribing to that character certain beliefs or views that Plato has placed in Socrates' mouth, as Brickhouse and Smith insist.

Now Brickhouse and Smith might reply that not all dialogues are aporetic in a strong sense—e.g. *Crito*, and that it is not the case that Socrates never argues *for* anything, or makes positive claims within his arguments *against* other things. From an *aporia* taken by itself it is admittedly difficult to draw positive conclusions, they might argue. However, these can be supplied from the many commitments and positive claims that Socrates makes along the way.

But even if a Socratic philosophy is said to exist, constructed from Plato's dialogues, it cannot with justified confidence be asserted that it belongs to the character Socrates in the sense that it represents his philosophically substantive beliefs and views. The reason for this, again, is that the dialogue form Plato selected does not permit readers to tease out a difference between Socrates' investigation of a philosophical problem versus his development of this or that aspect of his "philosophy" of this or that beyond perhaps methodological considerations. Whether or not one is licensed to take Plato's Socrates at his word, it matters what this might amount to. If by this it is meant that we can be justified in attributing to Socrates this or that belief or view, this is unclear because of the reasons given above. Brickhouse and Smith clarify their assumption that what is placed in Socrates' mouth by Plato is what Socrates believed or held as they do. (Brickhouse and Smith 2010: 16–17) But this begs the question as to whether or not such ascriptions are justified in more than some minimal sense.

While Brickhouse and Smith do not subscribe to a crude version of the Socratic Mouthpiece Interpretation which states that the words placed in the character Socrates' mouth by Plato truly represent in part what the historical Socrates believed, amounting to his views on a range of topics, they do assert that "…there is a philosophy worth trying to interpret and study contained and expressed by Socrates in the relevant Platonic dialogues and that this is distinguishable from the philosophy we find in other Platonic dialogues not included in the 'Socratic' group." (Brickhouse and Smith 2010: 16) What I challenge is the claim that there is a substantive *philosophy* or set of substantive philosophical beliefs in any of the Platonic dialogues that can be confidently and justifiably ascribed to even the character Socrates.

Brickhouse and Smith do not define what counts as a "philosophy." I assume what they mean is something of a set of beliefs or a viewpoint, a set of philosophically substantive propositions to which Plato's Socrates sincerely assents and accepts in the higher-order deliberative sense. Brickhouse and Smith "believe that Plato's Socrates is portrayed as holding certain *views*; these may come together into something more like a theory, or they may form enough of a pattern that we are prepared to explain the pattern they form as indications of a broader theory of some sort. Whether we wish to attribute *views or theories* to Socrates would depend on the nature of the textual evidence."[3] But what the reader of Plato's dialogues finds in Socrates' discussions are incisive dialogues about various important topics the contents of which hardly amount to, say, treatises wherein it is straight-

---

[3] Written correspondence from Nicholas D. Smith on 21 July 2010.

forward to know what the author's or character's intentional states were vis-à-vis what is said in the dialogues by Socrates. This is not the same as hyperbolically implying that we cannot ever know what any dialogical figure meant or believed by anything. However, Plato's use of the dialogue form conceals from readers the knowing with any reasonable confidence what Plato or Socrates or any other Platonic character believes about philosophically substantive matters. And if such beliefs are not manifest to us by way of the dialogues of Plato, then there seems to be no reason to have confidence that we can discover "the beliefs of Socrates," though perhaps we can have some degree of justified confidence in rationally reconstructing a Socrat*ic* philosophy which is based on what is ascribed to Socrates by Plato. By this it is not meant to convey what Brickhouse and Smith insist, namely, that we can take Plato's Socrates at his word and that he believes what he says (for the most part) in at least some of Plato's dialogues. Rather, it is that whatever is found in the "mouth" of Socrates in Plato's dialogues can be said to be Socratic in a looser sense, without the presumption that even the character Socrates believes what he argues therein or has a view about the topic under discussion. In this way, what is either Socratic or Platonic is congruent with what is found in the corpus of Plato's works in terms of the *philosophizing* that occurs therein.

For instance, a study of Plato's *Theaetetus* shows that Socrates investigates what has since been dubbed the traditional justified true belief analysis of human propositional knowledge. Argument after argument, Socrates eventually gets his interlocutors to accept the fact that these conditions are not sufficient for knowledge. But what we do not find in Plato's dialogue is Socrates' holding to a certain theory of knowledge (foundationalist, coherentist, externalist, etc.) or even a belief about it. Why not? That Socrates uses an argument to refute a point here or there does not imply that he believes that point, as he might be arguing *ad hominem*, assuming certain claims that his interlocutors accept for the sake of discussion in order to demonstrate the difficulties with the beliefs that they articulate. The same can be said for Socrates' discussion of justice in Plato's *Republic*, or his discussion of mimetic art in the same dialogue, and his discussion of love in the *Symposium*, etc.. There and elsewhere are found discussions of various issues and topics, but this does not entitle one to presume, as

Brickhouse and Smith appear to do, that we can take Plato's Socrates at his word in the sense that he believes what he says in the dialogues. For while this is a possibility, it is just as possible that Socrates is arguing *ad hominem*, making certain assumptions for the sake of argument. Plato's choice of the dialogue form makes it too difficult for one to infer with any meaningful degree of non-question-begging and justified confidence what Socrates believes therein.

One of the arguments given by Brickhouse and Smith for the reasonableness of their version of Socratic studies is the "very robustness" of Socratic studies. (Brickhouse and Smith 2010: 17–18) I take it that by this they mean that much has been gained over the centuries by way of Socratic studies that it itself is not threatened by certain objections to the very idea of attempting to build what Brickhouse and Smith and other experts on Socrates are attempting to build.[4] However, it will not do for Brickhouse and Smith to reply, as they do, that their principles "…are justified precisely because that scholarly work meets the standards required of a successful research program: again, the standards met when an inquiry results in 'an interesting or useful larger system of knowledge or information'" (Brickhouse and Smith 2010: 39) and "Even if the skeptics can plausibly show that the claims made in these foundational principles do not pass the high evidentiary standards of critical inquiry all on their own, the principles enjoy further support from the research program they motivate." (Brickhouse and Smith 2010: 40) For again, the fact that many astute scholars have attempted to articulate, complete with primary textual evidence from Plato's dialogues themselves, "the philosophy of Socrates" is a questionable reason to think that what they are engaged in is unproblematic in light of the points made above. While appeals to authority are often unproblematic, their appeal to such authorities must withstand the points of criticism of precisely the interpretive tradition in question. That a dominant group of scholars supports X does not mean that X is plausible—no matter how astute and distinguished those scholars might be. This has been proven to be the case beyond reasonable doubt with respect to the Mouthpiece Interpretation concerning the Platonic Question (see the previous chapters of this book). History is

---

[4] In their own words, Brickhouse and Smith state that on the basis of the principles they have articulated, "a very substantial body of research has been produced." (Brickhouse and Smith 2010: 39)

replete with examples of cases wherein the majority of experts in a field do not see that the path they have chosen is implausible or problematic. I for one find the "Socratic studies" scholars' works to be informative and incisive, assuming that they are sufficiently responsible to admit what Brickhouse and Smith admit: namely, that they are *presuming* that there is a Socratic philosophy in the pages of Plato's works, that is, that we can take Socrates at his word in the sense that Socrates believes what he says and that it is possible to construct a view of Socrates that is roughly Socratic.

In closing their defense of Socratic studies, Brickhouse and Smith write:

> For critics to provide adequate grounds for ending Socratic studies, accordingly, they must be prepared not just to cast doubt on its foundational principles. Either they must disprove such principles decisively, or explain why the research founded on such principles is so without value or promise of such as not to be worth pursuing or refining, or else they must provide a way of understanding Plato's writings that makes better sense of them than Socratic studies does. (Brickhouse and Smith 2010: 41)

Brickhouse and Smith are correct to state that to win the battle of how to interpret Plato's dialogues one must win the war on how to approach them. But this requires more than refuting the arguments of the Brickhouse and Smith interpreters. It also involves setting forth and defending a plausible alternative approach to the dialogues. However, they present a false dilemma.

I am not sure what exactly counts as a decisive disproof of something. However, I believe that I have rendered their Philosophical Identity Thesis sufficiently problematic by exposing that Brickhouse and Smith have not met their burden of argument in support of the idea that the dialogue form Plato's uses even permits one to confidently extract the character Socrates' philosophy from Plato's works. Nor must one choose the way of explaining why the research founded on Brickhouse and Smith's principles is so without value or promise of such as not to be worth pursuing or refining, as that would be plainly disingenuous and inconsiderate of the contrary fact that Socratic studies has been a rather immensely informative enterprise. Indeed, that an interpretive approach to Plato is problematic hardly implies that it has nothing much to inform us about the content of Plato's writings. Rather, what can be done is to provide at least an alternative picture of how to approach Plato's dialogues, explaining why it is overly problematic to think that one can discern the philosophy of Socrates from it. It is to this task that I shall turn shortly in reply to Brickhouse and Smith's challenge.

Brickhouse and Smith further argue that "We have long conceded that we cannot be sure whether the philosophical views we expose and explicate really do belong to the historical Socrates, which is the only concession the anti-historicists can claim their own arguments merit." (Brickhouse and Smith 2010: 39–40) Indeed, in *Plato's Socrates*, they write:

> We do not, in this book, intend to answer the question of whose philosophy we are actually interpreting. The title, *Plato's Socrates*, reflects that it is Plato's portrait of Socrates we wish to explore. In some sense or senses the philosophy we are attempting to bring to light is both Platonic *and* Socratic: Platonic at least insofar as Plato is the author of those texts in which this philosophy is expressed, developed, and explained, and Socratic because it is the character, Socrates, whose words this philosophy motivates and expresses. It might be a philosophy that both Socrates and Plato accepted, at some time or times in their lives. It might be one that neither ever—or fully ever—accepted. We claim only that a distinct philosophy can be found consistently portrayed as Socrates' in Plato's early dialogues, and that the philosophy so portrayed is itself consistent. Both of these claims have been matters of controversy. We hope our book provides some additional ground for accepting both claims. (Brickhouse and Smith 1994: viii)

If what they state in the Preface to *Plato's Socrates* is their true intent, and I believe it is, then why the ambiguous and misleading language about "the philosophy of Socrates" instead of something akin to the "beliefs of Plato's Socrates"? And why is the language of Socrates' "doctrines" (Brickhouse and Smith 2010: 33) or beliefs so prevalent throughout most of those working in Socratic studies? This is especially the case insofar as "doctrines" commonly means something akin to "deeply held beliefs." If it is difficult enough to discern the character Socrates' beliefs that make up his "philosophy," how much more problematic is it to determine which of those constitute his doctrines or theories? Yet Brickhouse and Smith provide no account as to whether or not there are meaningful differences between these categories ascribed by them (and so many others) to the character Socrates. Instead, why not use the locution, "Socratic philosophy" without the frequent use of "the philosophy of Socrates"? This alternative usage is consistent with their remarks, quoted above, and evades the problem of confusing what philosophy might be based on much of what Plato places in Socrates' mouth with "the philosophy of Socrates," consistently or not. And this does not assume or imply anything about the "fictional" nature of Plato's works. "Fictional" is rather vague and ambiguous, perhaps used here to convey a negative connotation toward those views that do not seek to interpret Plato's dialogues the way Brickhouse and Smith do. In any case, one need not hold to the so-called fictional nature of Plato's works to hold a rather different and unproblematic approach to them.[5] It need not make Socrates out to be a non-entity or lacking in philosophical importance. Nor does it make Plato's works out to be something less than deeply rich in philosophical content.

Moreover, is it true, as Brickhouse and Smith claim, that the proposition that we cannot be sure whether the philosophical views that Brickhouse and Smith and others expose and explicate really do belong to the character Socrates is the *only* concession the anti-historicists can claim their own arguments merit? The answer to this question is negative. There are other important propositions that can be reasonably held by those who do not adhere to the Brickhouse-Smith approach to Plato's dialogues. One is that it is unclear that there is a "philosophy" of Socrates to be found in the dialogues, whether it belongs to either the historical Socrates or Plato's Socrates.

---

[5] For instance, one can even hold that every word put in Socrates' mouth by Plato throughout the Platonic corpus is indeed actually what Socrates said at one time or another, yet still maintain without absurdity that the dialogue form of Plato prohibits readers from legitimately having adequate confidence in thinking that the person or character Socrates actually believed what he said in the dialogues. For the aim of Plato in writing the dialogues may well not have been to communicate his mentor's views, but rather to reconstruct some of Socrates' many dialogues in order to teach readers how to think philosophically. One reason for this interpretation is that even though Plato's dialogues are rather many in number, they would, realistically speaking, represent presumably only a small fraction of Socrates' actual philosophical encounters, thus making Plato's dialogues a rather small sample on which to have confidence in rationally reconstructing even a "Socratic philosophy." More will be covered below on this way of approaching Plato's dialogues.

Another proposition open to the detractors of Brickhouse and Smith-style Socratic studies is that, as noted above, Plato's dialogue form prohibits our extracting such a "philosophy" of anyone's, much less Socrates'. Again, it is not that there is nothing real or truth-seeking about Plato's works. It is, rather, that Plato's Socrates can be understood well as arguing hypothetically instead of doxastically.[6] Now Brickhouse and Smith might counter that these are not positive arguments, but considerations that render their approach to Socratic studies problematic. Perhaps this is the case. But this does nothing to discount the questionable nature of the Brickhouse-Smith approach to Socratic studies and their reasons grounding their approach.

Brickhouse and Smith make an appeal to secondary evidence in support of their approach to Plato's dialogues. Like so many before them, they appeal to Aristotle, Plato's most famous student in the Academy. Not unlike many other Plato scholars, Brickhouse and Smith state that "…Aristotle would have been in an excellent position to question others who knew the historical Socrates and who knew how well Plato characterized the views of his great predecessor." (Brickhouse and Smith 2010: 28) But as we found in Chapters 2 and 3 and as discussed in Appendix I, there are problems with this kind of statement as it might be applied to the Platonic Question, some of which I shall briefly repeat here in revised form relative to the Socratic Question. First, "the views of his great predecessor" begs the very question at hand. It assumes that Socrates had a philosophy, view or standpoint to begin with. Begging this question fails to answer the critics who argue in favor of a very different way of approaching Plato's works and what he has Socrates express in them. Second, as noted in the previous chapter, Harold Cherniss (1945), among others, has argued that Aristotle was not always a reliable witness of Plato's views. And if Cherniss is correct about this matter, then there is reason to doubt whether Aristotle would be a reliable witness of Socrates' alleged views insofar as it is plausible to believe that Plato's views, whatever they were, somewhat tracked his mentor's views, whatever they were. To be sure, Brickhouse and Smith state that "…the best evidence of how those in Plato's Academy read the dialogues must

---

[6] By "doxastically" I mean that Socrates believes (or sincerely assents to) what he says in the dialogues such that one can thereby attribute to him a view or philosophy based on what he states.

surely be the evidence we get from Aristotle." (Brickhouse and Smith 2010: 37) But "surely" they mean by "best evidence" the best *available* evidence or the best *extant* evidence of a secondary kind. But it is not even clear that the testimony of Aristotle, as controversial as it is, represents good extant evidence of how Plato's other students interpreted the dialogues. For it is unclear that the dialogues of Plato even existed in anything akin to the form we possess them for any of Plato's students in the Academy.[7] And if this is true, then it is dubious that "...the best evidence of how those in Plato's Academy read the dialogues must surely be the evidence we get from Aristotle," as Brickhouse and Smith claim. For "the dialogues" in Brickhouse and Smith's statement commits an equivocation fallacy in seemingly assuming that the dialogues of Plato that were at Aristotle's disposal sufficiently resemble the ones we possess. For neither Aristotle nor his contemporaries in Plato's Academy had access to the versions of Plato's dialogues we have today, and vice-versa. This makes it troublesome for anyone to rely on Aristotle or any of his contemporaries to serve as our guides to either Plato's or Plato's Socrates' views as they are alleged to be "in the dialogues" as the two respective versions of his dialogues (Plato's students' and ours) might well have been so different concerning their respective informational contents that any reasonably accurate interpretation of the informational contents of

---

[7] As John J. Mulhern has pointed out, the difficulty here is that some of Plato's students may never have read the dialogues. Certainly at one point of the history of Plato's Academy there probably were none of his dialogues to be read. And even more certainly at one point not all of his dialogues were available to be read. If we assume that Aristotle arrived at the Academy around 367 BCE, what dialogues would have been available in the form in which we have them now, except for a few scribal errors? Not very many. The point is that we do not know exactly what was going on along these lines, and Plato's contemporaries might well have had a better view than we do. Aristotle's testimony has been impugned on the assumption that what he was discussing in many cases was contained in the dialogues as we have them now, as if he were reading from some edition available today. Yet this is a problematic assumption. At about 325, the dialogues as we have them now were only beginning to become available and that there may have been some disagreement about how good the editions were. In short, it is highly controversial to base one's views of what Plato's contemporaries thought on the text of the dialogues as we have them, since the text of the dialogues as we have them probably came later (personal correspondence, 26 February 2012).

one set of dialogues might be quite different from the informational contents of the other set of the same. Is it not possible that in composing and revising his dialogues Plato removed and inserted entire sections thereof, including entire discussions of various philosophical issues? Indeed, the set of dialogues available to Plato's students might be importantly different, and thus containing different discussions and issues, from our "canonical" set of Plato's works. And if this is true, then it is still plausible for the Socratic Interpretation to hold, as it does, that none of Plato's students, including Aristotle, was in a position to serve as reliable guides to either Plato's or Plato's Socrates' alleged views as they are said to be found in his dialogues. By "Plato's dialogues," I mean the set of dialogues the authorship of which is attributed to Plato today and as we possess them. In particular, I assume that the Thrasyllean collection as it is found in the translations in Cooper and Hutchinson (Cooper and Hutchinson 1997) is the best or at least an adequate collection of Plato's extant works. And this line of thought makes (for the sake of argument) the mouthpiece assumption that either Plato meant to communicate his own or his Socrates' substantive philosophical views to his readers in the first place. So even if one assumes for the sake of the mouthpiece interpreter's argument that Plato intends to communicate either his own or the character Socrates' substantive philosophical views in his dialogues, it is highly problematic to think that Aristotle serves as an adequate witness to either Plato's or the character Socrates' views based on the informational contents of those dialogues.

Furthermore, have we not had the experience of having a popular and self-appointed authoritative-sounding intelligent student who believed she knew our views but did not? Furthermore, since when did the secondary testimony of one single author count as strong evidence for the views of another? Did not Plato's other students think for themselves about what they read in Plato's dialogues? And ought not the reasonable interpreter to allow them even that much authority with regard to Plato's views? And if so, then why should Aristotle's controversial testimony count so heavily in terms of how Plato's dialogues ought to be read in attempting to glean Socrates' "philosophy"? So even if Aristotle serves as the "best" available secondary evidence of "the philosophy of Socrates" in Plato's early dialogues, it is not obvious that Aristotle serves as *adequate* evidence of the same.

For generally speaking, genuine and reliable primary evidence trumps secondary evidence, especially when there is reasonable doubt concerning the congruence of the two. Matters might be different, in favor of the Mouthpiece Interpretation, if there were extant and genuine texts of at least a few of Plato's students so that their respective informational contents might be compared and contrasted, providing scholars with an opportunity to see which, if any of them, best and adequately interpreted what Plato wrote. But we are not afforded that luxury at this point of history. Until then, appeals to Aristotle in assisting one in deciphering Plato's, the historical Socrates' or even Plato's Socrates' views, runs into the problems noted herein.

The undeniable fact is, as evidenced by the vast literature in Socratic studies, broadly construed, there is more than one way to approach Plato's works. Aristotle represents the perspective of Brickhouse and Smith and most others in philosophical Socratic studies within the analytic tradition. But it is quite possible and reasonable to approach Plato's dialogues in a way that Aristotle does not consider, namely, in a way that does not attribute any philosophically substantive belief or view to the character Socrates because Socrates is best understood as arguing hypothetically, and this is justified on the basis of the primary evidence of the dialogue form in which Plato writes.

Thus far I have rendered implausible the statement that:

> It follows that, unless the critics of Socratic scholarship have better criticisms to make than the ones we have surveyed in this chapter, there is no reason for Socratic scholars to give any ground at all to such critics. Even if we do not and cannot know whether Socratic scholarship understands Socrates or Plato's dialogues rightly, we have certainly been provided with no plausible reasons in the criticisms we have addressed in this chapter for thinking that such scholarship is as naïve or as wrongheaded as its critics have claimed. (Brickhouse and Smith 2010: 37)

While it may be true that Brickhouse and Smith have rebutted various claims and charges they have examined in *Socratic Moral Psychology*, they hardly provide sound replies to my concerns which do not fit so neatly into the paradigms which they address.

What I shall now provide is a sketch of a more detailed analysis of an approach to Plato's dialogues and understanding Socrates' words therein that is not anti-historicist in the sense Brickhouse and Smith attempt to rebut, nor is it a fictional account of Plato's works. Rather, it is deeply Socratic, and one that I believe they show some signs that they want to adopt as a more cautious approach to Plato's Socrates given phrases they use such as "As Plato has Socrates tell us in the *Apology*…" (Brickhouse and Smith 2010: 41) Unlike locutions such as "Socrates' doctrine of…" or "the philosophy of Socrates" or "Socrates' theory of…" etc., this way of putting matters is in line with my Socratic approach to Plato's dialogues. (See Chapters 2–3 of this book)[8]

Additionally, a concern must be raised regarding Brickhouse and Smith's use of "Socratic studies" to refer to their particular method of approaching Plato's dialogues in order to extract Socrates' philosophy of this or that. In point of fact, "Socratic studies" properly refers less narrowly to the (in this case, philosophical) study of Plato's dialogues insofar as they pertain to what is portrayed to reflect Socrates' expressions on a variety of topics—regardless of which dialogues in which the Socratic expressions are found. To use "Socratic studies" to refer to only a narrow sense of how Plato's dialogues might be approached is parochial at best, and misguided at worst. Let us now consider a more plausible approach to the Platonic corpus with special attention paid to what Plato puts in Socrates' mouth in dialogue with various interlocutors.

Fortunately, one is not forced to choose sides between the hyperbole of Charles Kahn, on the one hand, or the methodology of rational reconstruction of Brickhouse and Smith, on the other. There is another option concerning the manner in which Plato's dialogues can be approached, and how the words of Socrates can be best understood. It is, of course, the Socratic (Anti-Mouthpiece) Interpretation. And what I set out to do in the remainder of this chapter is to expand the Socratic Interpretation to address not only the Platonic Question, but also the Socratic Question.

The Socratic Interpretation of Plato's Dialogues and the Socratic Question

The approach to Plato's dialogues adopted (assumed) by Brickhouse and Smith is what might be called the "Socratic Mouthpiece Interpretation" in that it holds that some or all of Plato's dialogues

---

[8] Also see Corlett (2005: Chapter 3).

contain "the philosophy of [the character] Socrates." It is a dominant approach to Socrates and Plato studies within the analytic philosophical tradition. But recall what I have been referring to as the "Socratic (Anti-Mouthpiece) Interpretation" of Plato's dialogues as it pertains to the Socratic Question. This position takes as axiomatic the depth of Socrates' influence on Plato in Plato's composing the dialogues and in Plato's very choice of the dialogue form to write what he did. Instead of construing Plato's works as having the purpose of teaching us his own or even Socrates' beliefs, doctrines or theories as the Socratic Mouthpiece Interpretation insists, the Socratic (Anti-Mouthpiece) Interpretation understands Plato's works as conveying the manner in which the philosophically examined life ought to be lived. And what better way of communicating this than by employing the dialogue method and placing Socrates (paradigmatic of excellence in philosophical method) as the main character in most of the dialogues? In light of Brickhouse and Smith's lack of a convincing argument in favor of their own interpretive approach and the problems I pose for it above, the Socratic (Anti-Mouthpiece) Interpretation refuses to accept their approach, pending further and stronger evidence and argumentation for the position that Plato's works reveal, or even attempt to reveal, Plato's Socrates' beliefs, doctrines or theories.

The philosophical profundity of Plato's works lies not in the misascriptions of this or that belief, doctrine, or theory to either Plato's Socrates or Plato, but rather in the philosophical enlightenment that readers derive from a careful study of Plato's works, and in our further developing incomplete or unclear arguments and analyses found in them. As A. D. Woozley writes of the *Crito*:

> ...I believe that the dialogue...was intended to be a substantially faithful representation of the actual Socrates, but even more because the purposes of the book do not demand that the authorship of this view or that, even if it could, should be established. The views are presented, and the reasons advanced for them, are what here matter; it is more important that they be correctly interpreted and fairly assessed than that they be properly attributed to 'Socrates' rather than to Socrates, or *vice versa*. (Woozley 1979: 5)

Moreover, part of the philosophical depth of Plato's works is that they not only contain certain arguments and analyses which are problematic or not, as the case may be, but that those who study them are urged to consider the problems they raise for themselves and, in taking up the torch of philosophical investigation, attempt to resolve them. As John M. Cooper writes, "It was characteristic of philosophy before Socrates and Plato that philosophers usually put themselves forward as possessors of special insight and wisdom: *they* had the truth, and everyone else should just listen to them and learn." (Cooper and Hutchinson 1997: xix) But as we know, throughout many of Plato's works Socrates makes claims to his own ignorance.[9] While some have made an attempt to construe Socrates' words here (and often elsewhere) to be ironical (Vlastos 1991), it is also plausible to take them on their face value without committing some version of the fundamental attribution error.

Now the facts that there is no formal Socratic method (Brickhouse and Smith 1994), on the one hand, and Socrates' insistence on his own ignorance, on the other, together support the Socratic Anti-Mouthpiece Interpretation's idea that the philosopher who had most influence on Plato was one who hardly fits the description of one who propounds one's own beliefs, doctrines or theories as both Socrates' predecessors and his contemporaries did. Thus we ought not to expect, nor should we attempt, to locate Socrates' own views in his dialogues. This is especially true in light of the various features of what we might informally refer to as Socrates' method of doing philosophy, including open-mindedness (*Euthyphro* 14c; *Phaedo* 82d; *Laws* 667a; *Protagoras* 349c–d; *Gorgias* 506c), persistence[10] and courage (*Euthyphro* 15c; *Phaedo* 84a; *Theaetetus* 155d; *Republic* 450e; *Phaedo* 83e, 90e; *Statesman* 260b), sincerity (*Protagoras* 331c; *Republic* 349a; *Protagoras* 348c; *Gorgias* 357e-358a, 489d, 515b–c; *Theaetetus* 151d, 191a; *Second Alcibides* 150e; *Republic* 535d–e; *Phaedo* 67d-68b, 82c), humility (*Apology* 21d, 29b; *Theaetetus* 150c; *Meno* 86b, e; *Cratylus* 428d, 436d, 440d; *Theages* 128b; *Phaedo* 107b), and justice (*Theaetetus* 167e-168a). In light of these factors, the informal Socratic method is a common search for truth and wis-

---

[9] As Anthony Kenny writes: "The man who is, as it were, the patron saint of philosophers, Socrates, claimed that the only way in which he surpassed others in wisdom was that he was aware of his own ignorance." (Kenny 2006: 13). As noted in Chapter 3 of this book, Socrates' proclamation of self-ignorance is argued not to discount the idea that Socrates knew "small" things, just not "big" ones, as articulated in Peterson (2011).

[10] What I refer to as Socratic open-mindedness and persistence is called "double open-endedness" in Nails (1995: 20).

dom. And if it is true, as the Socratic Anti-Mouthpiece Interpretation states, that Plato, in writing the dialogues and other works of the Platonic corpus, was influenced primarily by his mentor Socrates, then it would make good sense to think that Plato was in turn influenced by Socrates' "method" of philosophical inquiry, which is not, so far as the evidence and arguments go, dogmatic or theory-laden. If this is true, then it makes insufficient sense to think, as Socratic mouthpiece interpreters do, that Plato wrote to communicate to readers the beliefs or views of Socrates. And if this is true, then it would appear to follow that the primary purpose of Plato's works is not to communicate even Plato's Socrates' views, but to encourage readers to engage in philosophical dialectic as did Socrates, and to attempt to utilize philosophical method to attain truth, avoid error, and to become better persons in the process so that we may in turn be better for the rest of our lives. (*Euthyphro* 16)

The words of the previous paragraph indicate that it is not part of the Socratic Interpretation that reading Plato's works is a matter of subjective interpretation, as noted in the previous chapter. That the nature of the dialogues obscures attempts to discover Socrates' own views and that the aim of the dialogues is to engage readers in a dynamic way in no way rules out the possibility of doing philosophy analytically and without adopting some strong form of skepticism. In particular, it does not rule out the possibility that a student of the *Theaetetus* might discover the most plausible analysis of human knowledge, or that a reader of the *Republic* might arrive at the truth about the nature of justice. Nor does the Socratic Anti-Mouthpiece Interpretation deny that Plato had beliefs of his own with philosophical content. What it refuses to accept pending stronger evidence and argument is that extant primary and secondary evidence in dialogue form is sufficient evidence of Plato's Socrates' "philosophy" or "view," as Brickhouse and Smith suggest.

Further, the Socratic Interpretation may involve rational reconstruction. But all the while the interpreter of Plato's dialogues must not fall prey to the temptation to attribute this or that view found in the dialogues to either Plato or his character Socrates, especially since Plato nowhere writes or "speaks" in his own person and we have no reliable record wherein it is stated that Plato's dialogues contain

Socrates' philosophy.[11] There is nothing wrong with interpretations of Plato's texts as long as they are not presented as representing "the philosophy of Socrates" or his beliefs. The Socratic Mouthpiece Interpretation, at least in the Brickhouse and Smith version, understands Plato's dialogues as texts that represent the character Socrates' views, yet it lacks sufficiently good reason for ascribing such views to Plato's Socrates. Perhaps they put it best when they readily admit that they "presume" these things to be true. That being the case, they are hardly in a position to complain when their presumption is called into question.

Objections to the Socratic Anti-mouthpiece Interpretation, and Replies

Having outlined and clarified some of the main points of my argument for the Socratic Interpretation of Plato's dialogues in response to Brickhouse and Smith's challenge to their critics, I now turn to some concerns that might be raised about it. One worry about the Socratic Interpretation might be that there seems to be no philosophical significance to my criticism of Brickhouse and Smith's Socratic Mouthpiece Interpretation and defense of my Socratic Anti-Mouthpiece Interpretation. For instance, Brickhouse and Smith argue that:

> Perhaps notes would be added to scholarly works, acknowledging the historical non-identity of Plato's Socrates with the historical Socrates. But then the rest of the book or article would proceed almost exactly as it would have without such proof, since the historical identity and characteristics of the flesh-and-blood Socrates really never made any difference to the enterprise in which such books and articles were intended to play a part. After all, the goal is only to explicate the philosophical contents of the relevant dialogues of Plato. (Brickhouse and Smith 2010: 16–17)

I concur that one worthy goal of Socratic studies is to "explicate the philosophical contents of the relevant dialogues of Plato." But it is unclear what Brickhouse and Smith mean by "proceed almost

---

[11] As noted in the previous chapter, the only primary textual evidence that we possess along the lines of Plato's views is the clear support for the Socratic Interpretation found in the *Seventh Letter* the authenticity of which, however, has been called into question.

exactly..." For this might point to the very issue at hand. Whereas I want Socratic studies to adopt a more cautious approach insofar as ascriptions of beliefs and views to Socrates are concerned, Brickhouse and Smith seem to be less concerned about this caution. Furthermore, to the point about the overall significance of this issue I would reply that the accuracy of the very history of philosophy is at stake. And if for no other reason, we ought to have enough respect (as I believe most philosophers of Plato and Socrates do) for the history of philosophy to get it right. And this means, among other things, not question-beggingly ascribing a view to a philosopher—even if only a character in a dialogue--what we have inadequate reason to attribute to him or her. It is also a matter of precision in scholarship. To do as mouthpiece interpreters such as Brickhouse and Smith often do and use locutions such as "Socrates believes..." "Socrates' doctrine..." "Socrates' theory...." "the philosophy of Socrates" and the like without providing sound arguments for doing so is, if my objections to the arguments given for the Socratic Mouthpiece Interpretation are plausible, akin to attributing to any historical figure a belief without sufficiently good reason.

What I am referring to as "the Socratic Question,"[12] is not an issue having little or no consequence for philosophical studies. For it is vital that we get both the person and character Socrates right instead of being insufficiently cautious concerning what Plato's dialogues are about. By "right" in this context I mean, of course, as accurately as possible given the available evidence.

Thus there are numerous problems with this general approach to "discovering" Socrates' philosophy in the works of Plato, and it does little or nothing to demonstrate how we are to come to understand which of Socrates' words are "his own," doxastically speaking. To insist that we can take Socrates at his word in a strong sense is a bit naïve as his words are sometimes ironical. So Brickhouse and Smith owe us a theory of interpretation that would plausibly distinguish which words of Socrates are "his own" in the sense that they reflect his beliefs or views, and which are not.

---

[12] As mentioned above, this is the question of what substantive philosophical beliefs, if any, can be attributed to either the historical Socrates or Plato's Socrates from the contents of Plato's dialogues.

Finally, it might be argued that the crucial point is that the question whether, in any particular case, Socrates is represented as expressing his own belief or arguing *ad hominem* cannot be settled *a priori*, but must depend on examination of the particular text. That, of course, is what Brickhouse and Smith do, but I (it might be argued) do not examine any particular passages in support of my Socratic Interpretation. Ultimately, it is argued, I do no more than assert that it is always impossible to determine whether Socrates is represented as expressing his beliefs.

In reply to this concern, it is important to point out that it is Brickhouse and Smith who are making the claim that it is possible, in examining certain of Plato's dialogues, to legitimately ascribe this or that belief to Socrates. Epistemically, they bear the burden of argument in supporting such a claim. I pose challenges to it. And I do so without committing myself or the Socratic Interpretation to some strong version of skepticism about the claims that Plato or Socrates in fact had beliefs. This strategy is different than one wherein one would programmatically insist *a priori* that it is impossible to establish such doxastic claims about Plato or Socrates. I am engaged in the more modest task of pointing out that the ascriptions to Socrates of this or that belief even by the likes of such sophisticated and distinguished philosophers as Brickhouse and Smith fall short of adequately establishing their Socratic ascriptions. And this criticism need not, and in my case is not, based on some perfectionist notion of what would justify the said ascriptions.

The attempt to apply the Mouthpiece Interpretation to Socrates, then, fails for similar reasons that it fails in the case of misattributing Socrates' words to Plato. And we are left with the fact that there has been not one persuasive argument provided in favor of the Mouthpiece Interpretation in terms of Socrates' "philosophy." Again, as I stated in the previous chapter, perhaps it is time to put to rest an approach to Socrates (and Plato) that has run its course as not even the brightest minds who have tried have been able to provide unproblematic arguments to support this dominant approach to Plato's works.

As also stated similarly in the previous chapter on the Platonic Question, my point is not that the Socratic Interpretation has answered all there is to answer about problems related to the Socratic and Platonic questions. It is, rather, that in light of the implausibility of the

Socratic Mouthpiece Interpretation, the Socratic Anti-Mouthpiece Interpretation of Plato's dialogues stands as the least problematic of all competing approaches to Plato's works. As noted earlier, just as in legal interpretation there is an all relevant things considered best interpretation of law, there is an all relevant things considered best interpretation of Plato's works. Given the arguments provided thus far by Brickhouse and Smith, it is evident that there is better reason to accept the Socratic Anti-Mouthpiece Interpretation over the Socratic Mouthpiece Interpretation concerning the Socratic Question, just as it is more reasonable to accept the Socratic Interpretation over the Mouthpiece Interpretation when it comes to the Platonic Question.

References

Brickhouse, Thomas C., and Nicholas D. Smith. 1994. *Plato's Socrates*. Oxford: Oxford University Press.
———. 2010. *Socratic moral psychology*. Cambridge: Cambridge University Press.
Cherniss, Harold. 1945. *The riddle of the early academy*. Berkeley: University of California Press.
Cooper, John C., and D.S. Hutchinson, eds. 1997. *Plato: Complete works*. Indianapolis: Hackett Publishing Company.
Corlett, J. Angelo. 2005. *Interpreting Plato's dialogues*. Las Vegas: Parmenides Publishing.
Guthrie, W.K.C. 1969. *A history of Greek philosophy*, 3 (Cambridge: Cambridge University Press.
Kenny, Anthony. 2006. *What I believe*. London: Continuum.
Nails, Debra. 1995. *Agora, academy, and the conduct of philosophy*. Dordrecht: Kluwer Academic Publishers.
Peterson, Sandra. 2011. *Socrates and philosophy in Plato's dialogues*. Cambridge: Cambridge University Press.
Vlastos, Gregory. 1991. *Socrates: Ironist and moral philosopher*. Ithaca: Cornell University Press.
Woozley, A.D. 1979. *Law and obedience: The arguments of Plato's <u>Crito</u>*. London: Duckworth.

Chapter 5
Socrates and Distributive Justice

> A man who really fights for justice must lead a private, not a public, life if he is to survive for even a short time—Socrates, *Apology* 32a.

Having rendered implausible the Mouthpiece Interpretation of Plato's dialogues, and having defended the Socratic (Anti-Mouthpiece) Interpretation from various criticisms of its extremist cousin approaches thereby distancing the Socratic Interpretation from other anti-mouthpiece approaches, it is important to further defend the Socratic Interpretation by demonstrating precisely how it approaches Platonic texts. After all, it is one thing to answer objections with plausible replies, yet quite another to be able to show how an approach to Plato would in fact interpret various texts of Plato's dialogues on this or that substantive philosophical matter without having to employ the Mouthpiece Interpretation. If I succeed along these lines, I will have shown that the Mouthpiece Interpretation is not only absent a plausible argument in its favor, but that it is also unnecessary in approaching Plato's corpus of writings.

Given (a) the straightforward intolerance expressed toward atheists in both the *Laws* and the *Epinomis*; (b) the attitude of censorship found in much of the *Republic* regarding mimetic poetry and painting; and (c) Athens' ultimate intolerance of Socratic inquiry (drummed up as atheism and corruption of youth); it is important to ask what views, if any, Plato's Socrates and other characters in Plato's works might have expressed on justice in the distributive sense. As with other concepts discussed in Plato's corpus of writings, discussions of concepts of justice are found in a variety of his dialogues. The problem, however, is that there is no theory of justice found therein, despite what many mouthpiece interpreters want to assert to the contrary. Or, only slightly more cautiously, Richard Kraut argues that in Plato's *Republic* there is a specific, though sometimes indirect, defense of justice (as opposed to injustice) therein. (Kraut 1992) However, what we discover instead (both in the *Republic* and elsewhere in various other of Plato's writings) is a plethora of statements made by Plato's Socrates and other characters on what justice is in the ideal and non-ideal senses. As I argued in Chapters 2 and 3, it is controversial for one to assert, as mouthpiece interpreters often do, that such statements amount to Plato's theories, doctrines or beliefs about justice. In fact, as I argued in Chapter 4, it is unwarranted to insist without adequate supportive evidence that Plato's Socrates sincerely assents to (i.e., believes) the words that Plato puts in his mouth. Rather, what readers of Plato's corpus ought to do is consider such statements in their own right and critically examine them for plausibility. What we find in Plato's writings are statements about some of the particulars of justice, such as rights, equality, freedoms and the like. I shall refer to these as "distributive justice concepts" in that they are concepts falling under the more general category of distributive justice.

Is there a theory of distributive justice in Plato's corpus of writings? Is there a theory of justice in even one of his dialogues? If so, it would be reasonable for a certain set of questions to be answered in such writings. But in order for such a determination to be made on reasonable grounds, the following sorts of considerations must be taken into account. Only if such considerations are met can it then be decided whether or not such a theory, if it does exist therein, belongs to Plato as mouthpiece interpreters want to insist.

In order for there to be a theory of distributive justice in one or more of Plato's writings, there must at least be a definition of "justice" in this sense, a justification provided for the particular theory offered, an explanation of the importance of it, and also of the manner(s) in which distributive justice relates to other forms of justice. More systematically, there is no manner in which to discern if Plato's alleged theory of justice is in his dialogues, and if so, how it might be extracted unproblematically given the dialogue form in which Plato wrote most of his works. But for there to be such a theory in his dialogues, early, middle or late, whatever is plausibly taken to represent Plato's ideas amounting to a theory of distributive justice must at least do the following. First, it must provide an answer to the question "What is justice?" in the distributive sense. While the *Republic* and the *Gorgias* ask this question (or ones like it), they fail to answer it except only to criticize the views of Socrates' interlocutors on the nature of justice. Second, Plato's alleged theory of justice in the dialogues must answer the question "How, if at all, ought society to be governed?" Again, as with the question of the nature of justice, this question does not admit of an answer in Plato's works that address it, except again to criticize various proposed answers to questions like it. The discussions between Socrates, Thrasymachus, Glaucon and Adeimantus in the *Republic* exemplify this point rather clearly. Third, for there to be a theory of distributive justice that is Plato's that is contained in his dialogues, the dialogues must answer the question as to which laws ought to govern the just *polis*. The *Laws* proposes several such legal rules, though it is hardly obvious that Plato endorses any of them. Fourth, such a theory must also exhibit in Plato's dialogues an answer to the question "Is there a moral obligation to obey the law?" But as we shall see in the next chapter, there is no answer to this question in the *Crito* that is unproblematically attributable to Plato. Fifth, if there is a theory of distributive justice in Plato's works, then we should expect to see clear definitions and either defenses or repudiations of the concepts of freedom, equality, and rights, among other concepts related to distributive justice. Sixth, a theory of justice more generally that is plausibly ascribable to Plato must also answer the question "What, if anything, ought one to face if one violates the law?" While as we shall see, Socrates expresses (but does not necessarily endorse) a clearly and mostly retributivist attitude toward wrongdoing of various kinds, including legal wrongdoing, it is unclear what Plato's views on punishment amount to. Finally, related to the question of punishment is one concerning compensatory justice. If there is a theory of justice to be plausibly attributable to Plato, then it must include a coherent conception of compensatory justice. Plato's Socrates has much to say about such matters, but is it plausible to attribute to Plato such a view? Unfortunately, we find in Plato's works little, if anything, of positive use along the lines of answering such questions, rendering false or misleading claims that include locutions such as "Plato's theory of justice…"

The problem with studies on Socrates and justice is that, while so many of them ascribe a theory of justice to Plato, none of them seem to address the above requirements of a theory of justice such that one might know whether or not whatever is said in Plato's dialogues about justice might amount to a theory of justice. Worse still is the fact that mouthpiece interpreters continue to ascribe to Plato such a theory. For example, David Keyt assumes both that "Socrates is Plato's spokesman in the *Republic* and that the Eleatic and Athenian Strangers speak for Plato in the *Statesman* and the *Laws* respectively." (Keyt 2008: 38) A rather different approach to Plato's dialogues is captured by A. W. Price:

> … in order at once to clarify the content of Plato's dialogues, and to realize Plato's purpose in writing them, we must do philosophy ourselves. We have to play the roles both of handmaiden, attending to all the details of the text, and of apprentice, not leaving the philosophy to Plato but joining in the argument. …
>
> If Plato intends his readers to share his own risks, the constructive interpreter must take on the perils of constructive philosophy. What *his* readers can reasonably expect is not that he play safe, but that he refresh their own reading of Plato. (Price 2008: 25)

In the *Statesman* 295a, the Visitor and the Young Socrates agree that what is sought and possible is approximate justice rather than ideal justice, and that lawmakers will legislate "according to ancestral customs." Equally general is their agreement that "…by always distributing to those in the city what is most just, as judged by the intelligent application of their expertise, they are able both to preserve them and so far as they can to bring it about that they are better than they were…" (*Statesman* 297b) One thing seems clear to them: The masses of people are unable to manage a city well; it takes experts in wisdom and virtue to do so. (*Statesman* 297b–c)

Socrates on Freedom and Rights

In the *Statesman* 300, Young Socrates makes a claim that would appear on the surface to contradict what mouthpiece interpreters attribute to him in the *Republic* wherein Socrates allegedly argues for the censorship of mimetic art and poetry: "It's clear both that we should see all the various sorts of expertise completely destroyed, and that they would never be restored, either, because of this law prohibiting inquiry; so that life, which even now is difficult, in such a time would be altogether unlivable." This passage seems to imply that the ability to inquire into matters, especially philosophically, is central to a life worth living. Of course, this in turn is consistent with the famous Socratic dictum that the unexamined life is not worth living. It is also valued by Plato's character Clinias in his discussion of legal authority with Megillus (*Laws* 642d), implying that the laws of a just *polis* ought to protect the right of freedom of expression (or, at least, they ought not to interfere with it). And whether or not the myth of the Ring of Gyges proves that the unjust would really prefer to live unjustly if not for coercive legal rules backed by the power of the state to enforce punishments (*Republic* 359c-360d), freedom requires good judgment (*Laws* 693e) unless unrestricted freedom leads to disgrace (*Laws* 662a) and analrchy. (*Republic* 572d–e and 560e) But in the context of military service in a just *polis*, "Freedom from control must be uncompromisingly eliminated from the life of all men, and of all the animals under their domination." (*Laws* 942c–d) That freedom is juxtaposed to control in political contexts (*Laws* 962e) hardly implies that Plato's writings do not recognize the value of human freedom. But a vast array of details are left out of the discussions, and it is left to the reader to grasp hold of the exchanges where they end and to develop them further. At least, this is what the Socratic Interpretation suggests.

Moving from freedom to rights in Plato's works, even less is spoken of the latter. About all we read can be summed up in two passages in the *Gorgias*. At 486c, the implicit idea of rights serves as the grounding for claims to compensatory justice for harms incurred by the wrongful acts of others, and at 508c, it is implied that without rights there is no protection for persons. But Socrates implies even more about rights:

> I deny, Callicles, that being knocked on the jaw unjustly is the most shameful thing, or that having my body or my purse cut is, and I affirm that to knock or cut me or my possessions unjustly is both more shameful and worse, and at the same time that to rob or enslave me or to break into my house or, to sum up, to commit any unjust act at all against me and my possessions is both worse and more shameful for the one who does these unjust acts than it is for me, the one who suffers them.

Thus to put it in the contemporary parlance of rights: It is those who suffer the abuse of rights violations who indeed suffer. But far worse, according to Socrates, are those who violate the rights of others. So goes the line of thought, at least. For while it may be true that, morally speaking, Socrates is correct about such rights violators, it is hardly obvious that they suffer sufficiently for their wrongdoings in this life, as many of them get away with benefiting, on balance, for their wrongs against others. One must be ever mindful to not fall into the pacifistic trap of inferring from Socrates' statement that it is not the moral obligation of the state to punish offenders in proportion to the harms they have caused to others, as complicated as the concept of proportionate punishment may be.[1] Just as vital is the fact that implied in Socrates' above words is the importance of the contemporary notion of the moral right of the innocent not to suffer harm, for instance. More shall be made of this below.

One of the areas in which human freedom in a just *polis* is said to be limited is with regard to birthing children. Several times various of Plato's characters speak in favor of limiting procreation. In *Republic* 372c, Socrates states of citizens of the just city that "They'll enjoy sex with one another but bear no more children than their resources allow, lest they fall into either poverty or war." Again, at 423b, he says that "As long as it is willing to remain *one* city, it may continue to grow, but it cannot grow beyond that point." Not only does the Socrates of the *Republic* address concerns of human population growth in the just *polis*, so too does the Athenian. While *Laws* 721b–e and 774a–b make the controversial claim that in a just city it is a crime to not have children and that such is to be punished by an annual fine, and the *Laws* 930c sets a legal minimum of children per household, 737c-d discusses methods of land distribution in the just state in a manner that is sensitive to overpopulation and general ecological concerns:

> First, one has to determine what the total number of people ought to be, then agree on the question of the distribution of the citizens and decide the number and size of the subsections into which they ought to be divided; and the land and houses must be divided equally (so far as possible) among these subsections. A suitable total for the number of citizens cannot be fixed without considering the land and the neighboring states. The land

---

[1] For discussions of the nuances of proportionate punishment, see Corlett (2014: Chapter 5); Davis (1992); Ryberg (2004).

must be extensive enough to support a given number of people in modest comfort, and not a foot more is needed. The inhabitants should be numerous enough to be able to defend themselves when the adjacent peoples attack them, and contribute at any rate some assistance to neighboring societies when they are wronged.

Even in the second best state, it is said of it that "if too many children are being born, there are measures to check propagation." (*Laws* 740d) And most importantly, it is vital "to keep the said number as long as you live; you must respect the upper limits of the total property which you originally distributed as being reasonable, and not buy and sell your holdings among yourselves." (*Laws* 741b) Surely these are claims which invite critical philosophical investigation.

Within various of Plato's works, freedom is often said to have its recognized limits. The real question is precisely what are those limits given this or that circumstance, all relevant things considered. This is a matter that each generation must consider for itself, if indeed it takes the rights and freedoms of its own offspring seriously. For an overpopulated *polis* is one that strains the natural resources available to it within its own territory, and often pressures itself to impose its will on others to fulfill even its most basic needs. Yet as John Rawls states, "People must recognize that they cannot make up for failing to regulate their numbers or to care for their land by conquest in war, or by migrating into another people's territory without their consent." (Rawls 1999: 8. Also see 39) The above words, then, introduce the reader of Plato's *Laws* to some basic problems facing anyone seriously interested in freedom in the context of a reasonably just *polis*.

Equality

In *Phaedo* 74a-75d, Plato's Socrates asks, "What *is* Equal?" and spends some time trying to discover its true meaning. Of course, those interested in the genuine meaning of "equal" do not want to know the mere appearance of reality (with regard to the nature of equality), as we find mentioned in *Parmenides* 165a, but said reality itself. Socially and politically speaking, the *Laws* 805d seems to endorse equality between sexes in a just society, while the *Laws* 744b wherein "The whole point of our legislation was to allow the citizens to live supremely happy lives in the greatest possible mutual friendship" (743d), the state offers equality of opportunity" to all within its borders. Indeed, what the Athenian at *Laws* 668a refers to as "proportional equality" "does not depend on anyone's opinion that it is so, nor does it cease to be true if someone is displeased at the fact." *Gorgias* 508a also mentions "proportionate equality." But neither context provides a clue as to what this idea amounts. *Laws* 744b also mentions proportionate inequality. Again, however, there is no indication of its meaning. In either case, one might reasonably infer that whatever proportionate equality means, it seems to imply a kind of equality that is not strict. Perhaps it means that while people in a just regime are not to be treated equally in a strict egalitarian sense, they are rather to be treated equally insofar as some folk are relevantly similar, or are in relevantly similar classes: socially, economically, politically, etc.. It might mean, for instance, that those who have attained certain training or educational levels are to be treated equally, but they are not to be treated equally with regard to those who are not in those classes. While this would make good sense with regard to the economics of salaries and wages earned, it might not make sense insofar as the manner in which people are treated, say, in legal prosecutorial contexts wherein many believe that, say, the presumption of innocence ought to be accorded to all citizens. Other than this, it is difficult to discern what these passages mean when they mention, not discuss, proportionate equality.

For those, like Terence Irwin, who argue or imply that Athenian democracy requires "toleration and freedom of inquiry," that "this enormous debt to the Athenian democracy is acknowledged nowhere in the Platonic corpus," and that "we may be justifiably angry at Plato's attempt in the *Republic* (520a9-b4) to deny the debt he conspicuously owes" (Irwin 1986: 414), there are cautions in order. First, in the *Gorgias* 461e, Socrates says to Polus that Athens is "where there's more freedom of speech than anywhere else in Greece." Granted, this does not necessarily imply that Socrates thinks that whatever freedom of speech there is in Athens is adequate, all relevant things considered. And it is this point that might well explain in significant part the death of Socrates. For if I am correct in my interpretation of the *Crito* in Chapter 6 of this book, Socrates chooses to go to his death in part to reveal the injustices of Athens, including its intolerance of Socratic philosophy. This implies, contrary to Irwin's claim, that Socrates has no good reason to be grateful to Athens because it is Athens that is unduly intolerant of the Socratic mission. And if this is true, then why would we be "justifiably angry at Plato's attempt in the *Republic* (520a9-b4) to deny the debt he conspicuously owes"? Indeed, we have good reason to be angry with *Athens* and its failed attempt at democracy. It put to death one of its greatest citizens in Socrates, and for no reason other than trumped up charges! Socrates has no "debt"—much less a conspicuous one—to Athens. It is a city which punishes severely one of its best citizens and rewards its Meletuses.[2] Moreover, if there is no general moral obligation to obey the law (including that of a debt of gratitude), this implies that Socrates does not exhibit a "striking and treacherous ingratitude" as Irwin's baseless remarks beg the question as to whether or not there is a moral obligation (from gratitude) to obey the law. It is unfortunate that Socrates and Plato have been understood so uncharitably on this matter. Is it so absurd to think that Socrates was being ironic in stating that he owed so much to Athens? And is it so implausible to think that Socrates was simply stating arguments in favor of his having a moral obligation to obey his death sentence, when in fact he may have known quite well that it was Athens itself that owed him a debt of gratitude for what he has done in attempting to awaken its citizens out of their dogmatically unjust slumbers? And would this interpretation of Socrates' words about legal obligation fit well with the idea of the importance of the examined life? Why not interpret Socrates as suggesting that readers consider the idea that there is no moral obligation to obey an unjust law, or a legal system that is inadequate? Certainly this concept is not out of the realm of ancient Greek thought, especially for those who seek to live the examined life.

Indeed, the fact that Socrates and his interlocutors throughout the *Republic* state ideas that are absurd might provide us a clue, if we take seriously the Principle of Charity in Interpretation, as to what readers ought to challenge: the idea of banishing or censoring poets and mimetic artists, the idea of a class-based society, and in certain respects a communal one, etc.. On a Socratic Interpretation, such

---

[2] Furthermore, Irwin's unfounded remarks run afoul of Joel Feinberg's arguments against their being even a mere *prima facie* moral obligation to obey the law. (Feinberg 1992: Chapter 6).

ideas are put out there by Plato for readers to critically assess, each according to their best philosophical lights. And it would appear that such ideas do not withstand scrutiny, and for many reasons that a solid study of the philosophy of law would reveal. Indeed, such a study would at least bring to light Joel Feinberg's famous example of "Nowheresville" (Feinberg 1980: Chapter 7), a society having many duties, obligations, and privileges, but lacking rights altogether. It is a society that places value on social utility maximization rather than on respecting rights. Hence, it is one that can run roughshod over a poet's right to express herself, or an painter's right to do the same—all in the name of providing what appears to be an element of social stability. It is also a society, like Athens, that would think nothing of sentencing one of its greatest citizens to death primarily because his philosophical inquiry threatens the perceived stability of the *polis*. But a *polis* without rights is Nowheresville, lacking citizens' self-respect, self-worth, and dignity. So on a Socratic Interpretation, the words in Plato's dialogues are not taken to "speak" Plato's mind, or even Plato's Socrates' mind. Rather, they are taken to serve as challenges to various ways of thinking about a variety of matters. In this way, neither Plato nor Socrates, brilliant as they were, are not unnecessarily saddled with ideas that often lack even a modicum of plausibility. Thus the Principle of Charity of Interpretation is respected, as are Plato and his Socrates.

Perhaps equally problematic is Richard Kraut's idea that "Plato advises his readers to withdraw from politics in all but the most unusual circumstances…" (Kraut 2003: 153) While Christopher Rowe has pointed out that Kraut's interpretation fails to see that Plato is not discouraging active participation in politics, but rather emphasizing that there is more to political action, namely, care for one's soul (Rowe 2003), I see additional difficulties looming. First, as mouthpiece interpreters, both Kraut and Rowe presume that Plato is attempting to say something of philosophical substance in the dialogues related to politics and justice. This notion is problematic for reasons stated in Chapter 2 concerning the difficulties with the Mouthpiece Interpretation more generally. Secondly, pericopes that, according to Kraut, seem to suggest that the morally virtuous person ought to refrain from involvement in politics are just as easily understood by Socratic interpreters as those which encourage philosophical discussion about whether or not such a position is plausible. Common sense would suggest that the morally virtuous refraining from politics leaves politics to the less virtuous, posing problems for society more generally. On the other hand, the frustrations for those concerned with how matters ought to be can become rather overwhelming, causing one to re-think how to better spend one's time and energies. To saddle Plato, or even his Socrates, with such a simple-minded view of political participation (or lack thereof) seems a bit uncharitable, especially if one considers that perhaps Socrates has a much wider view of political participation. Perhaps for him, political participation just is living the morally virtuous life, whatever that amounts to. And if everyone did that, then politics would take care of itself, as would religion, economics, etc.. So on this wider notion of political participation, Socrates, insofar as he investigates the nature of moral virtue, is at least attempting to do what is morally virtuous at the level of moral analysis. And supposing that he can make significant philosophical progress along those lines, then that would constitute a meaningful contribution to the manner in which politics ought to take root in ancient Athens.

In sum, it is unclear that Socrates has much to say about matters of distributive justice, at least in a positive sense. What we are left with are cryptic statements or arguments that seem to constitute more in the line of propaedeutics for further analysis, which is precisely what we would expect to find in Plato's dialogues according to the Socratic Interpretation. It is understandable, however, since it was unlikely that there was available to Socrates or Plato a sophisticated concept of right, or of freedom, or of other justice-concepts. Those ideas were developed in the centuries that followed. But a bit more was said by Socrates concerning legal obligation, punishment, and compensation. It is to these matters that I now turn.

References

Corlett, J. Angelo. 2014. *Responsibility and punishment*. 4th ed. Dordrecht: Springer.
Davis, Michael. 1992. *To make the punishment fit the crime*. Totowa: Rowman & Littlefield Publishers.
Feinberg, Joel. 1980. *Rights, justice, and the bounds of liberty*. Princeton: Princeton University Press.

———. 1992. *Freedom and fulfillment*. Princeton: Princeton University Press.
Irwin, Terence. 1986. Socratic inquiry and politics. *Ethics* 96: 400–415.
Keyt, David. 2008. Plato on justice. *Philosophical Inquiry* 30: 37–53.
Kraut, Richard. 1992. The defense of justice in Plato's *Republic*. In *The Cambridge companion to Plato*, ed. Richard Kraut, 311–337. Cambridge: Cambridge University Press.
———. 2003. Justice in Plato and Aristotle: Withdrawal *versus* engagement. In *Plato and Aristotle's ethics*, ed. R. Heinaman, 153–167. London: Ashgate.
Price, A.W. 2008. Reasoning about justice in Plato's *Republic*. *Philosophical Inquiry* 30: 25–35.
Rawls, John. 1999. *The law of peoples*. Cambridge: Harvard University Press.
Rowe, Christopher. 2003. Reply to Richard Kraut. In *Plato and Aristotle's ethics*, ed. R. Heinaman, 168–176. London: Ashgate.
Ryberg, Jesper. 2004. *The ethics of proportionate punishment*. Dordrecht: Kluwer Academic Publishers.

Chapter 6
Legal Obligation in Plato's *Crito*

...it's a splendid thing to obey the law,...—Socrates, *Sisyphus*, 387c.

Let someone despise you as a fool and throw dirt on you, if he likes. And, yes, by Zeus, confidently let him deal you that demeaning blow. Nothing terrible will happen to you if you really are an admirable and good man, one who practices excellence....this way of life is the best, to practice justice and the rest of excellence both in life and in death."—Socrates, *Gorgias* 527d-e

Philosophical discussion of legal obligation traces back at least to Socrates as he is portrayed in Plato's works. What, if anything, in Plato's corpus of writings provides the moral grounding for an obligation to obey legal authority? I shall not trace and assess each of the arguments for legal obligation proffered in Plato's *Crito*, whether they are taken to amount to one complex argument,[1] two arguments, or three.[2] Nor shall I assess the many reasons that Crito provides in favor

---

[1] See, for instance, Allen (1980: 112): "The *Crito* does not, as has often been thought, present a series of independent arguments for the conclusion that it is wrong to escape. It presents one argument with two interlocking premises."

[2] Woozley (1979). Also see Young (2006), Soper (1996), where it is argued that the three arguments are those of consent, fair play, and the harmful consequences of disobedience. The arguments are called those from agreement, piety and injury in James (1973: 119–120). David Bostock believes it is possible to construe the *Crito* in three possible ways concerning the number of arguments provided by Socrates for obedience to law. (Bostock 1990) That Socrates presents four such arguments is argued in McLaughlin (1976: 190). Also see Young (1974) for a discussion of what are said to be four such arguments given by

© Springer International Publishing AG, part of Springer Nature 2018 133
J. A. Corlett, *Interpreting Plato Socratically*,
https://doi.org/10.1007/978-3-319-77320-9_6

of Socrates' escaping his death sentence.[3] Instead, I shall provide a new way to construe the contents of the *Crito* without falling prey to either the unitarian fallacy[4] or the developmentalist fallacy.[5] While

---

Socrates. That the speech of the *nomoi* contain the "Argument from Harm to Athens and its Laws (*Crito* 50a), the Argument from Benefits, the Argument from the Special Status of the State-Citizen Relationship (*Crito* 50d-51c), and the Argument from the Citizenship Agreement (*Crito* 51c-53a) is found in Panagiotou (1987: 37).

[3] Seven such arguments are discussed in Greenberg (1965: 48 f.).

[4] The unitarian fallacy is the error one makes in assuming that it is a legitimate method of textual interpretation to piece together various statements of Socrates' throughout Plato's works into a (relatively) unified and coherent theory or view of this or that. It might be construed globally insofar as it is believed that certain ideas through most or all of Plato's works can be interpreted in a unified manner. Or, it might be understood moderately wherein certain concepts between some of Plato's works are coherent. Or, it might be believed that there is local unity of some concepts within a particular work of Plato's. This sort of method is often employed as a means of making best sense of what Socrates expresses in a particular dialogue, though an argument is required to ground the method as it implies that Socrates had somewhat of a systematic or mature view of this or that, when indeed he may not have had anything of the sort. An example of this kind of approach to the *Crito* is found in Kraut (1984). Kraut exemplifies a complex approach to Plato that is Socratic, unitarian, theoretical, mouthpiece variety that draws on the *Apology*, *Euthyphro* and other dialogues to understand Socrates' "political theory." While Kraut's approach is sophisticated, it is essentially circular as it depends for its own reasonableness on the very hermeneutical legitimacy of unitarianism itself. While his account is internally coherent, it rules out *a priori* anti-mouthpiece interpretations of Plato as well as developmentalist approaches. For a review of Kraut's book, see Irwin (1986). A critical review of Kraut's attempt to reconcile Socrates' attitude toward legal obligation in the *Apology* with Socrates' attitude, as expressed by the personified *nomoi* in the *Crito*, is found in Calvert (1987). As I will argue below, it is a violation of the Principle of Charity in Interpretation to ascribe to Socrates so unreasonable a view as that expressed by the *nomoi*. Recognizing this fact leads to a different interpretation of how the two seemingly inconsistent views are indeed not inconsistent.

[5] The developmentalist fallacy occurs to the extent that an interpreter of Plato believes fallaciously that there is a development in "Plato's thought," or in the thought of Socrates. What makes this a fallacy is that inadequate evidence is adduced in favor of the claim that Plato's works contain ideas that are discernibly those of Plato's or Socrates'. Global developmentalism is the approach to Plato that sees the development of certain ideas throughout Plato's works, say,

many commentators seek to reconcile Socrates' proclamation in the *Apology* that he would disobey the law insofar as it might banish the life of the philosopher with what many commentators believe is Socrates' bold support of legal obligation in the *Crito*, I shall reconcile these two seemingly contradictory attitudes of his by answering the question: "Why does Socrates go to his death and refuse Crito's attempt to save him?" In answering the question of why Socrates refuses to escape his death sentence, one is not forced to think that there is a contradiction between Socrates' attitudes concerning legal obligation between these works of Plato. I shall argue thusly without committing the error of thinking that what Socrates states in the *Crito* amounts to a belief, doctrine, or theory,[6] of either Plato's or Socrates'. For that would commit some variation of the "mouthpiece fallacy" which construes Socrates or some other character in Plato's dialogues as being a mouthpiece for the expression of Plato's theories, doctrines or beliefs.[7] Having repudiated the Mouthpiece Interpretation of Plato's dialogues in Chapters 2 and 3 of this book, I assume for the sake of this discussion and the chapters that follow that that approach to Plato's works is implausible. My interpretation of the *Crito* is consistent with the claim that "Plato's *Crito* is not a treatise on obedience to

---

from the early, to the middle, to the late dialogues. Moderate developmentalism holds that there is development of this or that concept between a couple or a few of Plato's works, while local developmentalism is the approach that sees development of some concept in a particular work of Plato's.

[6] One example of this kind of approach to the *Crito* is the idea that "…in the *Crito* Plato has produced a theory of an entirely different sort." (Kahn 1989: 29) Also see Mulgan (1972).

[7] "Mouthpiece fallacy" first occurs in Mulhern (1971). Relative to the *Crito*, the mouthpiece fallacy is committed, for instance, in Murphy (1974), where it is asserted without supportive argument that the *Crito* contains "an elaborate theoretical defense…of a political theory, the social contract theory…" (Murphy 1974: 15) and "the Socratic theory of legal fidelity." (Murphy 1974: 16, also see 22, 25) It is also found in Bostock (1990: 17), where Bostock claims "…that Plato did indeed mean to argue for the strong conclusion that one should always obey any and every law." Among others, it is also found in West (1989: 76). While we will see that this interpretation of the *Crito* and the attribution of it to Plato (or to Socrates) is rather uncharitable, it also exemplifies the intentional version of the Mouthpiece Interpretation of Plato's works.

the law" (Weinrib 1982: 85),[8] though it adds considerable philosophical importance to this idea. It also recognizes that there is a complex structure to the *Crito*, as it comprises both logical and dramatic elements. (Gomme 1958)

Legal Obligation in the *Crito*

Throughout the history of philosophy, much has been written about legal obligation. Receiving its fair share of discussion in philosophical circles is the attitude that Socrates, in his own person in his defense in the *Apology* and in the *Crito* by way of the personified *nomoi* of Athens, expresses concerning legal obligation.[9] In *Apology* 19a, Socrates declares that he must obey the law and defend himself from the accusations made against him by Meletus. What follows is an eloquent defense. Included in Socrates' speech to the Athenian court was his statement that he would rather align himself with the law and justice than to become unjust out of some fear of punishment. (*Apology* 32c) Perhaps overly confident in the fairness of the jurors, Socrates bids them to uphold the law rather than provide a favor to his enemies. (*Apology* 35c)

However, arguably the most primary Socratic source on legal obligation is Plato's *Crito*. Visiting Socrates in prison after his trial and conviction, Crito accuses Socrates of cowardice because he could save his own life and raise his sons well. (*Crito* 45c) Part of the reply to Crito is that genuine courage does not concern itself with what

---

[8] Those who treat the *Crito* as precisely such a treatise include Vlastos (1974).

[9] A. D. Woozley writes of Socrates presenting his own views about legal obligation in Woozley (1979, 1980). For another example of the interpretation that the laws of Athens in the *Crito* represent Socrates' own views on legal obligation and are in need, for the sake of unity, of reconciliation with Socrates' words in the *Apology* is found in James (1973). Also see Daniel M. Farrell who assumes that the speech of the *nomoi* are actually Socrates' own views and interprets the speech in deontological terms of universalizing maxims and social contract theory. (Farrell 1978) Other such attempts to reconcile the views articulated in the *Apology* and the *Crito* on legal obligation include Stephens (1985), wherein a questionable dilemma, fraught with all manner of dubious interpretive assumptions, is said to face Socrates.

others think of us, but rather what justice and injustice are, and the truth itself. (*Crito* 48a) And at *Crito* 49b, it is argued that "one must never do wrong," perhaps implying that it would be wrong for Socrates to disobey the legal authority of even a wrongful conviction. However, "wrong" in this context is ambiguous, as it might refer to either what is against the law or what is against true morality (or reason), a distinction that pervades discussions of moral, social, political and legal philosophy to this day. At *Crito* 50a it states: "…if we leave here without the city's permission, we are mistreating people whom we should least mistreat? And are we sticking to a just agreement, or not?" So the implied argument here is that, as a citizen of Athens, Socrates is bound to the court's ruling against him, even if he knows it to be incorrect, because of a just agreement he has made with the people of Athens.

At *Crito* 51c, Socrates and Crito concur with one another that "the laws speak the truth." What many commentators[10] on this matter seem not to notice is that this is a crucial assumption, as whatever else is argued by Socrates in the dialogue about legal obligation appears to be predicated on this claim. And since the fallibility of law is a given, it becomes unclear exactly what Socrates' view amounts to concerning legal obligation. Is it true, as so many commentators assert about this passage,[11] that there is, as Immanuel Kant famously argued,[12] an absolute moral obligation to obey the law? Or, rather, is it that there is an absolute moral obligation to obey a just law, a true law, e.g., the law insofar as it tracks moral truth?[13] These are two different positions. The first represents a moral obligation to obey the law, come what may, regardless of the content of the law, while the second amounts to a version of natural law theory which states that there is a moral obli-

---

[10] For example, see Feinberg (1979).

[11] Bostock (1990), Martin (1970), Young (1974). Bostock argues for what he calls the "authoritarian interpretation" which holds that "Plato did indeed mean to argue for the strong conclusion that one should always obey any and every law" (Bostock 1990: 17) and "that the good man will never intentionally disobey the law." (Bostock 1990: 20)

[12] Recall Immanuel Kant's famous statement that "It is the people's duty to endure even the most intolerable abuse of supreme authority…" (Kant 1965: 86)

[13] Dixit (1980), Wade (1971). For a discussion of Wade (1971), see James (1973).

gation to obey only just laws. Another way of understanding this position is to state that there is a *prima facie* moral obligation to obey the law. However, if the law is not worthy of obedience (e.g., it is unjust), then it may be disobeyed.[14] It is with this understanding, then, of the stated view (in the *Crito*) on legal obligation that we can approach these arguments with sufficient clarity regarding their meaning. What the *nomoi* personified argue is that there is an absolute moral obligation to obey the law. But quite apart from what the *nomoi* assert,[15] Socrates and Crito concur that the obedience of which they speak is conditional on the *nomoi* being just. Thus a question arises for Socrates, Crito, and readers of Plato's dialogue as to whether there is a *prima facie* moral obligation to obey the law in general, assuming it is just.

It is important to consider that many philosophers who seek to interpret the concept of legal obligation in the *Crito* believe it is necessary to square what is said therein with what is said of the matter in the *Apology*. But as David Gallop argues, this approach is problematic:

> The authoritarian view of the *Crito*, then, makes it teach something which virtually no one would accept as true, which the Platonic Socrates disavows, and which Plato elsewhere attacks. [*Republic* 338e] We should not, therefore, begin by accepting the authoritarian view as Plato's, and then ask how to square it with other Platonic works. Rather, we should ask whether the *Crito* really does teach that one must always obey the law, unless one can persuade the authorities to change it. For that is a perfectly preposterous doctrine. (Gallop 1998: 256)

I concur with the general gist of Gallop's statement, namely, that the interpreter of the *Crito* ought first to ask what the content of the *Crito* means concerning legal obligation before one begins to compare and contrast its contents on the subject with what is said about legal

---

[14] Of course, there are the further questions of, assuming that there is no absolute general moral obligation to obey the law, what is civil disobedience, under what conditions is it morally justified to disobey the law, and what is the role of civil disobedience in a reasonably just society. For discussions of these questions, see Feinberg (1979), Rawls (1971: 363–391).

[15] For an interpretation of the content of the speech of the *nomoi* and how its contents cannot be used to "bolster" the idea of civil disobedience, see Dyson (1978). It is noteworthy that my argument below that Socrates has a moral right to civil disobedience does not depend on anything said by the *nomoi*.

obligation elsewhere in Plato's works. However, it is unclear that the "view of" the *Crito* is "authoritarian," as Gallop asserts. Instead, it is the view of the *nomoi* in the *Crito* which is authoritarian. For it is quite reasonable to think that the authoritarian view is used as a rhetorical device[16] in an attempt to remind Crito of the problematic thinking of "the many" relative to Socrates' conviction and sentence. This is especially likely since, as Gallop himself argues, such authoritarianism "is a perfectly preposterous doctrine." The absurdity of the statements made by the *nomoi* is used by Socrates to bolster his decision to go to his death, thereby exposing the injustice of his legal conviction and sentence. So one must be careful to not attribute to either Plato or Socrates such an absurd position so as to avoid violation of a viable Principle of Charity in Interpretation as noted in previous chapters of this book.

Moreover, it is important also to bear in mind that there are at least two related questions here. The first is whether or not there is a moral obligation to obey the law as a corpus of rules and regulations, i.e., as an institution, while a second question is whether or not there is a moral obligation to obey a particular rule or ruling of law issuing from that institution. The discussion with Crito seems to focus on the moral question of legal obligation as it pertains to Socrates' sentence. Yet the general and particular questions are clearly related, as there can hardly be a moral obligation to obey the law if its particular laws are unjust, and there cannot be a moral obligation to obey a particular law if the moral soundness of the legal system is in serious question. I ignore the legal positivistic question of whether there is a legal obligation to obey the law or particular laws, as that seems to have no normative moral relevance. It is an odd legal system indeed which would not require obedience to it by its constituents. Kant points out that such a view countenances self-contradiction in the law.[17]

In recent philosophical discussions of civil disobedience, a distinction is drawn between direct and indirect civil disobedience. While the former constitutes that civil disobedience which by its very nature is aimed at changing a particular law that is perceived to be unjust

---

[16] It is referred to as an "unusual fiction" in Dybikowski (1974: 521).

[17] Kant makes the claim that it is "self-contradictory" for the law to permit one to disobey the law. (Kant 1965: 86)

(e.g., ethnically integrated sit-ins at segregated lunch counters in the U.S. south pre-1970 protesting Jim Crow laws), the latter amounts to civilly disobedient activity that does not directly challenge the particular aspect of the law that is perceived to be unjust (e.g., marching without a permit in protest against a legal rule or ruling that has nothing to do with legal rights or permissions to march). If Socrates were to escape in civil disobedience to the ruling against him including his death sentence, it would appear that he would have engaged in direct civil disobedience as he is immediately challenging his verdict and sentence. In so doing, Socrates is not so much challenging the general legal system of Athens, but rather he is challenging the justice of the particular ruling relative to himself. (Bertman 1971)

While it might be objected that Socrates' escaping his death sentence would not constitute a public[18] act in the Rawlsian sense and thus fail to satisfy the publicity condition of his act being a civilly disobedient one, presumably his life thereafter as a philosopher would be rather public, especially should he seek to live it as he did prior to his trial. That Socrates' escape really could not be public under the circumstances does not rule out that the end result of his escape could not and would not be. Recall that he is obedient to the oracle of Delphi that has commissioned him to engage others in the search for truth. (*Apology* 31d; 40a–c) This would be difficult to do if he were to do it only privately. So while the initial act of bribing the guard and escaping from prison is not much of a public act, Socrates' life thereafter would likely constitute a public protest as he would continue doing philosophy while refusing to drink the hemlock while in legal custody.

---

[18] This point is made in Vlastos (1974: 531), where Vlastos makes the claim that in the *Crito* Socrates would engage, not in civil disobedience but in fraudulently averting his death sentence, while in the *Apology* his words, if carried out in action, regarding disobedience to the laws of Athens would constitute civil disobedience. As Vlastos admits regarding whether or not Socrates ought to escape in order to save his own life: "It is taken for granted that what it would exemplify would be subverting a just law to save one's skin, not breaking an unjust law to protest injustice." (Vlastos 1974: 532) However, as I argue below, the arguments of the *Crito* and many commentators merely assume that the only options available to Socrates are to submit to death or to flee into exile and away from public life. But there is yet another option, namely, *that he escape to practice philosophy until he is captured and finally punished.*

It is also important to understand that posing questions concerning the moral justification of Socrates' engaging in civil disobedience to his legally imposed sentence is not the same as asking whether or not he ought to have escaped. As I shall argue below, he may have had a moral right to such disobedience while having overriding reasons to go to his death, whether or not he does so heroically.[19]

The *nomoi* offer various arguments for there being a moral obligation to obey the law, assuming the law is just. I shall construe them as constituting two such arguments: the argument from gratitude and the argument from promise-keeping. And much philosophical discussion has taken place about these arguments. But it seems to have taken place without the recognition of the assumption, made by both Socrates and Crito, that the law is just and the pivotal role that this assumption plays in a charitable understanding of the words of the *nomoi* on legal obligation. This failure on the part of many commentators points to their misunderstanding of the position on legal obligation expressed in the *Crito*.

Furthermore, Socrates himself considers and rejects the retaliatory argument for disobedience to the law. (*Crito* 50d-51b) Then we are asked, not by Socrates in his own person but by the *nomoi* of Athens, to consider an argument from gratitude: the law has given birth to us, nurtured us, educated us, shared goodness and wealth with us. A sign of gratitude is that we respect the law rather than disobey it. (*Crito* 51d) After all, any adult has the freedom to take her property and leave the confines of the law to another *polis*. (*Crito* 51e) A complex reason is provided for legal obligation in terms of gratitude. To disobey the law is to disobey those who nurtured us. Moreover, it is to fail to remain under the law and change it for the better. (*Crito* 51e-52a) While Joel Feinberg has noted that the first part of this argument from gratitude seems to be based on a *feeling* of gratitude instead of a moral duty thereto (Feinberg 1979), it is also questionable whether there is a moral obligation to obey the law in order to improve it.

Contrary to the sentiments of the *nomoi* in Plato's *Crito*, there is no general absolute moral duty to obey the law, but rather a moral right to disobey contingent on the extent to which the law serves as an

---

[19] That Socrates ought not to have escaped and that he goes to his death heroically is found in Greenberg (1965).

oppressor and thereby creates and sustains a violation of a social contract that might exist between citizens and their state. Implied here is the idea that fair play serves as a bond between the state and its citizens such that oppressed people have no contract to honor as they are not treated as members of a fair contractual situation. For the conditions of fair play do not exist for them, and it is unreasonable to expect them to honor an explicit or implicit agreement to obey a legal system that oppresses them. Generally speaking, those who are seriously oppressed or discriminated against by the law have less of an obligation to remain faithful to its rules in order to, say, improve it, while those who are discriminated against by the law in minor ways may have some moral duty to attempt to improve it.

Implied in the argument from gratitude, as stated by the *nomoi*, is the idea that the longer one remains under the law as an adult who can indeed freely move elsewhere without unreasonable burden to herself or those about whom she cares, the greater the moral duty to remain under the law in order to improve it. Since Socrates had plenty of opportunities to depart Athens but never took advantage of them (except for military service), he chose to remain one of its citizens. (*Crito* 52c)[20] Any attempt to escape the dictates of law, including a death sentence, stands in embarrassing conflict with this agreement made with Athens throughout his life. (*Crito* 52d) So say the *nomoi* of Athens as they are placed into the mouth of Socrates by Plato in order to address Crito's plea for Socrates to escape imprisonment and death.[21]

---

[20] Also see *Phaedrus* 230d where Phaedrus tells Socrates, "Not only do you never travel abroad—as far as I can tell, you never even set foot beyond the city walls." Socrates' reply is that "I am devoted to learning; landscapes and trees have nothing to teach me—only people in the city can do that."

[21] Other reasons for the injustice of Socrates' sentence are that capital punishment violates proportionality considerations, it was applied arbitrarily in ancient Athens, and that Socrates was not really being tried for atheism or for corrupting the Athenian youth. (James 1973: 125) That "…the city's authority to administer capital punishment is not questioned" is pointed out in Ray (1980: 53). It is a curious fact that commentators on Plato's *Crito* seem not to raise questions concerning the justice or ethics of Socrates' sentence—even if he were duly found guilty of atheism and corrupting the youth. This is an especially interesting oversight given that elsewhere in numerous of Plato's works Socrates expresses retributivist sentiments (even some in favor of capital

But if it is true that Socrates was treated unjustly by Athens, including its legal system, then the question arises as to whether he has a genuine obligation to accept his death sentence. In what sense should Socrates be grateful or feel gratitude if he was treated unjustly by the laws of Athens? Here is where questions must be posed regarding whether or not, Athenian law aside, Socrates indeed insulted the gods and corrupted the youth. And if such charges are false, then on what grounds does he have an obligation to obey the laws of Athens, especially as they pertain to the ruling imposing his death sentence? In such a case, would not the social compact requirement of fair play stand in the way of his legal obligation? For if there is a significant violation of considerations of fair play, then what would morally bind Socrates to obey his sentence?

The Role of the *Nomoi* in the *Crito*

It seems reasonable to think that the <u>nomoi</u> is a sarcastic literary device used by Plato to engage his readers in philosophical dialectic concerning questions of legal obligation in general and Socrates' legal obligation in particular. But what further role might the speech of the *nomoi* play in the *Crito*? Might the *nomoi* voice Socrates' views of legal obligation? If not, then there is no reason to think, as many do, that there is even a *prima facie* discrepancy between what Socrates states in the *Apology* about legal obligation and what is stated in the *Crito* by the *nomoi*. While G. X. Santas asserts that "Socrates puts his arguments in the mouth of the law of the city…" (Santas 1979: 15), Charles Kahn suggests that Plato uses the speech of the *nomoi* as a rhetorical device, but in so doing it got out of hand due to "an authoritarian streak in Plato's own political temperament." (Kahn 1989: 40) However, as it has been observed, "Socrates is not pressing the argument in his own right, but through a personification, he achieves a certain distance between the laws' arguments and himself" (Dybikowski 1974: 522), and that Socrates nonetheless "accepts the fundamental premises and conclusion of the laws'

---

punishment!). Is capital punishment a proportionate punishment for atheism or corrupting youth?

argument" in order to avoid a pointless cynicism about legal obligation, while another scholar suggests that Socrates' use of the personified *nomoi* "is drawing attention to the status of the Laws as an hallucination, and he is thus denying the reality of their words." (Weinrib 1982: 101)[22] Yet this is not necessary to postulate if Socrates uses the *nomoi* as a sarcastic literary device, a "performance by Socrates" (White 1996: 114), to reduce to absurdity (for Crito) the very position on legal obligation the *nomoi* espouses. For "…the laws' contention is so sweeping that arguments purporting to support it will lack plausibility." (Dybikowski 1974: 524) Perhaps what Socrates is attempting to get Crito to understand is that there are questions of ethics which must be faced beyond those of gratitude and the law. And this reading of the use of the *nomoi* by Socrates makes good sense if it is construed as Socrates' rhetorical use of sarcasm.[23] Perhaps this is, "drown out by the oratory of the Laws, an unheard Socratic perspective on the question of his possible flight from execution…" (Miller 1996: 128) As N. A. Greenberg notes: "…the device of personification is dubious, for it embodies exactly the conviction which it is meant to oppose: what counts are the claims of people, not things." (Greenberg 1965: 78–79) It would be sarcastic of Socrates to speak in the name of the *nomoi* when he himself was not in favor of anything that did not conform to the rule of reason and often against the voice of the many: "…at all times I am the kind of man who listens to nothing within me but the argument that on reflection seems best to me." (*Crito* 46b) Furthermore, the deontic statement at *Crito* 49c–d regarding never rendering evil for evil seems, as any other absolute judgment, problematic and intrinsically unsocratic.[24] It is not as if Socrates does not engage in

---

[22] I concur with Weinrib that Socrates does not accept the arguments of the *nomoi*, as the arguments of the *nomoi* "are not enunciated directly by Socrates because they are not consistent with his philosophical position." (Weinrib 1982: 102) Also see White (1996: 114): "It is here not a serious statement of Socrates' own views." However, I do not see why it is necessary to think, as Weinrib does, that Socrates thought anything hallucinatory regarding them.

[23] That Socrates' use of sarcasm as a device is mentioned, but not developed, in Greenberg (1965: 47).

[24] This point is found in Greenberg (1965: 60). Greenberg adds that Socrates' use of the *nomoi* personified seems to be mostly emotive, contrary to Socrates

sarcasm elsewhere in Plato's writings. In *Gorgias* 497c, Socrates states: "You're a happy man, Callicles, in that you've been initiated into the greater mysteries before the lesser. I didn't think it was permitted."

Moreover, as Gregory Vlastos points out of Plato's use of the personification of the *nomoi* in the *Crito*:

> There is no dialectic here: no definition of terms, no facing up to obscurities and perplexities, no consideration of counterexamples. Time and again we see the diction running into hyperbole and the thought blown about by gusts of feeling. ...Plato would have served us better by leaving this kind of art to the rhetoricians.... (Vlastos 1974: 519)

And it is obvious that the legal ruling against Socrates, along with its sentencing of him, was morally unreasonable. Essentially, Socrates is ruled to be guilty of practicing philosophy (dressed up as charges of atheism and corrupting the youth), manifestly unreasonable charges in light of Socrates' speech in the *Apology*. So it is as if Socrates is attempting to get Crito to understand that what the many (who determine the rule of law) think is hardly what matters, especially in terms of doing what is morally right.

It is also reasonable to think that the nomoi *are used by Socrates to expose his injustice at the hands of Athens.* Another reason Socrates makes use of the *nomoi* in this manner might be that he wanted to force Athens to assume responsibility for his wrongful treatment, either directly upon his death or thereafter. And in reply to the idea that Socrates might have lived his life and died in vain, there are Socrates' haunting words from the *Apology* 39c-d: "...You are wrong if you believe that by killing people you will prevent anyone from reproaching you for not living in the right way. To escape such tests is neither possible nor good, but it is best and easiest not to discredit others but to prepare oneself to be as good as possible." In so doing, Socrates seeks to make Athens better by setting an example for how

---

constant reliance on the use of and reliance on *logos* (Greenberg 1965: 61), and they are easily refuted. (Greenberg 1965: 62) That the speech of the *nomoi* is "unsocratic" is also noted in Vlastos (1974: 519), Quandt (1982: 238), and in Weiss (1998: 5). For a defense of part of the speech of the *nomoi* as characterizing a serious and sound deontological argument as to why Socrates ought to obey his sentence in order to always avoid doing wrong regardless of the consequences of the act, see Barker (1977).

Athenians ought to live, and die, namely, by "radical reflection" on each.[25]

It is also likely that the <u>nomoi</u> are used by Socrates to prod readers to reflect philosophically on legal obligation in general, and about Socrates' case in particular. Whether or not Socrates' confidence underlying his approach to his life and death is motivated by a considered judgment or faith in an afterlife is unclear. Nor is it obvious that, as one commentator thinks, Socrates employs the personified *nomoi* in order to evade either Crito's arguments or Crito himself. (Rosen 1973) Regardless, it is unreasonable to think that Socrates' own views on legal obligation are stated directly in the *Crito*. What is most important is that readers of Plato's dialogue are compelled to think critically about the issues associated with the problem of legal obligation.[26]

The argument from gratitude leads to the argument from promise-keeping. Socrates understands fully the moral dilemma facing him by his imagined critics of his contemplated escape from his death sentence:

> "Surely," they might say, "you are breaking the commitments and agreements that you made with us without compulsion or deceit, and under no pressure of time for deliberation. You have had seventy years during which you could have gone away if you did not like us, and if you thought our agreements unjust. You did not choose to go to Sparta or to Crete, which you are always saying are well governed, nor to any other city, Greek or foreign." (*Crito* 52e-53a)

Does this not imply the cowardice of Socrates should he seek to disobey the court's verdict in his own case? Would it not reveal that he is not a person of his word, that he wants life on his own terms? And if Socrates is unconcerned with himself should he face ridicule for attempting to escape, would not his escape result in the harsh treatment of his family and friends who are linked to him by association? (*Crito* 53b) And if he were to escape Athens' judgment of him,

---

[25] The contents of this paragraph are borrowed from Miller (1996: 135), though Miller opts for an interpretation of the *Crito* which construes them as Socratic irony which involves Socratic self-suppression of his views on legal obligation. Also see, Dybikowski (1974: 531).

[26] That the *Crito* also involves matters related to death and the relationship between Socrates and Crito is found in White (1996).

anywhere he would go in Greece would treat him as an "enemy." (*Crito* 53b) Further, Socrates would lead many in the jury to deem their sentencing of him as right, which it surely was not for the reasons Socrates himself so eloquently expresses in the *Apology*. While Socrates might avoid some or all of these problems by settling in a town of ignorant folk who do not know him, would his life be worth living? What could a great mind like Socrates' possibly have in common with benighted fools? (*Crito* 53c) And if that is the case, what is the probability that Socrates would not suffer a worse fate than in Athens? In short, escaping his death sentence in Athens would disgrace his name. (*Crito* 53e) Beyond that is the likely alienation he would endure due to his being forced to live without the immediate presence of his family while he is in self-imposed exile from Athens. (*Crito* 53e-54a)

But more than all of these practical matters, the *nomoi* put forth the argument that one ought never to value any practical matter in life more than goodness (*Crito* 54b), implying that it is intrinsically right to obey the law, as it is always the right thing to do. For it is wrong to disobey the law because of what some people have done in using the law unjustly and unfairly. It is even under such circumstances best to obey the law and their perverted use of it in sentencing than to disobey the law itself. Indeed, this is of what the laws remind Socrates regarding his belief that god is instructing him. (*Crito* 54e) It is noteworthy here that the question Socrates faces as the result of being awakened from his sleep by Crito is whether or not *he* ought to disobey the law regarding his being unjustly convicted and sentenced. This raises an interesting interpretive quandary: "But the question which the Laws put to him concerns not his private complaint against a single act of theirs but his charge against Athenian laws in general. The question of Socrates' charge against Athenian laws in general is raised but not answered in the *Crito*." (Strauss 1984: 61) This provides further reason to think that Socrates employs the personified *nomoi* as a sarcastic rhetorical device to render the conservative position of the *nomoi* absurd in that it is off point.

As noted earlier, in assessing the arguments that the *nomoi* set forth in *Crito* 54e, we must bear in mind that it is assumed at the outset of his imagined dialogue between the laws and Athenian citizens that the laws are in fact just.[27] This argument does not, as stated, assume that the *application* of the law is just. This seems to imply to some that there is an absolute moral obligation to obey the law as it is stated, though not always its application.

Yet the application of the law is quite relevant to whether or not there is a moral duty to obey it. This suggests that whether or not the law rightly demands our obedience is transitive: If there is a moral obligation to obey the law and a particular part of the law issues a ruling, then there is a moral obligation to obey that ruling. Yet if there is no obligation to obey a ruling of law because it is unjust, then there is no moral obligation to obey the part of the law that issued the unjust result. In other words, if whatever issues from the law is unjust, there is no obligation to obey the part of the law that eventuated in the injustice. An example of this is when a people is oppressed under either the misapplication or non-application of generally just constitutional laws, as was the case especially for U.S. blacks and American Indians under Jim Crow. What Martin Luther King, Jr. and many other civil rights workers often argued was that the principles of law stated or latent in the U.S. Constitution ought to be applied uniformly throughout the country, regardless of the ethnic or sexual status of persons under the law. While many in the civil rights movement, including King himself, protested the law within the limits of fidelity to it often by engaging in non-violent direct action instead of civil disobedience and did not always break a law in protest, others engaged in civil disobedience. To the extent that they satisfied the conditions necessary and sufficient for morally justified law-breaking, they were morally justified in breaking the law in protest, whether directly or indirectly. This is especially the case given the levels of oppression experienced by such persons under Jim Crow.

Consider also what the Visitor asserts in Plato's *Statesman* 294d, where the imperfection of the law is acknowledged: "Why then is it ever necessary to make laws, given that law is not something completely correct?" Socrates answers, "Certainly." This supports the idea

---

[27] That Socrates thought the laws of Athens were just is stated in Wade (1971: 317), though it is unclear whether this amounts to the same thing as Socrates assuming the laws to be just, for the sake of argument. That Socrates assumes the laws of Athens to be just for the sake of argument is recognized in Allen (1972: 562).

that in the *Crito* Socrates is assuming the justness of the law when considering whether or not there is a moral obligation to obey it. Furthermore, it must be borne in mind that the *nomoi* themselves admit Socrates' innocence (*Crito* 54c) and that he was wronged not by them, but by a miscarriage of justice.

It is, moreover, reasonable to think that the <u>nomoi</u> are used by Socrates to embarrass the Court of Athens for its outlawing the examined life. A related reason for interpreting as sarcastic Socrates' use of the *nomoi* in the *Crito* which express reasons for his not escaping his punishment is to embarrass Athens, especially the Court of Athens and Meletus, for doing Socrates and themselves a grand injustice in essentially outlawing the examined life, ironic given that, if Socrates is correct, Athens is "where there's more freedom of speech than anywhere else in Greece,..." (*Gorgias* 461e) Furthermore, by not escaping, Socrates forces the hand of Athens to inflict a grave injustice on him and itself, which is "the worse thing there is" as it is the lesser harmful wrongdoing to be the victim of such injustice. (*Gorgias* 469b–c; also see 474b, 475c–d; 508e; and 509b–c) This is so, on Socrates' considered judgment, because the unjust are wicked and miserable (*Gorgias* 469e; those, like Meletus, who accuse Socrates of wrongdoing when he is innocent are "wicked" in *Gorgias* 521d) whose souls are sick and discordant. (*Sophist* 228b) And he is even more miserable to the extent that he does not "get his due punishment for the wrongdoing he commits, the less so if he pays and receives what is due at the hands of both gods and men." (*Gorgias* 472e; also see 473b; 509b-c) Even more miserable than that is "the one who avoids getting caught and becomes a tyrant." (*Gorgias* 473e) Hence "...the one being disciplined is being acted upon justly when he pays what is due..." (*Gorgias* 476e) in that harmful wrongdoers are ridding their souls of something bad. (*Gorgias* 477s)

It seems, then, that Socrates is going to his death consistent with the idea that it will expose to people the injustices of Athens and its most miserable condition both in condemning Socrates to death and banning the examined life. Indeed, if it is true to say that Athens has a soul, it would be true to infer that its soul is corrupted and that the corruption of its soul is "the most shameful thing." (*Gorgias* 477d; also see 477e) In exposing this sad fact about Athens, Socrates seeks to benefit it in the hope that it will improve itself by way of the examined life that it has outlawed with its condemnation of Socrates. In this way, then, Socrates is urging his fellow Athenians to make the difficult trek out of the cave and into the light. (*Republic* 7) For though Socrates loved philosophy first (*Gorgias* 481d), he also loved Athens which Socrates refers to as his "other beloved." (*Gorgias* 482a) Recall his words to Callicles: "Shouldn't we then attempt to care for the city and its citizens with the aim of making its citizens themselves as good as possible?" (*Gorgias* 513e)

In fact, Socrates makes it a condition of a good civic leader that he makes citizens better. (*Gorgias* 513e-521) Unbeknownst to Athens, then, it has just condemned to death perhaps[28] its most morally distinguished citizen! And it appears that the very same ignorance which condemned Socrates in court is the very same attitude which prohibits Athens from comprehending the wrongness of its act. Clearly, it prefers the stylings of Meletus over the tough-minded challenges of the Examiner. Why? Perhaps it is because if the things Socrates says in his philosophical quest are true, as Callicles asks of Socrates, "won't this human life of ours be turned upside down, and won't everything we do evidently be the opposite of what we should do?" (*Gorgias* 481c)[29] After all, the examined life does not kowtow to the opinions of the many. (*Gorgias* 512e-513a) It takes courage to live the examined life, and it is prone to loneliness, as Socrates states: "I think it's better to have my lyre or a chorus that I might lead out of tune and dissonant,[30]

---

[28] "Perhaps" in that, as Socrates notes, he is "one of a few Athenians…to take up the true political craft and practice of true politics." (*Gorgias* 521d)

[29] Also see Callicles' statements that too much philosophy will ruin a person by rendering him inexperienced at other matters of life (*Gorgias* 484c-d), and that philosophy is "ridiculous and unmanly, deserving a flogging" when practiced by older men. (*Gorgias* 485c; also see 485a-d) Assuming that Callicles' attitude reflects the *demos* of Athens more generally, it is no wonder that Socrates was convicted and sentenced to death. Ironically, Callicles even suggests to Socrates that philosophy, as opposed to oratory, would do him no good if he were to find himself accused of the most serious of crimes. (*Gorgias* 486a-c) That there was a wide range of attitudes (many negative) toward philosophers during Socrates' day is also reflected in the *Sophist* 216c-d. Perhaps, since Socrates was also charged with a kind of atheism relative to the gods of Greece, there was a pervasive lack of latitudinarianism throughout Athens at the time.

[30] At *Gorgias* 521e, Socrates states that his speeches "don't aim at what's most pleasant" because he is "not willing to" employ the clever rhetoric of Callicles and other orators in order to appease the many. Also see *Gorgias* 521e-522d.

and have the vast majority of men disagree with me and contradict me, than to be out of harmony with myself, to contradict myself, though I'm only one person." (*Gorgias* 482c; also see 522e)

Another reason for thinking that Socrates does not himself believe the arguments for legal obligation articulated by the *nomoi* is that, not only are they baldly problematic in that to impute them to Socrates constitutes a violation of the Principle of Charity of Interpretation, but in the *Greater Hippias* 284d, Socrates states that "So when people who are trying to make laws fail to make them good, they have failed to make them lawful—indeed, to make them law." If this is true, then it is plausible to hold that Socrates thinks there is only a moral duty to obey the law insofar as it is just. But when the law is unjust, then the law is, as Thomas Aquinas argued centuries later,[31] no law at all in the sense that it morally binds no one to it. We have, then, perhaps a philosophical precursor to this Thomistic natural law proclamation.

I suggest, then, that Plato's Socrates' employment of the *nomoi* personified constitutes his sarcastic rhetorical device to inform Crito that Socrates has no moral obligation to obey the ruling against him. For the tenability of the reasoning of the *nomoi*, authoritative as it is, is highly questionable to Socrates, especially in light of the other passages cited (above) concerning his attitude on the subject. This is not inconsistent, moreover, with thinking that in the end Socrates chooses to die in order to expose publicly the injustice of his sentence, and perhaps Athenian society in general insofar as it criminalized the examined life in the guise of charges of atheism and corruption of youth.[32] For Socrates may well have believed, with whatever concepts available to him, that he had a right to disobey the ruling against him, though as a right holder he need not exercise that right. Generally, being in possession of a right does not coerce one to exercise or enjoy it, as good judgment is required in such matters.

That *good* law, e.g., that which commands our respect and obedience, is just is made emphatic in the *Minos*, where Socrates says to his friend: "Law, then, is not what is accepted." (*Minos* 313c) After a discussion of whether or not the nature of law is revelatory or a matter

---

[31] For a discussion of this point, see Kretzmann (1988).

[32] Nor is it inconsistent with Socrates' proclaimed love of Athens.

of discovery, Socrates argues that law is discovery of reality. (*Minos* 315a; 317d) This implies that the law ought to contain rules concerning how we ought to live, providing additional evidence of Socrates as a forebear of natural law theory concerning the nature of law. Accordingly, Socrates seems to assume that the law is just. On this supposition, then, it makes sense for him to think that there is an absolute moral duty to not disobey just law—even to the point of not disobeying an unjust death sentence! To the extent that the law is just, it ought not to be disobeyed. It is no wonder Socrates thinks we "should always cooperate with it." (*Laws* 645a) It is no surprise, then, to find Socrates exclaiming to Sisyphus: "…it's a splendid thing to obey the law,…" (*Sisyphus* 387c) Thus to the extent that the law is just, Socrates believes that it ought to be obeyed. But it is not to be obeyed because it is the law, but rather insofar as it is just. However, it is reasonable to assume that Socrates is aware of the injustice of his sentence. Thus it is reasonable to suppose that he does not believe that he has a moral duty to obey it. Yet if he has a right to disobey it, he need not exercise that right. Rather, he may choose to go to his death in order to, say, expose Athenian injustice at least relative to his own case. This implies the falsity of John M. Cooper's claim that Socrates "must,…abide by the laws' final judgment and accept his death sentence." (Cooper and Hutchinson 1997: 38) To the extent that Socrates has a moral right to disobey his death sentence due to its injustice, he need not opt to escape, but choose to act otherwise. Others, then, would have a moral duty to refrain from preventing him the exercise of his right given the general (but not absolute or perfect) correlation between rights and duties. But Socrates chooses instead to underscore the fundamental injustice of his sentence, and of Athenian society for allowing Meletus to influence such an unjust verdict and sentence on such an innocent person, guilty only of seeking truth and avoiding error and assisting others in doing so in order that they would be better for the rest of their lives. (*Euthyphro* 16)

So Socrates might have escaped and would have been morally justified in doing so. But he could also have done exactly what he did do and was morally justified in doing so. All the while, he listened only to arguments that, on reflection, seemed best to him. (*Crito* 46b) Socrates valued principles he has articulated on other occasions, presumably, in certain of the other dialogues of Plato. (*Crito* 46b) It is reasonable to attribute to him, then, values such as those articulated above about following justice and not injustice, never doing wrong (*Crito* 49) or not following the opinion of the many, but rather valuing true beliefs and not false ones. (*Crito* 47a) But attributing to Plato's Socrates such general views is not what truly separates Socratic Mouthpiece Interpretation from the Socratic Anti-Mouthpiece Interpretation. For these are broad views that presumably most would say they adopt. Making such ascriptions to Socrates is hardly the same thing as attributing more particular ideologies to him such as that he believes in a theory of forms, or in a theory of art, or that he is an oligarch, anti-democratic, communistic, totalitarian, etc..

Thus for Socrates, assuming that the law is just, we have a moral obligation to not disobey it.[33] For we have a moral duty to do what is just, and the law is, on his assumption in the *Crito*, just. However, it might be a mistake of grand proportions to conflate Socrates' statements in his own person in the *Crito* with his sarcastic (or otherwise) expression of the *nomoi* personified in the same dialogue. For on his considered view, to the extent that the law is not just, there is no obligation to obey it, as arguments from gratitude and promise-keeping seem to be problematic, as seen in the *Crito*. Or, at least, it does not follow from Socrates' claim that assuming the justice of the law that there is a moral obligation to not disobey it that there is a moral obligation to obey the law, come what may. A path is left open, then, for morally justified disobedience to the law insofar as the law is unjust. However, and unfortunately for those who resent Socrates' death because of its injustice, this avenue is not explored by Crito, and thus not addressed by Socrates in the pages of Plato's *Crito*.

In light of what Thomas C. Brickhouse and Nicholas D. Smith refer to as "Socrates' famous absolute prohibition of injustice" (Brickhouse and Smith 1994: 141) in *Crito* 49d, why ought one to suffer punishment for something, even if it were legitimately ruled a crime, one did not commit? Why should one suffer, that is, what one does not deserve?[34] Or, as R. E. Allen puts it: "Can it conceivably be true that a man ought to abide by his own death sentence, given that the sentence

---

[33] The distinction between reasons for obedience to the law and those against disobedience to it is found in Martin (1970: 22), Woozley (1980, 1979: 22–26).

[34] That these are Socratic notions is articulated in Chapter 7 of this book.

was rendered according to law and that he is not guilty?" (Allen 1972: 558) Not unlike the bulk of Plato's other writings, the *Crito* is apparent in its lesson that good reasons, sound arguments, are what one ought to abide by in theory and in life. Good ones sometimes make the difference between life and death, certain other circumstances obtaining. So that Socrates rejects Crito's arguments for disobeying the legal sentencing of Socrates in no way implies that either Socrates had no good reason to escape, or that there was (unbeknownst to Socrates, Crito, or anyone else) a good reason to escape. And this is apparent especially in light of the flaws in Socrates' reasons for not disobeying the law, not to mention the fact that there is "…nothing in the dialogue between Socrates and the Laws which explicitly states, or requires, that the basic agreement cannot be abrogated." (Martin 1970: 29) This implies that there was at least one good reason for Socrates to escape and thereby to disobey the law.

However, "Socrates went to his death on the basis of a *logos*, an argument. He chose to die because he was convinced by reasoning that it was wrong to escape." (Allen 1972: 558)[35] The *Crito* is an aporetic dialogue that bids readers to delve more deeply into its contents and discover possible reasons why things might have turned out differently for Socrates. In large part, it is about the "sovereignty of reason" in everyday life, and death. (Allen 1972: 567; Allen 1980: 113) This reflects Socrates' "unflagging commitment to the rational pursuit of truth even when it is his own life that is at stake." (Quandt 1982: 238) But this is consistent with my point that Socrates chooses to waive his moral right to flight in order to draw attention to his unjust conviction and sentence.

Contrary to what some others have interpreted Socrates to believe about legal obligation in Plato's *Crito*, it turns out that, even on the dubious assumption that the speech of the *nomoi* reflect Socrates' own views, Socrates does not believe that there is an absolute moral duty to obey the law. Assuming that the law is just, then we have a duty to obey it. But, again, it is not merely because it is the law that we must obey it. Rather, it is because it is just that we must obey it. Most

---

[35] Allen continues: "Whether Socrates should escape has nothing to do with what people think, their praise and ignorant blame; it is a question to be settled by *logoi*—arguments, accounts, reasoned conclusions. The issue rests with 'he who understands things just and unjust,' the Truth itself." (Allen 1972: 561)

importantly, what determines whether or not the law is just is a matter of the balance of human reason, all relevant things considered. A life lived according to the best dictates of reason is a life well-lived. For "the unexamined life is not worth living." (*Apology* 38a) Socrates abided by the sentence from the Athenian court, even though it was unjust as he neither corrupted the youth nor was he an atheist.

Socrates obeyed the law, unjust as it was. But to the very end, he encouraged Crito and, as it turns out, readers of the *Crito*, to think more deeply about whether or not Socrates really did have an obligation to obey the law, and why. Moreover, he seeks to expose the absurdity of the reasons given as to why one might think Socrates ought to obey the court's decision, and the injustice of that decision itself.

As for the alleged inconsistency between what Socrates states in the *Apology* wherein he translucently states his refusal to stop practicing philosophy even if the laws condemn it (32a-b), and where in the *Crito* it is argued that Socrates argues against disobedience to the law, there are several problems. First, as I have noted above, while the *Apology* consists in the speech of Socrates speaking on his own behalf, the *Crito* (from 51c and following) consists of Socrates not speaking his own words, but those of the *nomoi* of Athens. This means that while there is an inconsistency between the informational contents of the two works of Plato, it is not one facing Socrates himself as many commentators think.

Secondly, even in light of the first difficulty, important consistency remains concerning Socrates' behavior vis-à-vis the *nomoi* and his attitude toward them. Just as in his speech to the Athenian court he refused to resort to begging, crying and the like to win leniency, he goes to his death willingly because, it is reasonable to suppose, the unexamined life is not worth living, and "the most important thing is not life, but the good life." (*Crito* 48b) If living in Athens prohibits him from "the good life" of engaging others philosophically, then life in Athens, his beloved city, is not worth it because it is not good. For "in condemning Socrates the Athenians condemned philosophy as a way of life." (Weinrib 1982: 92)[36] As Vlastos notes:

---

[36] Indeed, the speech of the *nomoi* and the basic message of the *Crito* itself constitutes a "shrewd observation about Socrates' future inability to practice philosophy." (Colson 1989: 37) Under such circumstances, then, for Socrates, "death is preferable to mere life, that is, to living without examining." (Colson 1989: 40)

...to obey *this* command [of the Athenian court to not practice philosophy] he would have to give up something he had prized more than life, and which the state should have valued more than obedience: his moral identity. The character Socrates had created for himself—the person he had come to *be* for his own and all subsequent generations—would have been shattered had he now chosen to muzzle himself at the behest of the state; by prolonging his physical existence on those terms he would have committed moral self-destruction. (Vlastos 1974: 533)

Why, then, ought Socrates to resort to bribery and escape in order to live an *un*examined life? This interpretation of the contents of the *Apology* and the *Crito* is congruent with the following perspective:

...Socrates' first allegiance is to justice and philosophy; he is man first and citizen second; and he refuses to escape because he believes that escape would violate the moral principles to which he has always adhered. The views espoused by the Laws are the views of the laws—not of Socrates; indeed, the moral perspective reflected in the laws' arguments stands in stark opposition to the Socratic point of view. (Weiss 1998: 3)

It is plausible to think that Plato creates the speech of the *nomoi* "for Crito's benefit," and that Socrates in the end fails to benefit Crito's soul. (Weiss 1998: 4) However, this not only fails to rule out my suggestion that Socrates employs the speech of the *nomoi* out of sarcasm (and as a rhetorical device of Socrates' or Plato's[37]) in order to expose how ridiculous the argument(s) of the *nomoi* (are), but they end up, given their transparent implausibility, showing that not only does Crito's set of arguments fail to persuade Socrates, but Socrates courageously chooses death rather than to be controlled by the injustice of his sentence.

It is, furthermore, reasonable to think that the <u>nomoi</u> are used by Socrates as a reductio ad absurdum of the view of "the many." The arguments of the *nomoi* are indeed, I further suggest, a kind of *reductio ad absurdum* of the idea that Socrates ought to consider what the many will think of him should he not escape as he would hasten his own death just as his enemies wish for him (*Crito* 45c), and that he would fail his sons by not being able to father them in his permanent absence. (45d)

---

[37] Weiss (1998: 6). This runs counter to R. E. Allen's idea that the words of the laws of Athens represent Socrates' own [Allen (1984: 107), cited in Weiss (1998: 57)].

And while it is plausible to assert that the informational contents of the arguments of the *nomoi* are fundamentally unsocratic, the method and motivation for Socrates' (or Plato's) employment of them is quite Socratic indeed, as it turns the argument against Crito. Perhaps, then, it is not Socrates who fails to benefit the soul of Crito as much as it is Crito's failure to benefit his own soul by doing more to grasp Socrates' words. This is congruent with Socrates' consistent insistence on the rule of reason in thought and in life. As noted above, the result is that Socrates, following the arguments wherever they lead him, chooses death. Why? Because "Socrates will not...obey Crito unless Crito produces a principle superior to his." (Weiss 1998: 60) Thus one good-making feature of my interpretation of the *Crito* is that it retains the importance of the Socratic "persuade [*peithô*] or obey" attitude toward legal rules and rulings. It is not, however, that one must indeed succeed in persuading others that it is justified to break the law, or obey it instead. Rather, it is that one must engage others in the process of persuasion, even if one fails to convince others of the truth of one's own position. (Young 2006: 84)[38]

While "Perhaps...flight would be justified for Socrates, as it was for Achilles, ... that departure will be frustrated by supervening considerations." (Weinrib 1982: 90) In the end, Socrates chooses to accept his death sentence perhaps in a heroic gesture to expose some of the injustices of Athenian society, especially those concerning his plight. The injustices include not only the conviction of Socrates for the crimes he did not commit, but in its essentially criminalizing Socratic philosophy. While he attempted with all his might to persuade the court of his innocence relative to the charges leveled against him, the court (perhaps unsurprisingly) failed to heed his wisdom. In the midst of the injustice of the court, Socrates knows that he has a moral right to disobey his sentence if for no other reason than he complied with the "persuade or obey" dictum (in the requisite sense of "persuade"). But the absurdity of the argumentation of the personified *nomoi* suggests that Socrates is aware of further difficulties with such an authoritarian standpoint on legal obligation. Nonetheless, he goes to his death (perhaps unintentionally) as a hero who is respected by those

---

[38] Charles Young's point is intended as a corrective to the idea that a complainant must actually convince others, or obey the law, an interpretation found in Panagiotou (1987: 44).

who love wisdom and hate injustice. Having a moral right to disobey the court's unjust ruling, Socrates instead chooses to go to his death in order to expose the injustice of the court of Athens, unjust at least relative to his particular case.[39] For the discussion of legal obligation in the *Crito* is, as Vlastos argues, not so much one about the general question of obedience to political authority, but one about whether or not *Socrates* ought to comply with his unjust sentence. (Vlastos 1974: 534)[40] And insofar as the dilemma facing Socrates seems to be of his facing either exile or hemlock, "It is impossible to overemphasize the infeasibility of exile for the Socratic life." (Colson 1989: 47) And while it is true that "we can only understand why Socrates chooses not to escape Athens by taking seriously his claim that the unphilosophical life is not worth living…" (Colson 1989: 52), it is also plausible to think that Socrates, in not disobeying his sentence, seeks to expose its fundamental injustice, morally speaking, by stating (in the guise of the *nomoi*) the reasons why he ought to obey, and what this implies for the examined life. For Socrates, life without philosophy renders unthinkable the fundamental meaning of his life insofar as that life values centrally a certain kind of critical inquiry. (White 1996: 121)

Objections and Replies

Having set forth a coherent and novel approach to the notion of legal obligation in the *Crito* which does not attribute to Socrates contradictory beliefs (in the *Apology* and the *Crito*, respectively) concerning his own legal obligation, it is important to consider some concerns that might arise regarding it. First, it might be objected that my analysis of the *Crito* fails to take into consideration Socrates' explicit and

---

[39] It is noteworthy that my interpretation of the *Apology* and the *Crito* on legal obligation sidesteps the debate about how to reconcile two apparently opposing positions espoused by Socrates on the matter: Brickhouse and Smith (1984), Colson (1986). This discussion centers on whether or not the facts of ancient Athenian law would have made Socrates' verdict justified, and hence Socrates' possible disobedience to it unjustified. Of course, this discussion assumes a kind of legal positivistic stance on whether or not Socrates would have been morally justified in disobeying his sentence.

[40] Also see White (1996: 109).

repeated claims that "...one must never in any way do wrong willingly..." and "...wrongdoing and injustice is in every way harmful and shameful to the wrongdoer" and "nor must one, when wronged, inflict wrong in return." (*Crito* 49) In light of these statements, it is implausible, it might be argued, to suggest that Socrates would have been morally justified to escape in light of his being treated unjustly by the Court of Athens.

However, this objection begs the moral question against Socrates had he engaged in civil disobedience against his death sentence. If indeed Socrates would have disobeyed the ruling of the court in his case while satisfying the conditions of morally justified civil disobedience, then had Socrates escaped he would not have acted wrongly in response to the Court's wrongful sentence. In that instance, he would not have violated his own dictums "...one must never do wrong" or "Nor must one, when wronged, inflict wrong in return." For he would in that case have performed an act that was morally permissible, or justifiable. What would have violated such Socratic pronouncements is if he were to engage in civil disobedience regarding his sentence while *not* satisfying the conditions of morally justified civil disobedience. So the discussion then must focus on exactly what those conditions are, and why.

John Rawls has devoted much attention to the nature, justification and role of civil disobedience. (Rawls 1971: 363f.) For Rawls, civil disobedience is a public, conscientious, non-violent, political act contrary to law, and it is morally justified when it is directed against a severe form of injustice, when good faith attempts have been made to use other non-violent methods to address the sense of justice of those in power, when the act is generalizable, and when the civil disobedience is well-designed to best achieve its goals. The role of civil disobedience is to maintain and strengthen just institutions in a reasonably just society. Whether it is the Rawlsian or some other plausible theory of civil disobedience which wins the day, there is in principle a manner by which to determine the moral status of Socrates' possible act of disobedience had he decided to engage in it. It turns out that if Socrates had chosen to escape his death sentence, then it would have satisfied the Rawlsian conditions of civil disobedience as it would have been a public act (not clandestine as he would not have hidden from the authorities but continued instead to practice philosophy openly once he escaped). It would also have been a conscientious act in that it would have been for a just cause. Moreover, it would have been a non-violent act contrary to his legal sentence. Furthermore, Socrates' disobedience to the law would have been based on his unjust death sentence and after he made sincere attempts to dissuade the Court of Athens. His act would have been generalizable as it was done out of principle rather than egoism, and was well-designed to meet its goals of exposing the injustice of his sentence. So one ought not to assume that his escaping his death sentence would have constituted a wrong in the relevant sense. Thus it is plausible to think that there is a scenario in which Socrates might have escaped without committing a wrong against anyone, all relevant things considered.[41]

A second concern with my interpretation of the *Crito* might be that, while it evades the alleged problem of how to square its informational contents on legal obligation with that of the *Apology* (a difficulty said to exist by those who take the laws as representing Socrates' own view on legal obligation), it might be argued that this rhetorical interpretation fails to make sense of Socrates' theory of political obligation. (Soper 1996: 5)

However, this concern begs the question in favor of the Socratic Mouthpiece Interpretation of Plato's works which has already been proven (in Chapters 2 and 3 of this book) to be dubious. Why must it be assumed that words placed in Socrates' mouth by Plato always reflect what Socrates believes? Moreover, why must Socrates have a theory of political obligation, or of anything else for that matter? Why not think instead, as I argue above, that Socrates uses the words of the *nomoi* personified in the *Crito* in a rhetorical manner in order to attempt to get Crito to understand the absurdity of the position it enumerates? Moreover, it is at the same time reasonable to think that Socrates is attempting to articulate for Crito the dilemma he himself confronts. On the one hand, Socrates (he might believe) has a *prima facie* moral obligation to Crito and friends, while at the same time he has *prima facie* moral duties to the law provided they are just (assumed here is the supposition that obligations and duties are the same).

---

[41] This analysis differs significantly from that found in Weiss (1998: 67f.), wherein it is assumed that had Socrates escaped he would have violated his charges to do no (legal?) wrong. Socrates may well have committed a crime, but not necessarily a moral wrong.

(Soper 1996: 10) Thus this second concern with my position is not telling.

A related concern is articulated by Brickhouse and Smith in their assessment of what they term the "separation thesis." Separationists, they argue, believe that the quandary regarding the apparent contradiction between what Socrates says in the *Apology* about legal obligation and what he states by way of the personified *nomoi* of Athens about them in the *Crito* can be explained only in terms of arguing that what Socrates says via the personified *nomoi* is not what he really believes about legal obligation. Hence separationists seek to alienate from each other what Socrates says about legal obligation in these two dialogues. In the *Apology*, according to separationism, Socrates really does believe what he says about his willingness to in a certain kind of circumstance disobey the law, while in the *Crito* Socrates in no way believes what the personified *nomoi* state. As evidence against the separationist stance, Brickhouse and Smith argue that separationism runs afoul of *Crito* 46b: "I'm not just now but in fact I've always been the sort of person who's persuaded by nothing but the reason that appears to me best when I've considered it." According to Brickhouse and Smith, the separationist interpretation has Socrates contradicting his own commitment to the examined life. (Brickhouse and Smith 2006: 4; Brickhouse and Smith Forthcoming) Even more recently, they add that separationism makes it seem as if Socrates gives up on his long-time friend Crito who is deemed by separationists to be overly unintelligent to grasp the meaning and cogency of Socrates' arguments, which then interprets Socrates resorting to "deception" in order to "manipulate" Crito, "his befuddled friend." (Brickhouse and Smith Forthcoming) All of this is to misunderstand the texts in question, as they make Socrates out to be someone who is irrational, deceptive, manipulative, and disloyal to his friend.

While I concur that it is possible to hold the separationist interpretation of Socrates on legal obligation in such a way as to make him out to be all that Brickhouse and Smith charge separationism with, it is unclear that the separationist position must make (or even imply) these morally unattractive attributions to (or about) Plato's Socrates. In particular, my interpretation of the texts, namely, that the personified *nomoi* are Socrates' use of sarcasm in order to communicate to Crito just how absurd their content is hardly makes Socrates out to be one who has turned his back on either the examined life or Crito. Nor does it interpret Crito as one who is too unintelligent to grasp what Socrates has to say. Rather, my account construes Crito as one who is sufficiently astute to comprehend the use of sarcasm in this context. After all, who but a friend who knows Socrates would better understand Socrates' use of sarcasm in this context, especially subsequent to the dialogue between them prior to the injection of the personified *nomoi* earlier in the *Crito*? Thus there is on my interpretation no attempt by Socrates to either deceive or manipulate Crito.

Brickhouse and Smith go on to argue that:

> Those attracted to the separationist view understand Socrates as committed to a very radical form of individual moral autonomy,...It is hard to see, however, how this view can give the state *any* authority to command action from the citizen. The injunction, "Obey the law, just in case you believe the law is just" reduces to "Always act in the way that you personally regard as just, no matter what the law commands." (Brickhouse and Smith Forthcoming).

They cite *Crito* 54d and insist that the "obvious implication of this passage [is] that Socrates does, indeed, accept what the Laws have said." (Brickhouse and Smith Forthcoming)

Now there are several problems with the reasoning of Brickhouse and Smith on this matter. First, it is a straw man argument to saddle the separationist view with the idea that one ought to "Always act in the way that you personally regard as just, no matter what the law commands." This is not a charitable interpretation of the separationist account of Socrates on legal obligation. Rather, one might think that Socrates, in rejecting an absolute obligation to obey the law, urges instead what we know today as a Rawlsian position that there is a *prima facie* moral duty to obey it. Yet this is hardly the nuanced position that Brickhouse and Smith have chosen to attribute to separationism. But it is precisely the one I as a separationist ascribe to Socrates, making sense of why disobedience to legal authority is a moral issue in the first place.

Furthermore, it is not obvious, despite the assertion of Brickhouse and Smith that it is "obvious," that *Crito* 54d implies anything like Socrates' acceptance or endorsement of the informational content of the speech of the *nomoi*. They provide no textual evidence for such a claim. Nor have they ruled out on conceptual or logical grounds why theirs has to be the only reasonable or even best interpretation of the passage vis-à-vis the Socratic notion of legal obligation. While the passage might reasonably be construed "as a very emphatic endorsement [by Socrates] of the persuasiveness of the Law's arguments" (Brickhouse and Smith Forthcoming), a separationist disinclined to accept what Brickhouse and Smith foist upon her might reasonably deny their traditionalist and literalist explanation of the passage in question in favor of an interpretation that holds that Socrates believes, as a reasonable person would, that there is a *prima facie* moral duty to obey the law, but that reason might justify disobedience to it on occasion. Additionally, this view squares with the idea that Socrates thought that the informational content of the speech of the *nomoi*, particularly the very notion of there being an absolute moral duty to obey the law, is self-serving of the *nomoi*, and it is an *argumentum ad baculum* to boot! Socrates, it might be argued, thought so badly of the reasoning behind such a view that it brings out the sarcasm in him, to wit, in order to reduce to absurdity (for his friend Crito to plainly see) the argument of the *nomoi*.

Perhaps Brickhouse and Smith have defeated a rendition of separationism that understands Socrates as a "radical libertarian" (Brickhouse and Smith Forthcoming) when it comes to legal obligation. But they have hardly provided reasons sufficient to discount a more nuanced version of separationism which succeeds in giving a coherent account of why Socrates does not believe the substance of what the *nomoi* assert. We have no solid textual evidence that Socrates was a radical libertarian about legal obligation. Whatever he was, he was one who did not take lightly disobedience to the law, as the *Crito* demonstrates. But it hardly follows from this that he was an absolutist on this important issue, as some of his words to the Athenian court in the *Apology* speak against. He will never give up on doing philosophy so long as he is able—even if that means disobeying legal authority that would disallow, even criminalize, his living the examined life. This hardly makes Socrates a "radical" political libertarian even on this narrow issue.

The general difficulty with Brickhouse and Smith's otherwise valuable take on this problem is that it is overly literalist in its approach to Plato's works. In failing to recognize by way of a more charitable interpretation of Plato's dialogues that Plato might well have employed the personified *nomoi* as a literary device in the form of sarcasm, Brickhouse and Smith, in defending the traditional interpretation, do not see the plausibility of, say, something like my version of the separationist standpoint. If Vlastos is correct in arguing that sometimes Socrates uses irony to make this or that point (Vlastos 1991), then is it not reasonable to think that he would sometimes use sarcasm as he did in *Gorgias* 497c? And if that is true, then why would it be unreasonable for him to have employed it in *this* context? My reply is not intended as a 'knock-down" rebuttal to the Brickhouse and Smith challenge. Instead, I believe that my interpretation of the apparent differences between what Socrates says about legal obligation in the *Apology* and the *Crito* is at least as reasonable and as coherent as the traditional and literalist interpretation defended by Brickhouse and Smith. Hence I do not have sufficiently good reason to think that the Brickhouse and Smith complaints with separationism count decisively against my particular version of it for the reasons stated.

My interpretation of the Socratic problem of legal obligation, then, appears to withstand some leading concerns it faces. Unless there are other such concerns, it appears to be, on balance, a reasonable interpretation of what Socrates has said on this important moral problem.

Without committing the numerous fallacies that pervade Plato scholarship regarding the *Crito*, I have made sense of Socrates' choice to go to his death rather than to follow Crito out of jail. But it was not Crito's arguments which influenced Socrates' decision. Crito's arguments were as poor as the ones offered in the name of the *nomoi* of Athens! What means most to Socrates is his ability to practice philosophy. So unless Socrates can be dissuaded by Crito's, or someone else's, reasons, he must go to his death as even his successful escape, civilly disobedient or not, would only land him back in a society that is intolerant of philosophy in the manner in which Socrates practices it. He has discovered the hard way that Athens refuses to permit the practice of philosophy as it poses too many challenges to nescient minds. Socrates, the ultimate philosopher and pursuer of truth and wisdom, would rather die than to continue at his age to do battle with the anti-philosophical folk of Athens. This is consistent with Socrates' expressed attitude that those who practice philosophy have no reason to fear death. For "the unexamined life is not worth living." Socrates has become a tragic and heroic figure, to be sure.

But from the perspective of Socrates who loved Athens, it was a tragedy for Athens itself.[42]

This implies that it is somewhat hyperbolic to argue that the problem of the *Crito* "is not whether Socrates should go beyond the law to do something higher but whether Crito can get up to the notion of law from something lower." (Congleton 1974: 435)[43] Rather, it is that Socrates must follow the dictates of reason, which is higher than the law, while he attempts to persuade his friend Crito to understand the choice. In the end, Socrates chooses to expose the immoral underbelly of his beloved city perhaps in the hope that at least some citizens will follow reason and love wisdom, making Athens better.

According to the *Crito*, is there a moral obligation to obey the law? If so, it is surely not an absolute one, contrary to what some argue about Socrates and legal obligation.[44] Socrates has a moral right to disobey and escape his sentence, even if his escape would only eventuate in a rather quick capture of his practicing philosophy publicly. But Socrates already knows his eventual fate at the hands of the Meletus' of his world. He has lived his life as well as a fine philosopher could in ancient Athens. He has prepared himself for death. Why not forego his moral right to escape to a life not worth living and allow the entire world and history to see how morally inept ancient Athens really is in its criminalizing the examined life?

References

Allen, R.E. 1972. Law and justice in Plato's *Crito*. *The Journal of Philosophy* 69: 557–567.
———. 1980. *Socrates and legal obligation*. Minneapolis: University of Minnesota Press.
———. 1984. Translator, *The dialogues of Plato*, Vol. 1. New Haven: Yale University Press.

---

[42] This point is made in Congleton (1974: 445).

[43] On my interpretation, there are not two forms of lawlessness facing Socrates. Rather, Socrates faces a choice between two more or less morally justified forms of action.

[44] One such example is Panagiotou 1987: 49): "There is no room for disobedience to the law in the *Crito*."

Barker, Andrew. 1977. Why did Socrates refuse to escape? *Phronesis* 22: 13–28.
Bertman, M.A. 1971. Socrates' defence of civil obedience. *Studium Generale* 24: 576–582.
Bostock, David. 1990. The interpretation of Plato's *Crito*. *Phronesis* 35: 1–20.
Brickhouse, Thomas C., and Nicholas D. Smith. 1984. Socrates and obedience to the law. *Aperion* 18: 10–18.
———. 1994. *Plato's Socrates*. Oxford: Oxford University Press.
———. 2006. Socrates and the Laws of Athens. *Philosophy Compass* 1: 564–570.
———. Forthcoming. Persuade or obey. In *l'éthique de Socrate*, ed. P. Destrée and L.-A. Dorion. Paris: Vrin.
Calvert, Brian. 1987. Plato's *Crito* and Richard Kraut. In *Justice, law, and method in Plato and Aristotle*, ed. S. Panagiotou, 17–33. Edmonton: Academic Printing and Publishing.
Colson, Darrel D. 1986. On appealing the Athenian law to justify Socrates' disobedience, 133–151. XIX: *Aperion*.
———. 1989. *Crito* 51a-c: To what does Socrates owe obedience? *Phronesis* 34: 27–55.
Congleton, Ann. 1974. Two kinds of lawlessness: Plato's *Crito*. *Political Theory* 2: 432–446.
Cooper, John C., and D.S. Hutchinson, eds. 1997. *Plato: Complete works*. Indianapolis: Hackett Publishing Company.
Dixit, R.D. 1980. Socrates on civil disobedience. *Indian Philosophical Quarterly* 8: 91–98.
Dybikowski, J. 1974. Socrates, obedience, and the law: Plato's *Crito*. *Dialogue* 13: 519–535.
Dyson, M. 1978. The structure of the laws' speech in Plato's *Crito*. *The Classical Quarterly* 28: 427–436.
Farrell, James M. 1978. Illegal actions, universal maxims, and the duty to obey the law: The case for civil authority in the *Crito*. *Political Theory* 6: 173–189.
Feinberg, Joel. 1979. Civil disobedience in the modern world. *Humanities in Society* 2: 37–59.
Gallop, David. 1998. Socrates, injustice, and the law: A response to Plato's *Crito*. *Ancient Philosophy* 18: 251–265.
Gomme, A.W. 1958. The structure of Plato's *Crito*. *Greece & Rome* 5: 45–51.
Greenberg, N.A. 1965. Socrates' choice in the *Crito*. *Harvard Studies in Classical Philology* 70: 45–82.
Irwin, T.H. 1986. Socratic inquiry and politics. *Ethics* 96: 400–415.
James, Gene. 1973. Socrates on civil disobedience and rebellion. *The Southern Journal of Philosophy* 11: 119–127.
Kahn, Charles. 1989. *Problems in the argument of Plato's Crito*, 29–43. XXII: *Aperion*.
Kant, Immanuel. 1965. *The metaphysical elements of justice*, John Ladd, Trans. Indianapolis: Bobbs-Merrill.

References

Kraut, Richard. 1984. *Socrates and the state*. Princeton: Princeton University Press.

Kretzmann, Norman. 1988. *Lex Iniusta Non Est Lex:* Interpreting St. Thomas Aquinas (Laws on Trial in Aquinas' Court of Conscience). *American Journal of Jurisprudence*, 33: 99–122.

Martin, Rex. 1970. Socrates on disobedience to the law, 21–38. XXIV: *The Review of Metaphysics*.

McLaughlin, Robert J. 1976. Socrates on political disobedience: A reply to Gary young. *Phronesis* 21: 185–197.

Miller, Mitchell. 1996. 'The arguments I seem to hear': Argument and irony in the *Crito*. *Phronesis* 41: 121–137.

Mulgan, R.R. 1972. Socrates and Authority. *Greece & Rome* 19: 208–212.

Mulhern, John J. 1971. Two interpretive fallacies. *Systematics* 9: 168–172.

Murphy, Jeffrie G. 1974. Violence and the Socratic theory of legal fidelity. In *Violence and aggression in the history of ideas*, ed. Philip P. Wiener and John Fischer, 15–33. New Brunswick: Rutgers University Press.

Panagiotou, S. 1987. Justified disobedience in the *Crito*? In *Justice, law, and method in Plato and Aristotle*, ed. S. Panagiotou, 35–50. Edmonton: Academic Printing and Publishing.

Quandt, Kenneth. 1982. Socratic consolation: Rhetoric and philosophy in Plato's *Crito*. *Philosophy and Rhetoric* 15: 238–256.

Rawls, John. 1971. *A theory of justice*. Cambridge: Harvard University Press.

Ray, A. Chadwick. 1980. The tacit agreement in the *Crito*. *International Studies in Philosophy* 12: 47–54.

Rosen, F. 1973. Obligation and friendship in Plato's *Crito*. *Political Theory* 1: 307–316.

Santas, G.X. 1979. *Socrates*. London: Routledge & Kegan Paul.

Soper, Philip. 1996. Another look at the *Crito*. *The American Journal of Jurisprudence* 41: 1–21.

Stephens, James. 1985. Socrates on the rule of law. *History of Philosophy Quarterly* 2: 3–10.

Strauss, Leo. 1984. *Studies in platonic political philosophy*. Chicago: The University of Chicago Press.

Vlastos, Gregory. 1974. Socrates on political obedience and disobedience. *The Yale Review* 63: 517–534.

———. 1991. *Socrates: Ironist and moral philosopher*. Ithaca: Cornell University Press.

Wade, Francis C. 1971. In defense of Socrates. *The Review of Metaphysics* XXV: 311–325.

Weinrib, Ernest J. 1982. Obedience to the law in Plato's *Crito*. *The American Journal of Jurisprudence* 27: 85–108.

Weiss, Roslyn. 1998. *Socrates dissatisfied: An analysis of Plato's Crito*. Oxford: Oxford University Press.

West, E.J.M. 1989. Socrates in the *Crito*: Patriot or friend? In *Essays in ancient Greek philosophy III: Plato*, ed. J. Anton and A. Preus, 71–84. Albany: State University of New York Press.

White, James Boyd. 1996. Plato's *Crito*: The authority of law and philosophy. In *The Greeks and us*, ed. R.B. Louden and P. Schollmeier, 97–133. Chicago: The University of Chicago Press.

Woozley, A.D. 1979. *Law and obedience: The arguments of Plato's Crito*. London: Duckworth.

———. 1980. Socrates on disobeying the law. In *The philosophy of Socrates*, ed. Gregory Vlastos, 299–318. Notre Dame: University of Notre Dame Press.

Young, Gary. 1974. Socrates and obedience. *Phronesis* 19: 1–29.

Young, Charles M. 2006. Plato's *Crito* on the obligation to obey the law, 79–90. XXVII: *Philosophical Inquiry*.

Chapter 7
The Socratic Roots of Retributivism

So one must never do wrong [*adikein*]—Socrates, *Crito* 49b

...that he should accuse himself first and foremost, and then too his family and anyone else dear to him who happens to behave unjustly at any time; and that he should not keep his wrongdoing hidden but bring it out into the open, so that he may pay his due and get well; and compel himself and the others not to play the coward, but to grit his teeth and present himself with grace and courage as to a doctor for cauterization and surgery, pursuing what's good and admirable without taking any account of the pain. And if his unjust behavior merits flogging, he should present himself to be whipped; if it merits imprisonment, to be imprisoned; if a fine, to pay it; if exiled, to be exiled; and if execution, to be executed. He should be his own chief accuser, and the accuser of other members of his family, and use his oratory for the purpose of getting rid of the worst thing there is, injustice, as the unjust acts are being exposed—Socrates, *Gorgias* 480c-d

Many contemporary philosophers of law have followed M. M. MacKenzie in thinking that Plato had a theory of punishment as moral education. But a close look at what Plato's Socrates says about punishment reveals that not only did neither Plato nor Socrates express a theory of punishment in Plato's dialogues, but that neither expressed one of moral education. The vast majority of Socrates' words on punishment are retributivist in character, something overlooked by contemporary thinkers. Moreover, Socrates does express an element of utilitarian thinking when it comes to punishment, though it is overshadowed by his retributivist statements. Moral education plays a relatively minor role in Socrates' thinking on punishment.

Much has been made over the past several decades of the plausibility status of retributivism in punishment theory, especially in philosophical circles.[1] Indeed, there are about as many construals of retributivism as there are defenders and opponents of the view, or cluster of views, rightly called "retributivism." Whether pure or mixed versions of the theory, what all punishment theories worthy of the name "retributivism" share with one another is that the justification of both the institution and particular forms of punishment[2] are primarily matters of desert, however "desert" and its cognates (desert words) are understood by the various retributivists themselves. According to the standard retributivist line of thinking, those who are responsible for a harmful wrongdoing deserve to be punished (positive retributivism). The innocent are never to be punished for any reason whatsoever (negative retributivism). And the guilty ought to be punished in approximate proportion to the kind and degree of their harm wrongfully caused to others. Strong versions of retributivism, such as Immanuel Kant's, hold that the state has a perfect moral duty to punish all offenders, while weak retributivists[3] hold that the state has an imperfect duty to punish them. While some retributivist theories also admit (consonant with certain statements made by Kant) that considerations of social utility (deterrence, rehabilitation, etc.) might serve as secondary justifications of the institution and particular forms of punishment (Corlett 2014: Chapters 3–4), all retributivisms seem to hold that the notion of desert is central to why, if ever, punishment and punishments are morally justified.

And while what Kant wrote of punishment (especially in the *Rechtslehre*) surely counts as retributivist if only impurely,[4] he is hardly the philosophical founder of retributivism. This chapter will reveal the philosophical roots of retributivism in Socrates as "his" arguments and analyses are expressed in Plato's works, though no

---

[1] For a bibliography which contains such works, see Corlett (2014).

[2] The distinction between the justification of the institution of punishment versus the justification of particular forms of punishment is found in Stanley I. Benn, Anthony Quinton, and John Rawls, later "borrowed" by H. L. A. Hart. (Corlett 2014: Introduction and Chapter 2)

[3] See, for example, Corlett (2001, 2003).

[4] See Corlett (2014: Chapter 5), where Kant is quoted as stating that considerations of social utility count as secondary justifications for punishment.

argument is made herein that Socrates is the ultimate founder of the view. Focus in the expository section of this chapter will be given to what Plato's Socrates argues concerning desert and some related concepts in the context of punishment. And it may surprise many to know that Socrates' words in congruence with retributivism are not purist.[5] Instead, Socrates' words on punishment, like Kant's, are indicative of impure retributivism in important ways.[6] Indeed, most contemporary philosophers of law will be surprised to find that the idea that Plato's works reveal a kind of moral education "theory"[7] of "punishment"[8] is at best only a small part of what we find in Plato's corpus of writings

---

[5] Contrast Mackenzie (1981).

[6] The only philosophical work which has even hinted at this view of Socrates on punishment is Brickhouse and Smith (2007).

[7] I write "theory" here in that it is hardly obvious that what Socrates says in Plato's dialogues concerning punishment amounts to a theory in light of the criteria for a theory of punishment found in Murphy (1987). Using Murphy's criteria as a propaedeutic, one might argue plausibly that a theory of punishment requires at least the following: (a) a definition of "punishment;" (b) a statement of the moral and legal justifications of punishment; (c) a distinction between the justification of punishment as an institution and particular forms of punishment; and (d) an account of proportionate punishment. While Socrates' words on punishment seem to satisfy (a) and perhaps to a lesser extent (d), it seems implausible to think that they satisfy (b)–(c). However, this is not to say that a Socratic basis for a theory of punishment so construed cannot be constructed from what Socrates says of punishment and other Socratic statements made that might relate indirectly to punishment. Hence, it might be possible to piece together a Socratic theory of punishment, one that, it is cautioned, ought not to be confused with that (allegedly) of Socrates' given what he says in Plato's dialogues. Thus while the texts of Plato on punishment do not amount to a theory of punishment, especially regarding the words placed therein in Socrates' mouth, rational reconstruction might possibly provide something of a Socratically-based theory of punishment.

[8] Hampton (1984); Brickhouse and Smith (2002). I write "punishment," because it is unclear that such a view amounts to a belief about punishment if by "punishment" is meant "hard treatment" (Joel Feinberg) and treatment normally considered to be unpleasant (Rawls). (Corlett 2014: 26) For if *Laws* 728c is correct, then punishment is "suffering that follows a wrongdoing," just as capital punishment ensures the safety of others in society. It is unclear how moral education amounts to punishment in any significant sense of the term: "punishment." This confusion of moral education or curing wrongdoers with punishment as hard and unpleasant treatment is widespread among philosophers.

on the subject. And even those, such as A. D. Woozley, who recognize the impure status of the concept of punishment in Plato's works, seem to miss the strong retributive element in them: "For Plato, the purpose of punishment is twofold: making good to the victim the damage actually suffered, and encouragement to the offender to reform…" (Woozley 1979: 130) Indeed, it will be revealed that such a view--when attributed to Plato or Socrates--is misleading as it fails to understand the essentially retributivist leanings of the words of Plato's Socrates, that is, according to many of the arguments placed in his "mouth" by Plato. Thus not only is it unclear that Socrates expresses in Plato's dialogues a theory of punishment, it is unclear that what he says about punishment amounts to what some refer to as moral education. Whether or not Plato's Socrates expresses a theory of punishment, the content of most of what he does express about punishment is clearly retributivist. Furthermore, *if* there is a viewpoint on punishment that is to be attributed to Socrates in Plato's works, it is predominantly one of retributivism, standardly construed. Whether or not such words can be properly attributed to Socrates, they can be construed as Socratic in the sense that we find them placed in the mouth of Plato's Socrates. It is in this sense that I use the locution: "the Socratic roots of retributivism." The words in the Socratic epigraphs above speak clearly to a Socratic notion of retributive punishment. But as we shall see, several additional Socratic passages can be brought to bear that support a Socratic retributivism far greater than they support any other view of punishment.

Assumed in my approach to Plato's writings is neither a unitarian nor strictly developmentalist approach, but rather a hybrid of these approaches. While Chapters 2–3 argued that it is dubious that we can decipher Plato's own views from the content of the corpus of his writings, the problem of this chapter is what might be reasonably ascribed to Plato's Socrates as his arguments and analyses are depicted in Plato's corpus of writings, assuming that it is justified to ascribe anything at all to Socrates from the contents of Plato's corpus. And since even the most responsible ways to date Plato's works are fraught with difficulties (Cooper and Hutchinson 1997: xii-xviii), any claims to the unity or development of Socrates' arguments and analyses must be done with the understanding that such unity or development in his thinking is at best rather general and contingent on an unproblematic dating of Plato's writings. Moreover, it faces the fact that it is not always clear that what Plato places in the mouth of Socrates (especially in the "Socratic dialogues") represents something Socrates actually said, historically speaking, or whether it is Plato having the character Socrates express something that is nonhistorical. In the latter case, Plato might put in the mouth of Socrates ideas which only those closest to Socrates have heard him express, perhaps in order to enhance the philosophical level of such dialogues. In light of these seemingly insurmountable challenges, my approach to the Socratic roots of retributivism is to look closely at what can be found in Plato's writings along these lines, while respecting the possibility that the most that can be said with reasonable plausibility about such Socratic roots is that they are somewhat tenuous. Nonetheless, it is vital that such roots be explored both for the sake of accuracy in the history of philosophy and for the sake of correcting a common misunderstanding amongst philosophers in general and philosophers of law in particular both concerning the nature of retributivism and its conceptual roots.

It is noteworthy that the philosophical work on Plato or Socrates and punishment of which I am aware does not even mention the fact that desert words such as "*axios*," "*kalos*" and their cognates appear numerous times throughout Plato's works both in and aside from legal punishment contexts. Moreover, Plato's Socrates uses desert words in the context of legal punishment. When these facts are brought to light, it is believed that the entire framework of what most philosophers attribute to either Socrates or Plato concerning punishment is in need of rethinking. Whatever Socrates expresses in terms of moral education must take into account the fact that far more of what Socrates expresses in Plato's dialogues concerning punishment is indeed retributivist. But as I will argue, retributivism can accommodate the concerns of moral education as a by-product of retributive punishment. So the most that can be said of the standard interpretation of Plato on punishment is that it is mistakenly attributed to Plato, and that moral education is at most a sometimes byproduct of a predominantly retributivist notion of punishment, according to what Socrates states in various of Plato's works. But even so, if the Socratic Interpretation is correct, then even these words of Socrates' must be taken as those which seek to urge readers to further analyze such claims for their plausibility.

Since what characterizes retributivisms mostly is their commitment to the idea of desert in contexts of punishment and compensation, Socratic expressions of desert words in these contexts will be the focus of this investigation. And we might begin with Plato's *Apology* 38b, where Socrates, in addressing the court of Athens, says that he is unaccustomed to believe that he deserves to be punished. But his use of desert words does not only apply to his perception of his own innocence. Rather, it applies, as it does with typical retributivists, to whether or not others might deserve blame: "…but they thought they were hurting me, and for this they deserve blame." (*Apology* 41e) So in Plato's *Apology* where Socrates is defending his own life from Meletus' charges of corrupting the youth of Athens and of atheism, Socrates argues that he is not deserving of punishment, but that those who seek to do him harm deserve blame, presumably, for seeking to have him punished unjustly. Thus far, Socrates' use of desert words is quite consistent with any retributivism worthy of the name.

But retributivism is not only about what the guilty and blameworthy deserve in terms of punishment or forced compensation by the state. It is, as Socrates states in *Phaedo* 113e, also a matter of rewarding those who deserve praise: "…they are also suitably rewarded for their good deeds as each deserves." In fact, it is in this context that Socrates implicitly employs a notion of proportionate punishment, another primary principle of retributivisms:

> Those who have been deemed incurable because of the enormity of their crimes, having committed many great sacrileges or wicked and unlawful murders and other such wrongs—their fitting fate is to be hurled into Tartarus never to emerge from it. Those who are deemed to have committed great but curable crimes, such as doing violence to their father or mother in a fit of temper but who have felt remorse for the rest of their lives, or who have killed someone in a similar manner, these must of necessity be thrown into Tartarus, but a year later the current throws them out, those who are guilty of murder by way of Cocytus, and those who have done violence to their parents by way of the Pyriphlegethon. (*Phaedo* 113e-114a)

One thing to notice about what Socrates states here is the retributivist blending of the idea of proportionality with that of desert. In so doing, Socrates makes it rather difficult, if not embarrassing, for those who would seek to attribute to him some moral education "theory" of "punishment" as "Plato's theory of punishment." There is nothing of the sort in this passage, consistent with the ones from Plato's *Apology*.

In *Rival Lovers*, considered by many scholars to constitute one of the many apocryphal writings of Plato, Socrates asks the young polymath: "And isn't it also the case that cities are well governed when the unjust are punished?" (138b) This is an indication that even in the secondary[9] writings of Plato, there is confirmation of a retributive idea expressed by Socrates: In states that are reasonably just ones, the guilty deserve to be punished. It is noteworthy that there is no mention of moral education in this context, consistent with the previous ones from Plato's *Apology* and *Phaedo*.

So it is clear that Socrates argues for the punishment of the unjust because they deserve it, and in proportion to the gravity of the injustice. But it is not until Plato's *Protagoras* that the matter of the significance of such punishment is addressed. According to Protagoras, "… the true significance of punishment lies in the fact that human beings consider virtue to be something acquired through training." (*Protagoras* 324a-b) And it is Protagoras, not Socrates, who espouses what centuries later becomes known as a utilitarian view of the justification of punishment as found in Jeremy Bentham (1948): "Reasonable punishment is not vengeance for a past wrong—for one cannot undo what has been done—but is undertaken with a view to the future, to deter both the wrong-doer and whoever sees him being punished from repeating the crime. This attitude towards punishment as deterrence implies that virtue is learned,…" (*Protagoras* 324b-c) What is noticeable in Socrates' reply to Protagoras at 329f. is that, while Socrates compliments Protagoras on the beauty of his speech, he never concurs with the words on punishment and addresses only Protagoras' notion that virtue can be taught. While this in itself hardly makes Socrates a retributivist, it likewise hardly makes him a proponent of moral education as punishment for harmful wrongdoing.

Perhaps more than any other Platonic dialogue, the *Gorgias* has Socrates address issues of punishment and desert. There is Socrates' statement that the one who murders is to be pitied and is miserable because doing what is unjust "is actually the worst thing there is"

---

[9]"Secondary," because it is unclear on precisely what legitimate (non-ideologically driven) grounds such writings are to be denied canonical or primary textual status.

(*Gorgias* 469b), and the agreement between Socrates and Polus on the idea that it is sometimes better to put people to death and banish them and seize their assets as methods of punishment for certain kinds of wrongdoing (*Gorgias* 470b) so long as these punishments are meted out justly (*Gorgias* 470c), and the ultimately retributivist idea that those who are unjust are miserable, but those who do not get their just deserts are even more miserable—and the less so to the extent that those who deserve punishment pay their due "at the hands of both gods and men." (*Gorgias* 472e) It is clear to Socrates that the one who is worst off, morally speaking, is the one who escapes punishment. This is consistent with Kant's point that the state has a perfect moral duty to punish criminals. Why might this be the case? Socrates provides the answer to this question at *Gorgias* 479d: "…doing what's unjust is the second worst thing. Not paying what's due when one has done what's unjust is by its nature the first worst thing, the very worst of all." What is implied here is that harmful wrongdoers ought to have sufficient moral virtue to do the right things and undergo punishment without having to be punished by the state:

> …that he should accuse himself first and foremost, and then too his family and anyone else dear to him who happens to behave unjustly at any time; and that he should not keep his wrongdoing hidden but bring it out into the open, so that he may pay his due and get well; and compel himself and the others not to play the coward, but to grit his teeth and present himself with grace and courage as to a doctor for cauterization and surgery, pursuing what's good and admirable without taking any account of the pain. And if his unjust behavior merits flogging, he should present himself to be whipped; if it merits imprisonment, to be imprisoned; if a fine, to pay it; if exiled, to be exiled; and if execution, to be executed. He should be his own chief accuser, and the accuser of other members of his family, and use his oratory for the purpose of getting rid of the worst thing there is, injustice, as the unjust acts are being exposed. (*Gorgias* 480c-d)

Thus "…injustice is the worst thing there is for the person committing it" and "that person's failure to pay what's due is something even worse." (*Gorgias* 509b) Those lacking such moral virtue are indeed miserable, as Socrates argues, as injustice is a very bad thing, but not wanting to be punished for it is even worse. This is a clear statement in support of punishing those who deserve to be punished. At the very least, it is consistent with a common general justifying aim of retributive punishment and compensation. As with the previous passages, there is no indication in the *Gorgias* pericopes quoted herein that Socrates believes in moral education with regard to penal contexts. Instead, Socrates seems to be arguing repeatedly that punishment is required to achieve or retain moral virtue. And moral virtue is important for the moment of death: "For no one who isn't totally bereft of reason and courage is afraid to die; doing what's unjust is what he's afraid of. For to arrive in Hades with one's soul stuffed full of unjust actions is the ultimate of all bad things." (*Gorgias* 522d) And for third parties who seek to avoid getting involved with cases of harmful wrongdoing, Socrates urges them to demonstrate a genuine concern for the wrongdoer and attempt to pay the fine where fines are relevant to cover the cost of the injustice. (*Gorgias* 480a-b)

Aside from the fact that those who wrongfully harm others deserve to be punished in proportion to their injustice, Socrates adds at *Gorgias* 525b-c that "it is appropriate for everyone who is subject to punishment rightly inflicted by another either to become better and profit from it, or else to be made an example for others, so that when they see him suffering whatever it is he suffers, they may be afraid and become better." This utilitarian justificatory aim of punishment is immediately tied to a retributive one wherein "…the ones whose errors are curable;…their benefit comes to them,…by way of pain and suffering, for there is no other possible way to get rid of injustice." (*Gorgias* 525b-c) This latter point seems to be a retributivist one in that it appeals to a notion of paying one's debt for injustice that one has caused. The first quotation from Socrates here is our first putative indication that something akin to rehabilitation might serve a moral educational function in society where punishment is employed. But this is just one possible implication of the passage, as one can be rehabilitated without moral education accruing to her, just as one can serve as a deterrent to others without moral education having anything to do with the deterrent punishment in question.

Perhaps *Republic* 591a-c sheds light on the idea that Socrates has in mind some kind of moral education in the rehabilitative process of punishment when he states of lawbreakers:

> Doesn't the one who remains undiscovered become even more vicious, while the bestial part of the one who is discovered is calmed and tamed and his gentle part freed, so that his entire soul settles into its best nature, acquires moderation, justice, and reason, and attains a more valuable state

than that of having a fine, strong, healthy body, since the soul itself is more valuable than the body?

Yet there is a limit to the extent to which rehabilitation plays a role in dealing with the unjust, according to Socrates' words in this dialogue. Sure, the souls of the unjust "indeed die of injustice." (*Republic* 610d) But there are those who meet with death due to their injustice. (*Republic* 610d)

However, the bulk of statements on desert are found in Plato's *Laws*. In the *Republic* 337d, desert is linked to punishment. And at 349b-d, desert underlies what ought to happen to the just person, on the one hand, and to the unjust person, on the other. But in *Laws* 626d, naming one after a god or goddess, Clinias states, is a matter of merit. And considerations of philosophical discussion can deserve due attention at *Laws* 645c. And in *Laws* 657e-658c, prizes for competitions are said to be matters of merit, while whatever benefits people most deserves a most fitting honor or prize. (*Laws* 698d-e) Respect and offices in life are said to be deserved when they are merited. (*Laws* 738e) Politicians are said to deserve their positions of power when they are the right candidates for the positions. (*Laws* 751c-d; 917a) And those making their wills are to decide who deserves to be heirs. (*Laws* 923c) Parents deserve good treatment (*Laws* 931e), so much so that those who kill their parents will suffer death.

The Athenian declares at *Laws* 663a that some words deserve legal condemnation. Yet a society striving for genuine happiness will find it "necessary for it to distribute honors and marks of disgrace on a proper basis," argues the Athenian at *Laws* 697b. So long as one pays proper respect to the gods, she will receive the award she deserves from them. (*Laws* 718a) Furthermore, those who prevent others from committing a wrongdoing deserve to be highly respected. (*Laws* 730d) In fact, justice amounts to "granting the 'equality' that unequals deserve to get." (*Laws* 757d) *Laws* 762f. lists a number of punishments, not modes of moral education, that are linked to the commission of certain harmful wrongdoings, amounting to a kind of sentencing guide for the legal system. Severe beatings are mentioned for those who abandon their posts, and the right to have authority over the young is stripped from those who know of harmful wrongdoing but fail to do anything about it. (*Laws* 762c–d) Harshest punishments are saved for foreigners and slaves, while some citizens will be fined for their offences. (*Laws* 764b) Former husbands who violate court orders regarding their children can be beaten by *"anyone who wishes,"* and not suffer punishment for it. (*Laws* 784d) Whippings (hardly construable in terms of moral education the way most philosophers of law understand these terms) are also said to be deserved at *Laws* 949c for refusing to participate in a public ceremony. But certain "social evils" are deemed trivial and are indecent to punish by law. (*Laws* 788b) For as the Athenian states: "I maintain that serious matters deserve our attention, but trivialities do not." (*Laws* 803c) This is consistent with a retributivism that does not entail a perfect moral duty of the state to punish criminals, but rather a retributivism that is based on the state's imperfect moral duty to do so. (Corlett 2014: 85) Dances of peace and war are examples of serious matters, as stated in *Laws* 815d. A person's lifestyle can make her deserving of her fate as being slothful and fat. (*Laws* 807a-b) For boys and their tutors who misbehave, punishment is in order, according to *Laws* 808e. It is noteworthy that the picking of "'dessert' grapes or figs" from another's trees is to be met with punishment to amount to a lash with a whip for the number of fruits taken. (*Laws* 844e-845a)

Perhaps the most interesting feature of Plato's *Laws* is at 846b, where judges who judge poorly (say, out of bias), are to be punished such that they receive twice the damages that the plaintiff deserves. Thus not even judges are above the law. And punishment and moral education are conjoined at *Laws* 844d–e, where temple thieves are to be punished with whippings in order to, perhaps, "teach him restraint and make him a better man: after all, no penalty imposed by law has an evil purpose, but generally achieves one of two effects: it makes the person who pays the penalty either more virtuous or less wicked...." There is insufficiently good reason to think that there is some anti-retributivism being propounded here. Rather, it is consistent to hold that temple thieves deserve to be punished (on the one hand) and that "perhaps" the thief will learn a valuable moral lesson from her punishment (on the other). Capital punishment is again expressed for those who commit unspeakable offences against the gods, the state or parents. (*Laws* 854e) It is difficult to understand how this is not a statement in favor of retributivism, especially when it permits no moral education or curing of the perpetrator of such wrongdoings—even though it does allow for other citizens to learn from those who are banished from the state for their crimes. (*Laws* 855a) However, it is vital to note that punishment, on this view, never nullifies some of the rights of the criminal as a citizen of the state. (*Laws* 855c) This includes various procedural rights that such wrongdoers possess. All of these statements are consistent with any plausible version of retributivism.

The Athenian further argues that judges, when deciding who is to provide rectification to another, ought always to do so in a way that reconciles the parties as "friends" provided that "atonement" has been made by the wrongdoer. (*Laws* 862c) For whenever there is lawbreaking, the law will combine "instruction and constraint" both for reasons of deterrence and so that the wrongdoer will pay for the damages she has done. (*Laws* 862d) In cases of theft, criminals deserve proportionate punishment because of the probability of the thief's curability. (*Laws* 941d) For those criminals who are curable, any means necessary can be used to make him hate injustice and embrace true justice. Yet for the incurable, death is the best thing for everyone. (*Laws* 862e; 942a) But it is only the incurable who ought to receive death as a punishment for their crimes. (*Laws* 863a) Murderers must receive death, and the murderer's assets must be given to the family of her victim (*Laws* 866d), that is, if the murder is committed intentionally. For there are different kinds of murder (*Laws* 866e-867c), and some do not justify capital punishment, but rehabilitation. (*Laws* 867c-d) But there are even said to be cases where capital punishment is justified where the crime does not result in the death of a human being. (*Laws* 946d-e) When the topic of criminal recidivism is discussed, there is a double standard pertaining to the punishment of those who murder slaves versus those who murder citizens. (*Laws* 868)

Perhaps the most obvious retributivist passage in all of Plato's *Laws* is 869b-d, where it is stated that "if one man could die many times, the murderer of his father or mother who has acted in anger would deserve to die the death over and over again. To this one killer no law will allow the plea of self-defense; no law will permit him to kill his father or mother, who brought him into the world." The death penalty is further elaborated at *Laws* 871d-872c. In fact, there is even mention of vengeance in punishment for murder at *Laws* 871b and 872e, though of course no vengeance theory of punishment ought to be confused with any plausible version of retributivism, for reasons Joel Feinberg and Robert Nozick (respectively) have provided. (Feinberg 1995; Nozick 1981: 366–368)

The *Laws* 877a-b raises and answers the matter of failed criminal attempts, an issue which has gained the attention of the most respected twentieth-century philosophers of law.[10] And the answer which is given is quite nuanced: "If a man deliberately intends to kill a fellow citizen…and wounds him without being able to kill him, no pity should be wasted on the man who has inflicted a wound with that sort of intention: he should be treated with no more respect than a killer, and made to stand trial for murder. But we should have due respect for the luck that has saved him from total ruin…*He who* has inflicted the wound shall be spared the death penalty…" While a justification is not provided for why moral luck and intentionality are to play such pivotal roles in distinguishing the sentences of assassins from attempted assassinations, perhaps this is yet another reason to think that the Socratic Interpretation is correct in thinking that Plato wants his readers to reflectively analyze such positions. At *Laws* 877c-879b, further minutae are discussed concerning punishment and compensation.

Capital punishment, Plato's *Laws* 881a admits, is not always a (successful) deterrent. But Socrates has not embraced utilitarian justifications of punishment, including deterrence, as being primary. So appeal is made to "the sufferings said to be in store for these people in the world to come" which are "much more extreme than" capital punishment. This strikes the reader as being rather distant from either a moral education theory of punishment, on the one hand, or rehabilitation or deterrence theories on the other. Nonetheless, "…the punishments men suffer for these crimes here on earth while they are alive should as far as possible equal the penalties beyond the grave." (*Laws* 881b) If this is not a bold expression of retributivism, then there is no such theory as retributivism. Yet it astounds the serious student of punishment theory, and of Plato's works, why these passages never seem to be brought into discussions of "Plato's 'theory' of 'punishment'." The State's not being able to adequately punish certain offenders proportionally is not used as an excuse for not fulfilling what Plato

---

[10] For example, see Feinberg (2003: Chapter 4). For a discussion of Feinberg's views on failed criminal attempts, see Corlett (2006: 146–151).

(and later Kant) argue is the State's moral duty. Rather, inadequate punishments are said to meet with true justice in the world to come. Also important in this context is the fact that "deserves" is tied to the details of whippings, capital punishment, reprimands, etc., for various and sundry crimes. (*Laws* 881c-883c) And for those who still do not comprehend the fact that in Plato's works the notion of retribution is often central in punishment contexts, there is the distinction between different kinds of "prisons," including one "to convey the notion of 'punishment'." (*Laws* 908a) The key point here is that one of the other "prisons" is dubbed a "reform center." But the first is clearly not for reform, but (implicitly) for punishment! Underlying this point in Plato's *Laws* is the retributivist notion of proportionate punishment: the punishment must "fit" the crime, however approximately.[11] That centuries later a famous utilitarian Bentham devotes several pages of a major work of his to devising 13 principles of proportionate punishment is hardly sufficient reason to understand that the problem of proportionate punishment, though faced by both retributivist and utilitarian theories, is so important to retributivists that some notion of proportionate punishment constitutes part of the very core of retributivism. That proportionate punishment is a recurrent notion expressed in various of Plato's works suggests that important retributivist themes are argued for here and there throughout them.

Plato's *Laws* 933d-934b details rules about capital punishment,[12] along with those of proportionate punishment—and even "an additional penalty appropriate to his crime, to encourage him to reform." Each of these notions is central to retributivism (except the reformatory one). And as noted earlier, reform is not in principle incongruent with retributivism. Even so, criminals can deserve sympathy in certain cases. (*Laws* 936b) Other details about deserved capital punishment are found at *Laws* 952d-958c.

Now if the words of the Athenian in the *Laws* are really those of Socrates, then the argument for their being a Socratic retributivism (in the sense noted above) is beyond reasonable dispute. However, even if the Athenian's desert words are not meant by Plato to reflect

---

[11] As opposed to Hammurabi's code, which includes the dictum: "An eye for an eye, a tooth for a tooth."

[12] Including for the fourth crime of perjury (*Laws* 937c) and frivolous law suits! (*Laws* 938c)

Socrates' convictions, the textual evidence for the Socratic roots of retributivism remains strong, far stronger in both number and tone than Socrates' words about prisoner rehabilitation and moral education.

The idea of deservedness is so important to Socrates that even aside from punishment contexts, he is unwilling to say anything about himself that would inflate or overstate his person. (*Lesser Hippias* 372d) Even in death, people ought to get what they deserve in terms of caring for the dead (*Menexenus* 236d), and in praising them for courageous service. (*Menexenus* 242d) Those who give in friendship deserve praise also, according to the author of *Letter XIII* 362b. In *Republic* 375d, Socrates believes that he deserves to be hit because of his inability to stay on track concerning an analogy that was used. And at *Republic* 382c, a question is asked about what is deserved concerning the use of false words. Sympathy and pity are said to be deserved (or not) at *Republic* 539a. And a question is asked about a child deserving to do better than her parents at *Republic* 574a. Finally, the title of being wise ought only to be bestowed on those who deserve it. (*Epinomis* 974b)

What these final uses of desert words seem to indicate are statements of oughtness. When Socrates says that someone deserves this or that, what he seems to mean at the very least is that they ought to be treated in such and such a way: Those guilty of harmful wrongdoing ought to be punished in proportion to their harmful wrongdoing; those who have performed supererogatory acts ought to be praised, presumably, in proportion to how well their action positively served the interests of others, etc.. However, the devil is in the details and Socrates' statements must be put to the critical test of reason. For it might turn out that the concept of desert is highly problematic even in its most plausible formulation. Whether or not Socrates believes what Plato puts in his mouth is not a question that can be settled with confidence, as the Socratic Interpretation insists. But that the retributivism articulated by Socrates deserves further serious philosophical attention is obvious.

Now all of this textual data from Plato's works renders rather dubious much of M. M. Mackenzie's study on "Plato's theory of punishment." (MacKenzie 1981: Chapter 11) After defining "retributivism" such that it is totally distinct from "benefit" or rehabilitation theories of punishment, Mackenzie reads into each passage from the few passages of Plato's works that she discusses Plato's putative theory of punishment. Mackenzie even goes so far as to interpret Protagoras' words in Plato's *Protagoras* as suggestive of Plato's theory of punishment: "This suggests that Plato, as a penologist, would not acknowledge the claims of retributivism—whether real or ideal." (MacKenzie 1981: 181) This is astounding given that, first, nowhere is there sufficient evidence, textual or otherwise, to indicate that what we find expressed in any work of Plato's amounts to Plato's own views, as argued in Chapters 2 and 3 of this book. Secondly, even if mouthpiece interpreters like Mackenzie could demonstrate that what we find in Plato's works amounts to what Plato believed, it is incumbent on them to explain which characters in Plato's works represent Plato's views and which do not. But in the passage quoted from Mackenzie, it is Protagoras who represents Plato's supposed denial of retributivism, as Mackenzie herself construes retributivism. Third, even if it could be shown which characters in Plato's works express Plato's views and which do not, it is surely a stretch beyond credulity to think, as Mackenzie does, that what we find in Plato's works is anything even akin to a *theory* of punishment. Perhaps there is the foundation of such a theory, but to think that what we have studied thus far from Plato on punishment and desert amounts to a theory is to grossly misunderstand the nature of a theory, or to use "theory" in such a fast and loose way that it loses its essential meaning. Finally, as we have seen, in nearly every work of Plato's in which the discourse of punishment is found in the mouth of Socrates, we find the expression of a desert-based retributivist idea of punishment, contrary to Mackenzie's above-cited assertion that Plato "would not acknowledge claims of retributivism…" Thus Mackenzie's claim that "that Plato, as a penologist, would not acknowledge the claims of retributivism—whether real or ideal" is false.

It is important to study Plato's works such that we permit them to speak for themselves, without infusing into them our own preconceived dispositions for or against this or that "theory" of punishment. When we study Plato's works with attention focused on notions of punishment and desert, we find inescapable expressions of retributivism. Whether or not this view belongs to Plato is difficult to know. But to assert as Mackenzie does that Plato's works express anything but a retributivist idea of punishment but instead a moral education theory of punishment is to misunderstand the plain reading of the Platonic texts on punishment, or perhaps it is to misunderstand the nature of punishment, moral education, and retributivism.[13]

For all that Mackenzie and others (Brickhouse and Smith 2002) point out regarding the reasons for Socrates' embracing something like the moral education of harmful wrongdoers and that Socrates might have supported some kind of moral education for those who are not beyond the pale of reform, this is in no way inconsistent with any plausible version of retributivism. And in light of the textual evidence, it is clear that the words of Socrates amount to both a kind of retributivism and reform. Judging by the number and tone of statements about punishment found in the mouth of Plato's Socrates, it is beyond reasonable question that according to the view expressed therein the primary justification of punishment is desert-based, while the secondary justifications are rehabilitation and deterrence, or even moral education. It is quite another question indeed as to whether or not such a view of punishment is morally justified. That such a view finds its roots in Plato's Socrates' discussions about punishment provides good reason to continue to explore its plausibility.

The expository section of this chapter has demonstrated that several passages in Plato's works contain explicit references to and uses of desert words in punishment contexts. If it is objected that Plato's *Laws* does not necessarily reflect either Plato's or Socrates' views, as the "Athenian" might not be meant to speak for either or because some find it dubious that Plato authored the *Laws*, then there remains sufficient textual evidence from the dialogues of Plato to support the attribution of various desert words of Socrates in punishment contexts to show that Socrates articulated (though did not necessarily accept) a version of retribution worthy of the name. That Socrates also here and there expresses moral education in penal contexts in no way discounts his obvious and consistent retributivist expressions, as both views of how the state ought to address criminal wrongdoing are compatible with one another. It is time that philosophers recognize that neither Plato nor Socrates was a singularly-minded moral education punish-

---

[13] This also applies to Hampton (1984) which attributes, however tentatively, a moral education theory of "punishment" to Plato as she supportively cites Mackenzie's work.

ment theorist. Whatever their respective particular views on punishment were, they are not so easily discernible from Plato's dialogues. But what is expressed about punishment therein is mostly expressive of retributive ideals of a mixed variety.

References

Bentham, Jeremy. 1948. *An introduction to the principles of morals and legislation*. New York: Hafner.
Brickhouse, Thomas C., and Nicholas D. Smith. 2002. The problem of punishment in Socratic philosophy. *Aperion* 36: 95–107.
———. 2007. Socrates on how wrongdoing damages the soul. *The Journal of Ethics* 11: 337–356.
Cooper, John C., and D.S. Hutchinson, eds. 1997. *Plato: Complete works*. Indianapolis: Hackett Publishing Company.
Corlett, J. Angelo. 2001. Making sense of retributivism. *Philosophy* 76: 77–110.
———. 2003. Making *more* sense of retributivism. *Philosophy* 78: 277–285.
———. 2006. The philosophy of Joel Feinberg. *The Journal of Ethics* 10: 146–151.
———. 2014. *Responsibility and punishment*. 4th ed. Dordrecht: Springer.
Feinberg, Joel. 1995. The classic debate. In *Philosophy of law*, ed. Joel Feinberg and Hyman Gross, 5th ed., 613–618. Belmont: Wadsworth Publishing Company.
———. 2003. *Problems at the roots of law*. Oxford: Oxford University Press.
Hampton, Jean. 1984. The moral education theory of punishment. *Philosophy and Public Affairs* 13: 208–238.
Mackenzie, M.M. 1981. *Plato on punishment*. Berkeley: University of California Press.
Murphy, Jeffrie G. 1987. Does Kant have a theory of punishment? *Columbia Law Review* 87: 509–532.
Nozick, Robert. 1981. *Philosophical explanations*. Cambridge: Harvard University Press.
Woozley, A.D. 1979. *Law and obedience: The arguments in Plato's Crito*. London: Duckworth.

Chapter 8
Socrates and Compensatory Justice

> ...doing what's unjust is the second worst thing. Not paying what's due when one has done what's unjust is by its nature the first worst thing, the very worst of all.—Socrates, in *Gorgias* 479d

This chapter explicates what amounts to a substantial gap in the articulations of the analyses and arguments of Plato's Socrates. It centers on what Socrates says about compensatory justice. The nature of compensatory justice is clarified, and the words of Socrates about it are made clear in their respective contexts. It turns out that the words of Socrates on compensatory justice are rather sensible indeed, serving as the basis for a more sophisticated understanding of the concept and practice in legal contexts.

While many a philosopher has turned her attention to the topic of Socrates and justice, most have focused on the subject of what Plato's Socrates has to say about matters of distributive justice. Few have devoted their attention to matters of either Socrates or Plato on retributive justice. And of those, like me, who have sought to clarify what Plato's Socrates discussed in terms of retributive justice (See Chapter 7 of this book), no philosopher seems to have devoted attention to what Socrates says regarding compensatory justice. It is this topic that concerns me in the present chapter. I shall explicate Socrates' words on compensatory justice as they are articulated in Plato's *Gorgias* and the *Laws*. I shall assume that what is stated by the Athenian in the latter work are Socratic in a loose sense. I make this assumption realizing that the journey depicted in the dialogue takes place outside Athens, which Socrates reputedly rarely left. However, the Athenian is akin to

Socrates in the way he investigates issues, leading me to believe that he might be, if not Socrates, somewhat representative of Socrates or at least Socratic in philosophical style and substance. What is expressed concerning compensatory justice in these important dialogues of Plato? And is it plausible? Moreover, are there differences or inconsistencies between what is said of this topic in these dialogues? And do these statements amount to a Socratic theory of compensatory justice? Do they constitute either Plato's or Socrates' doctrine or beliefs on the matter?

In order for me to answer these and related questions, it is helpful to note what a theory of compensatory justice requires. First, it needs to provide a definition of "compensatory justice" and its cognates. Second, it must explain why compensatory justice is important. Third, it must provide a legal and moral justification of compensatory justice as an institution within the overall institution of corrective justice. Fourth, it must explain under which conditions a party is liable to provide compensation to another. And fifth, it must explain which kinds or levels of compensation are appropriate for which cases of harmful wrongdoing, and why. It is clear that what Socrates says about compensatory justice fails to meet these conditions. Hence it hardly amounts to a theory. And whether or not he truly believes what he says about compensatory justice, it is important to understand what he expresses about it, as it seems to capture some of the basics of contemporary thinking about the subject.

Compensatory Justice in Plato's *Gorgias*

Socrates' statements on compensatory justice are couched in a narrow context of punishment within a broader context of the alleged virtues of oratory. (*Gorgias* 447–467) Several times throughout this dialogue Socrates states that to suffer wrong or injustice is far better for the soul than to do injustice or wrong to another. One such instance is found at *Gorgias* 469b:

POLUS: "Surely the one who's put to death unjustly is the one who's both to be pitied and miserable."
SOCRATES: "Less so than the one putting him to death, and less than the one who's justly put to death."

POLUS: "How can that be, Socrates?"
SOCRATES: "It's because doing what's unjust is actually the worst thing there is."

Why is this? Socrates answers: "...when one does these things [punishment] justly, it's better, but when one does them unjustly, it's worse." (*Gorgias* 470b; also see 475c) And this is so because the admirable person is happy while the wicked person is miserable. (470e) Precisely why this is so, Socrates argues, lies in the principle of deservedness. (472e) He explains: "On my view of it, Polus, a man who acts unjustly, a man who is unjust, is thoroughly miserable, the more so if he doesn't get his due punishment for the wrongdoing he commits, the less so if he pays and receives what is due at the hands of both gods and men."

Now it is this last claim which seems to suggest that, according to Socrates, the committing of a harmful wrongdoing to others should receive its just reward in the form of punishment or compensation, a point reiterated at *Gorgias* 476e: "So the one being disciplined is being acted upon justly when he pays what is due?" Otherwise, there is injustice, which corrupts the soul and is the worst thing there is. (477d-e) And it is the happy one whose soul is uncorrupted by badness of the most serious sort (478d),[1] namely, doing harm to others and not paying what is due to one's victims. It is "he who commits the most serious crimes and ... succeeds in avoiding...paying his due." (479a) That, says Socrates, is one whose "soul is rotten with injustice." (479c)

Thus committing injustice is a bad thing indeed. However, it is not the worst thing of all. Rather, Socrates states, "... doing what's unjust is the second worst thing. Not paying what's due when one has done what's unjust is by its nature the first worst thing, the very worst of all." (*Gorgias* 479d: also see 509b) Thus it is "paying what is due" that purifies the soul of the wrongdoer. (479d) Indeed, "...whoever avoids paying his due for his wrongdoing...deserves to be miserable beyond all other men, and that one who does what's unjust is always more miserable than the one who suffers it, and the one who avoids paying what's due always more miserable than the one who pays it." (479e) Because of this, Socrates continues, "...if he or anyone else he

---

[1] Indeed, "the one whose life is the worst." (*Gorgias* 478e)

cares about acts unjustly, he should go voluntarily to the place where he'll pay his due as soon as possible; he should go to the judge as though he were going to a doctor, anxious that the disease of injustice shouldn't be protracted and cause his soul to fester incurably." (480a-b) But unless one thinks that this ought to be done privately, he admonishes wrongdoers to rectify their wrongs publicly: "…he should not keep his wrongdoing hidden but bring it out into the open, so that he may pay his due and get well…" (480c) And for those who might think that Socrates is discussing payment only in terms of punishment (hard treatment), but not by way of compensation, he adds: "And if his unjust behavior merits flogging, he should present himself to be whipped; if it merits imprisonment, to be imprisoned; *if a fine, to pay it*; if exile, to be exiled; and if execution, to be executed" (480d, emphasis provided). Furthermore, for third parties (not the State) who seek to avoid getting involved with cases of harmful wrongdoing, Socrates urges them to demonstrate a genuine concern for the wrongdoer and attempt to pay the fine where fines are relevant to cover the cost of the injustice. (480a-b)

At *Gorgias* 525b-c, Socrates states that punishment has two main aims: rehabilitation and example-making. For those who are curable, punishment serves to provide them an opportunity to better themselves and avoid recidivism. But for those who "have committed the ultimate wrongs" and who are incurable, they are to serve as examples to others of the ultimate demise that awaits those who commit such atrocities. While in this context of punishment and wrongdoing Socrates makes no reference to paying what one owes, it is not inconsistent to think that compensatory justice can and should play an appropriate role in the institution of punishment. For surely one can learn from one's own wrongdoing if one is forced to compensate one's victims, just as compensatory justice can serve to make examples out of criminals.

It is important to note that while what Socrates expresses in the *Gorgias* concerning compensatory justice expresses mostly retributivist ideals, the passage from 525b-c is clearly utilitarian in substance. But what is also important is that the content of the dialogue regarding compensatory justice revolves around the question of the rightness of the institution of compensatory justice. The *Laws*, on the other hand, mostly pertain to issues of particular forms of compensatory justice related to particular crimes. One matter of significance here is what appears to be the foreshadowing of the famous distinction in philosophy of law between the justification of the institution of punishment versus the justification of the particular forms of punishment, an important distinction made by Anthony M. Quinton (1954), John Rawls (1955), and Stanley Benn (1958), respectively, and more a decade later re-stated less eloquently (without giving credit to either Quinton, Rawls or Benn on this point) by H. L. A. Hart.[2]

Compensatory Justice in Plato's *Laws*

While in the *Gorgias* Plato's Socrates makes statements which support not only retributive punishment of criminals and forced compensation to victims by criminals, the Athenian in the *Laws* does so with seemingly even more resolve. Not unlike Socrates in the *Gorgias*, the Athenian has some pointed things to say about justice, injustice, and the unjust life in general: "Injustice looks pleasant to the enemy of justice, because he regards it from his own personal standpoint, which is unjust and evil; justice, on the other hand, looks *un*pleasant to him. But from the standpoint of the just man the view gained of justice and injustice is always the opposite." (*Laws* 663c) To this he adds, "…the unjust life is not only more shocking and disgraceful, but also in fact less pleasant, than the just and holy." (663d) This forms part of the backdrop for what the Athenian expresses concerning compensatory justice as a means of criminal rectification.

The point of the following account of what might plausibly be deemed to be a Socratic view of compensatory justice is not to suggest that it is acceptable. While some aspects of it seem intuitively acceptable, others are odious, such as the differences in treatment between citizen-offenders and slave-offenders of the laws, and the fining of family members of "lunatics" who fail to keep them inside their homes. (*Laws* 934d) To suggest the differential treatment between slaves and citizens violates the idea of human equality under the law,

---

[2] This point is made in Corlett (2006: 1). H. L. A. Hart borrows the vital distinction without giving credit to either Benn, Quinton, or Rawls in Hart (1968: 8–12).

while the fining of family members of "lunatics" seems overly harsh given the complexities such family members face in living with such persons. Other punishments and compensations might appear disproportionate to the damages compensated, whether in terms of their being overly harsh or overly lenient. Nonetheless, it is important to understand what a Socratic account of compensatory justice looks like, warts and all. Once again, according to the Socratic Interpretation of Plato's works, such statements are meant by Plato to encourage readers to consider and critically evaluate them in order to further our understanding of the problems. There is inadequate evidence to attribute such claims to either Plato or to Socrates—even to Plato's Socrates, as argued in Chapters 2, 3 and 4 of this book.

According to the Athenian, Market-Wardens must punish citizen-offenders of temples and fountains by a fine up to 100 drachmas. (*Laws* 764b) Law 26 states that anyone found guilty of moving the boundary stones of another's property is to be punished in a way that includes a fine (843b), while encroachment onto a neighbor's land requires the payment for any damages including an extra payment to the victim of twice the amount of any damages incurred. (843c-d) Compensatory damages are also deemed appropriate for those who allow their cattle to graze on another's land without permission of the owner, for confiscating another's bees, for burning wood unsafely, and for planting trees that encroach on a neighbor's property. (843d-e) Even the mismanagement of the flow of rainwater onto another's property is to result in a fine "twice the value of the damage to the injured party." (844d) Those who consume any part of a crop of grapes or figs whether on one's own land or on another's are subject to fairly severe compensatory fines. (844e)

The deliberate spoiling of another's water supply by poisoning, excavation or theft is to be met with a fine, among other things (*Laws* 845e), and even judges who are deemed to have settled such cases in a biased way are to be fined double the damages in the relevant case. (846b) Where appropriate, temple defilement by a citizen is to be met with fines, if not much harsher punishment. (855c) In general, every thief must pay twice the value of the stolen item (857a), while the same law 42 states that if any thief has not the means to pay the fine for his crime, he must be cast into prison "until he pays up or persuades the man who has had him convicted to let him off." The same is true of those who steal from public sources, except that they must serve time in debtor's prison until "he has either persuaded the state to let him off or paid back twice the amount involved." (857b)

Not only does the Athenian articulate fines for various and sundry crimes and torts, he expresses a general view of compensatory justice. At *Laws* 862b-d, he states of the lawgiver:

> ...he must keep his eyes on these two things, injustice and injury. He must use the law to exact damages for damage done, as far as he can; he must restore losses, and if anyone has knocked something down, put it back upright again; in place of anything killed or wounded, he must substitute something in a sound condition. And when atonement has been made by compensation, he must try by his laws to make the criminal and the victim, in each separate case of injury, friends instead of enemies.
>
> ...when anyone commits an act of injustice, serious or trivial, the law will combine instruction and constraint, so that in the future the criminal will never again dare to commit such a crime voluntarily, or he will do it a very great deal less often; and in addition, he will pay compensation for the damage he has done.

Interestingly, the Athenian here provides a rather good account of what we refer to as "rectification." In either case, what we have here is a rather straightforward description of compensatory justice. It is stated in terms that are a mixture of retributive and utilitarian reasons. The retributive reasons find themselves in the overall context of the entirety of the *Laws* insofar as the concept of desert underlies the justification of compensatory justice throughout. Moreover, within this pericope, "He must use the law to exact damages for damage done..." seems to capture the retributivist and utilitarian notion of proportionate punishment and compensation, though the distinctively utilitarian notion of deterrence is quite obvious: "...so that in the future the criminal will never again dare to commit such a crime voluntarily, or he will do it a very great deal less often..." In any case, the Athenian's expressed view of punishment includes an obvious category of compensation which is rather robust: Those who wrongfully harm others according to the law are to be punished, and often forced to compensate their victims in proportion to the harm caused (and twice as much as the harm caused in some cases).

Indeed, "concerning wounding inflicted in anger," law 55 states that if the wound is curable, then the offender must pay double the damages incurred, while if it is incurable, the offender must pay quadruple the amount. If the wound causes embarrassment or shame to the victim (disfigurement, for example), the offender must pay triple the damages. (*Laws* 878c) But if one injures not only a private party but also the state by "rendering him unable to defend his fatherland against the enemy," the offender must, among other things, compensate the state, including the performance of military service on behalf of her incapacitated victim. (878c-d) However, only simple damages are owed to the extent that one harms another involuntarily. (879b) Maltreatment of an orphan requires double the compensation she would have to pay for the illicit harming of non-orphans. (927d) If a guardian of a child fails to treat that child as she would her own child, she is subject to "a fine of twice the damages as estimated by the court." (928b) If a guardian is guilty of "neglect or malpractice," "He must be fined four times the sum he is found to have taken, half the fine going to the child and half to the successful prosecutor." (928c) If a grown person seeks compensation for maltreatment while a minor under her guardian's care, and this suit is brought within 5 years of the incident(s), the court will estimate the damages owed to the child by the offending guardian(s). (928d) Finally, if a non-medical professional poisons someone, the court will decide the amount of the fine the offender owes to the victim. (933d-e)

In general, the Athenian proposes,

> …when one man harms another by theft or violence and the damage is extensive, the indemnity he pays to the injured party should be large, but smaller if the damage is comparatively trivial. The cardinal rule should be that in every case the sum is to vary in proportion to the damage done, so that the loss is made good. And each offender is to pay an additional penalty appropriate to his crime, to encourage him to reform. (*Laws* 933e-934a)

In essence, this is a basic rule of proportionate compensation. While it contains a primarily retributivist element of proportionate compensation with regard to "so that the loss is made good," it adds a secondary utilitarian feature of deterrence concerning "reform" of the harmful wrongdoer.

Whether or not the Athenian is Socrates or can rightly be said to represent Socrates' views on punishment and compensation, the *Laws* contain a set of loosely Socratic rules of proportionate compensation. It is a perspective that contains both retributive and utilitarian elements, a mixed position that is absent from Socrates' words on compensatory justice in the *Gorgias*.

Concerns with the Socratic View of Compensatory Justice

Having set forth what Plato's Socrates and the Athenian say about compensatory justice, it is important to ask whether or not their expressed claims are plausible, and why? One concern that might be raised is the point made regarding debtor's prison. While it makes some sense to force an offender to pay back her victim(s) in proportion to the wrongful harm caused to the victim(s), with the addition of a compensatory "kicker," at least two concerns arise. One is from a theoretically neutral standpoint. It is a practical concern that if an offender cannot afford to pay her fine in full and must then be cast into debtor's prison until she can pay-off the fine in full or persuade her victim(s) to have her released, how, if persuasion fails, is the offender to earn the fine to pay her victim(s)? Other than a prisoner release to work to compensate program, it is difficult to imagine how this might be feasible as a means of compensation to victims. Yet the cost of such a program in monitoring workers on release time might well outweigh a substantial amount of money the prisoner might earn in order to pay the fine in full. It would seem, then, that a debtor's prison, especially for minor to moderate-level crimes, stands to violate considerations of proportionate compensation, at least in some cases. Another concern here is that the fine itself, whenever "doubled" or "tripled" or quadrupled," is a violation of proportionate compensatory justice. While such a compensatory measure might be explained in terms of the extra "pain and suffering" of the victims, or the immeasurable factors the victims typically experience, it is unclear that proportionality is given sufficient attention when the statute for compensatory damages is so broad. Nonetheless, it might be argued by Socrates and the Athenian that this compensatory "kicker" just does seek to accommodate considerations of proportionality, however approximately.

Another concern that might be raised about the Socratic statements about compensatory justice is from a retributivist standpoint. It is one thing to argue that considerations of utility such as deterrence and rehabilitation of offenders might be seen as secondary aspects of the justification of compensation, whether it is the institution of compensatory justice or particular forms of compensation. This view is actually consistent with Immanuel Kant's view of punishment, as noted in Chapter 7. However, it is quite another thing to argue that such utilitarian considerations are part of the primary justification of compensatory justice. This is true for the very same reasons why it is problematic in the context of punishment. First, without qualification, a "mixed" view of compensatory justice, as Socrates states it, seems to run afoul of the problem of subsuming considerations of desert under those of social utility. But this seems to imply that the best compensation is only that which will maximize utility, which in turn seems to imply that considerations of desert and proportionality might well be ignored or not given their due. This of course is a problem that has long been a part of discussions of punishment and are not directly germane to this discussion. But the issues in compensatory justice appear to be parallel ones.

Imagine a case wherein society itself has committed a tremendous harmful wrongdoing against a group of its constituents. Imagine that the total damages are far greater than the society can afford to pay within a generation or two, and that even if the damages were paid in perpetuity they would cause great hardship for it. If compensatory justice is to be made contingent on the ability of the offender to pay what she owes to her victim(s), then such compensatory damages are likely to not end up being in proportion to what is truly owed the victim(s). Instead, compensatory damages ought not to be made to conform to the offender's ability to pay, as implied in the Socratic point about debtor's prison. Offenders owe to the extent that they have damaged others wrongfully, and must be forced to compensate victims accordingly. The fact that, as many would argue, such compensation would place society in great hardship is no excuse for decreasing the compensatory damages owed, or for ignoring compensation altogether. So there seems to be a difficulty some of Socrates' statements about compensation, though his point about debtor's prison might provide a possible way out of the problem.

In sum, this treatment of the words of Socrates on compensatory justice is largely consistent with the Socratic statements on retributive punishment discussed in Chapter 7. While it is not always clear what the precise meanings of such statements are, they serve as general ones on topics that readers are intended to pursue philosophically. At least, this is how the Socratic Interpretation might render such passages. But even if we take the statements on retributive punishment and compensatory justice as a mouthpiece interpreter would, attributing them to Plato and/or Socrates, the very idea that either Plato or Socrates is a staunch retributivist and strongly in favor of compensatory justice renders dubious the allegation that either one is a mere moral education theorist (and not a retributivist) in penal contexts. For *if* anything is able to be attributed to either such philosopher, it is, at the very least, that each believes in retributive justice. This excursion into several of the passages from Plato's works on punishment and compensation puts to rest any attempt by scholars to read into them and thereby misattribute to either Plato or Socrates some view about such matters that seems more palatable to certain contemporary philosophical minds which are often averse to considerations of retributive justice.

References

Benn, Stanley. 1958. An approach to the problem of punishment. *Philosophy* 33: 325–341.
Corlett, J. Angelo. 2006. *Responsibility and punishment*. 3rd ed. Dordrecht: Springer.
Hart, H.L.A. 1968. *Punishment and responsibility*. Oxford: Oxford University Press.
Quinton, Anthony M. 1954. Punishment. *Analysis* 14: 133–142.
Rawls, John. 1955. Two concepts of rules. *The Philosophical Review* 64: 3–13.

Conclusion

My main line of argument has proceeded as follows. First, in Chapters 2 and 3, I considered and rebutted various objections to the Anti-Mouthpiece Interpretation of Plato's dialogues, ones that were not considered in my previous book on the Platonic Question: *Interpreting Plato's Dialogues* and ones that can legitimately be aimed at my moderate Anti-Mouthpiece position. Various attempts during recent years to provide a foundation for the Mouthpiece Interpretation, along with various objections to some version or other of the Anti-Mouthpiece Interpretation, have been rendered problematic. However, in light of the several reasons offered in favor of the Mouthpiece Interpretation and against the Anti-Mouthpiece Interpretation discussed herein and in my book, *Interpreting Plato's Dialogues*, it is unreasonable to accept the Mouthpiece Interpretation. This is the case unless, of course, textual evidence is discovered which, being authentic, would render plausible the Mouthpiece Interpretation.

Moreover, not even the Socratic Mouthpiece Interpretation is unproblematic, as we saw in Chapter 4. That is, it is not even clear that it is justified to ascribe to either the historical Socrates or to Plato's Socrates whatever Plato puts in his mouth in the dialogues. While there are stronger and weaker versions of the Anti-Mouthpiece Interpretation, my Socratic Interpretation is a moderate one which does not state that it is impossible that Plato had beliefs that might be found in the dialogues. Rather, it states more modestly that given the reasons that have been offered in favor of such an approach to Plato's works, it is unjustified to accept the Mouthpiece Interpretation. For no unproblematic argument or piece of evidence, primary or secondary, has been provided in favor of that position.

But while it is one thing to render dubious the Mouthpiece Interpretation, it is quite another to provide a demonstration of the Socratic Interpretation in terms of how it approaches a Platonic dialogue or topic. Chapter 5 sought to delineate several passages in which Socrates discusses certain justice-concepts: freedom, equality and rights. While not much is said by him on such matters, what is said, according to the Socratic Interpretation, both encourages readers of Plato's works to take up the challenge of completing the analyses that Socrates starts therein, and also proves incorrect certain mouthpiece interpreters who loudly proclaim that Plato was a totalitarian, or a communist, or some other such extremist.[1]

In Chapter 6, I addressed one of the oldest topics in Plato/Socrates studies, namely, that of Socrates' words on legal obligation pertinent to his death sentence by the Athenian court. Legal obligation is one of the central concepts of justice. While there are a plethora of positions taken by numerous philosophers and other scholars over the past several decades, I develop a rather novel approach to the problem, one that sees no contradiction in Socrates attitude toward the law between the *Apology* and the *Crito*, and one that also makes reasonable sense on a charitable interpretation of his words. All this is done without ascribing to either Plato or Plato's Socrates substantial philosophical beliefs, doctrines or theories allegedly found in the dialogues. In the end, what I provide is a Socratic Interpretation of what Plato's Socrates states therein. In this way, further evidence is given in favor of the claim that the Socratic Interpretation is the most viable way to approach Plato's texts.

Chapters 7 and 8 further demonstrated how the Socratic Interpretation can make good sense of Plato's dialogues without committing a fundamental attribution error in the process regarding their contents and Plato himself. I not only refuted the simplistic claim that Plato held to a moral education theory of punishment, but I showed

---

[1] Here I have in mind Popper (1962). Yet to some extent, many a mouthpiece interpreter, while not as irresponsible as Popper in their interpreting Plato's works, nonetheless fall prey to the error of attributing to Plato this or that view of politics and society.

Conclusion

that it is quite possible to interpret whatever Plato's Socrates says on punishment and compensatory justice in Socratic terms, that is, according to the Socratic Interpretation. In so doing, I demonstrated some of the complexities of what Socrates said about such topics, and allowed what he said thereof to serve as a propaedeutic for further philosophical discussion of punishment and compensatory justice.

Appendix I provides a meticulous refutation of Lloyd Gerson's objections to Harold Cherniss' logical and textual disabling of the Mouthpiece Interpretation's idea that Aristotle serves as a reliable guide to the ideas of Plato with regard to Plato's dialogues. And Appendix II once more criticizes the Mouthpiece Interpretation and defends the Socratic Interpretation with regard to the concept of mimetic art in some of Plato's dialogues.

Thus it is possible to provide more along the lines of the "proof ... in the pudding" regarding the Socratic Interpretation of Plato's corpus. There is a viable alternative to the fallacious thinking which underlies the Mouthpiece Interpretation. I suggest that it is the Socratic (Anti-Mouthpiece) Interpretation. While the Socratic Interpretation does not deny that it is reasonable for interpreters to ascribe to Socrates a respect for philosophical analysis and argumentation (reason), and perhaps some other general beliefs, it denies that it is adequately justified to attribute to Socrates substantial philosophical beliefs, doctrines or theories. So the Mouthpiece Interpretation is found to be unacceptable given the problems it faces. But even more problematic is the Mouthpiece Interpretation's ascriptions of several substantial philosophical beliefs, doctrines and theories to either Plato or Plato's Socrates. That position I hope to finally have put to rest given the plethora of difficulties it faces and in light of the rather poor reasoning provided in its favor and pending further textual evidence that might evade my many concerns with the defense of the Mouthpiece Interpretation. Plato and Socrates deserve our greatest respect as philosophers. Perhaps one step in the direction of demonstrating such respect is to become open-minded about the lack of adequate reasons supporting the dominant tradition of how Plato's works are approached and interpreted.

Appendices

Appendix I: Gerson on Cherniss on Aristotle on Plato

> In modern times scholars have been concerned with Aristotle's remarks about Plato chiefly as evidence of what the latter said and meant; and yet no agreement has been reached concerning the weight and value to be assigned to this evidence.—Harold Cherniss (1962: ix)

Introduction

Lloyd Gerson provides replies to Harold Cherniss' objections to the use of Aristotle as a witness to "Plato's philosophy" as it is expressed in Plato's dialogues. (Gerson 2014) Gerson begins his attack on Cherniss' objections by drawing a distinction between what he refers to as the "Protestant" and "Catholic" approaches to the study of Plato. I shall refer to these approaches as "Platonic Protestantism" and "Platonic Catholicism," respectively. According to Gerson, the Protestant approach construes the texts of Plato's dialogues themselves as the sole manner by which to "access Plato's philosophy." (Gerson 2014: 397) While the strong version of Platonic Protestantism, I might add, would hold that only Plato's writings are to be used in determining the informational content of "Plato's philosophy," a weaker version of it would admit that secondary sources such as the testimony of Aristotle, other of Plato's students, some ancient historians of Greek philosophy, etc., might be used to understand "Plato's philosophy," but that such sources must be subordinated to the primary sources of Plato's own writings. As Gerson puts it in describing Platonic Protestantism more generally: "the contents of the dialogues always trump testimony." (Gerson 2014: 397) This holds, according to this weaker version, unless there is a sufficiently good reason to believe that in a particular circumstance secondary evidence outweighs primary evidence. Gerson classifies as "extreme Protestantism" the approach which

> contends that, given only the dialogues as a data set, there is no way to determine Plato's philosophy since in those dialogues Plato nowhere speaks in *propria persona*. …I call this position 'extreme' Protestantism because it reduces the *sola scriptura* principle to absurdity. It does this by claiming that the dialogues alone cannot tell us what their author thinks, which is one possible, albeit highly implausible, conclusion to draw from rejecting the Aristotelian testimony. (Gerson 2014: 398)

Without argument, Gerson dismisses this approach to Plato's dialogues as "highly implausible." I shall argue that it is not such an approach (or at least a particular version of it), but Gerson's own approach, which lacks adequate justification. That is, given Gerson's own attempt to either defeat or neutralize Cherniss' objections to the use of Aristotle as a witness to "Plato's philosophy," Gerson fails to adequately justify the use of Aristotle as a "key witness" to "Plato's philosophy." But worse still, the very informational contents of the dialogues of Plato themselves fail to adequately and uniquely support Gerson's approach. His approach to Plato's dialogues fails to support his claim that "Plato's philosophy" is discernible from said texts, much less by way of Aristotle. More is made of this point below.

According to Platonic Catholicism, Gerson writes,

> …the dialogues are only one means, albeit perhaps the best means available to us, for access to Plato's philosophy…the dialogues are not the ultimate authority for Plato's meaning. It is the Platonic tradition, beginning with the first generation members of the Academy, that provides significant, although not unimpeachable, "control" for understanding what is in the dialogues. In cases where the tradition and the dialogues stand in direct conflict, some further principle or principles must be adduced to resolve that conflict. The most important witness that the Catholics have on their side is Aristotle. His testimony regarding Plato's philosophy is extensive; his criticisms, based on his understanding of that philosophy, are penetrating and unrelenting. Aristotle is by no means the only witness. He is, though, the key witness. (Gerson 2014: 397)

For the sake of discussion of Gerson's replies to Cherniss' objections to the use of Aristotle as a witness to "Plato's philosophy," I shall assume Gerson's depiction of Platonic Catholicism. However, I should note some preliminary concerns with it. A Platonic Protestant, much like a Christian Protestant with regard to the authority of the Christian scriptures, might well concur that Plato's "dialogues are only one means, albeit perhaps the best means available to us, for access to Plato's philosophy." But one point where Platonic Protestants diverge from Platonic Catholics is on the matter of what constitutes the ultimate authority in deciphering "Plato's philosophy." Platonic Protestants will hold that it is Plato's writings alone which have such ultimate authority, while Catholics deny this, as Gerson points out. And Gerson is also correct to state that Platonic Catholics rest much of the basis of their approach to the study of Plato on the testimony of Aristotle.

The burden of proof concerning what constitutes legitimate authority pertaining to the interpretation of ancient philosophical figures and their alleged substantive beliefs rests on those who think, implicitly or not, that secondary evidence can constitute "ultimate authority" over primary evidence. If it can, then surely a justification for such an implicit hermeneutical principle can be adduced, and it would be possible to state and successfully defend the conditions under which such a hermeneutical principle obtains. It is noteworthy that nowhere in his article on Cherniss does Gerson refer to, state, or defend such a principle.

The general philosophical context of Gerson's discussion is the Platonic Question, which is the question of how best to approach Plato's works most of which are in dialogue form. Generally, there are two opposing ways to approach Plato's dialogues. The first is the Mouthpiece Interpretation called such because it holds that Plato composed dialogues in order to communicate his philosophy to readers. On this approach, it is usually Plato's Socrates who serves as the mouthpiece for Plato in explicating "Plato's philosophy" in terms of "Plato's theory of ideas," "Plato's theory of justice," "Plato's theory of art," etc.. The second general approach to the Platonic Question is the Anti-Mouthpiece Interpretation which denies that Plato's dialogues are an appropriate avenue by which to discern Plato's beliefs, doctrines or theories (that is, his substantive philosophy). While Plato likely had beliefs—even philosophical ones—they might have been more along the lines concerning the importance of critical philosophical reasoning exemplified throughout the dialogues. Each of these general approaches admits of variants. I shall focus on those most relevant to Gerson's replies to Cherniss' objections to the use of Aristotle's testimony about the alleged philosophy of Plato.

Cherniss and Gerson are each advocates of the Mouthpiece Interpretation, and Platonic Protestantism and Platonic Catholicism are species of it. For each approach affirms that Plato's philosophy can be found in his dialogues. Where they differ, given Gerson's taxonomy, is the extent to which a secondary source such as the testimony of Aristotle can ever trump or be on par with the primary sources of Plato's dialogues when the question is the nature of "Plato's philosophy." This matter is particularly important given Gerson's recognition, quoted above, that there can be conflicts between these two sources of "Plato's thought."

In what follows, I shall examine some of Gerson's main replies to Cherniss' objections to Aristotle's testimony. I argue that such replies can either be defeated or neutralized. In either case, Aristotle's testimony about what Plato allegedly believed philosophically is at best dubious, if not impeached, rendering problematic the Platonic Catholic approach to Plato's works and its insistence that Aristotle is "the key witness" to "Plato's philosophy."

If Cherniss is correct about the dubious nature of Aristotle's testimony about "Plato's beliefs," then there is serious doubt cast on the Mouthpiece Interpretation insofar as, Gerson admits, Aristotle's testimony is "the key witness" to "Plato's philosophy." The philosophical significance of this challenge to the Mouthpiece Interpretation is that it seems to undermine the debate between Platonic Protestants and Platonic Catholics concerning the extent to which Aristotle (or some other secondary source) might serve as a legitimate witness to "Plato's philosophy." So whereas Gerson is focused on Cherniss' objections to a Platonic Catholic approach and its reliance on Aristotle as the key witness to understanding "Plato's philosophy," Platonic Catholicism itself may be undermined. This appears to be true, that is, given that the content of most of Plato's works consists in dialogues instead of treatises and because of this Plato's substantive philosophy is not readily available to us. So much depends on the reliability (or not) of

Aristotle's testimony concerning Plato's alleged substantive philosophy. Has Gerson either defeated or neutralized Cherniss' objections?

Gerson on Aristotle on Plato: Do Aristotle's Words on Plato Represent "Plato's Philosophy"?

Gerson begins his discussion of why Aristotle should serve as "the key witness" to "Plato's philosophy" by arguing that one ought not to accept some of Aristotle's testimony, but not all of it, "…since Aristotle nowhere distinguishes either between testimony based on the dialogues and testimony that is, shall we say, conjectural or speculative." (Gerson 2014: 398)[2] Gerson makes this claim in the context of Aristotle's remarks on Plato's Socrates' discussion of "Form-numbers" in *Republic* 509b. Now this is a surprising argument in that Gerson seems to imply that a trustworthy witness to "Plato's philosophy" might be one who "…nowhere distinguishes either between testimony based on the dialogues and testimony that is, shall we say, conjectural or speculative." Yet if Aristotle is to qualify as a reliable witness to "Plato's philosophy," or, as Gerson insists, "the key witness," *would it not be reasonable to expect that Aristotle would at least differentiate between what can be found by a plain sense reading of Plato's dialogues, on the one hand, and what is Aristotle's mere speculation about "Plato's philosophy," on the other?* And would it not be reasonable to think that a witness who fails to make such a distinction is confused (even presumptuously so), or at least an unreliable one?

Indeed, this very problem in Aristotle seems to be indicative of the lack of an explicit and clear distinction made between what a historical philosopher actually states in his writings versus what a commentator thinks that that author means, in other words, between historical reconstruction and rational reconstruction. So given Gerson's admission on this matter with regard to Aristotle, it is unclear that Gerson has provided a good reason to think that Aristotle is a trustworthy witness to "Plato's philosophy." For the very reason Gerson provides

---

[2] Also, see Gerson (2014: 400): "…Aristotle does not generally distinguish between dialogue-based testimony and testimony that is based on orally transmitted communications…"

to support Aristotle as a witness to "Plato's philosophy" is undermined by Gerson's own assertion that Aristotle fails to make a distinction between what can be found in Plato's dialogues (a matter of historical reconstruction) and what is merely Aristotle's speculation about them (a matter of rational reconstruction). In turning Gerson's point against itself, his argument is hereby neutralized and as such does not uniquely support the thesis that Aristotle is a reliable secondary source for understanding "Plato's philosophy."

Cherniss on Aristotle on Plato: Gerson's Errors

After summarizing in one sentence Cherniss' hundreds of published pages of detailed exegetically-based objections to the use of Aristotle as a reliable witness to "Plato's philosophy" (Gerson 2014: 399), and subsequent to citing Léon Robin's work as a "polar opposite of Cherniss's approach" (Gerson 2014: 399, footnote 5), Gerson in only about two pages describes Cherniss' objections without providing quotations or citations from Cherniss' monumental scholarly and philosophical work on the subject. Readers are left to wonder if Gerson accurately portrays Cherniss' detailed study.

In studying Cherniss' work on this topic and Gerson's depiction of Cherniss' work, however, it is clear that Gerson provides an uncharitable summary of Cherniss' position, one replete with dismissive and inflammatory language, straw man portrayals, question-begging, and other varieties of fallacious reasoning. Since Cherniss is not available to defend his position, and in the spirit of both the hermeneutical Principle of Charity of Interpretation[3] and the epistemic Principle of Seeking Truth and Avoiding Error,[4] I shall examine some of Gerson's

---

[3] By the "Principle of Charity in Interpretation" I mean that where it is unclear what an author means by his or her written word, an interpreter ought never to ascribe to that author a less plausible understanding of such words when there is a more plausible one available unless a sound argument is provided to do otherwise.

[4] The basic content of this principle is found in Lehrer (2000: 26). A general version of it is provided by Plato's Socrates in the *Crito* 47 where Crito concurs with Socrates that "good opinions" ought to be valued instead of bad ones. See also the *Republic* 485c where it is said that philosophers "must be without falsehood—they must refuse to accept what is false, hate it, and have a love for the truth."

other main replies to Cherniss' objections in order to see if they are plausible. It turns out that they are not plausible and thus cannot serve as good reasons why Aristotle ought to be taken as an unproblematic and reliable witness to "Plato's philosophy." Fairness to Cherniss' position requires that I sometimes quote him at length, especially in light of Gerson's uncharitable summary of it.

First, it is unclear why Gerson makes reference to Robin's research in a positive manner ("…it is in line, as Robin emphasizes, with the later Platonic tradition's understanding of Platonism."),[5] except perhaps to raise doubt in the reader's mind about the plausibility of Cherniss' work. But Gerson fails to recognize that Cherniss devotes almost two pages to a criticism of Robin's work. [Cherniss (1962a: xix-xx); Cherniss (1962b: 26–27)] So if Gerson's aim in citing Robin's work is an attempt to discredit Cherniss' objections, then it does not succeed insofar as it ignores Cherniss' objections to Robin's work on the topic. Dismissiveness is not a legitimate substitute for sound argumentation.

Secondly, throughout Gerson's paraphrasing of Cherniss' objections are found inaccurate, inflammatory, dismissive, and question-begging rhetoric. Gerson describes Cherniss' view of the Platonic concept of "eternal divine intellect" as being dismissive "as having no relevance to Aristotle's account of the reduction of Forms to Numbers." (Gerson 2014: 401) But that this accurately reflects Cherniss' position on the matter is dubious: Why would what is written by Plato need to be relevant to anything thought by Aristotle? Would it not be more reasonable to ask the question of whether or not Aristotle's testimony is relevant to "Plato's philosophy" since the context of the discussion is the Platonic Question? That Gerson attempts to describe Cherniss' view in such unsophisticated hermeneutical terms by reversing the terms of relevance between Plato's works and Aristotle's remarks on Plato's works makes one especially suspicious of Gerson's grasp of Cherniss' detailed arguments. Gerson seems to have attempted to Aristotelianize Plato to such an extent that he implicitly believes (absent any quotation or citation from Cherniss as having "dismissed" the said passage from the *Philebus* 23c-26d) that Cherniss or any other professional scholar would dare think it appropriate that some

---

[5] Gerson (2014: 399).

of the contents of Plato's dialogues ought to be relevant to what Aristotle has to say about said passages. The reason why such an interpretive idea is problematic is because it begs the question in favor of the Aristotelianization of Plato's works. Moreover, said passages from Plato are not, on Cherniss' view, to be dismissed as "forgeries" and "denigrations" of written work, as Gerson alleges. (Gerson 2014: 402) Instead, Cherniss carefully argues the following with particular regard to Paul Shorey's rejection of Aristotelian evidence about "Plato's philosophy:"

> Such study, however, must take into consideration all the evidence, neither restricting itself to any part of Aristotle's testimony nor disregarding any of the available means of controlling that testimony. The diverse opinions hitherto pronounced have for the most part been the result of general impressions, and at best they are conclusions reached from investigations which were in one way or another fragmentary. It is true that we do not possess all the material which we could wish to have; it may even be that we do not possess enough to justify in some important matters a conclusion of high probability; but that too is a decision which can be fairly given only after weighing all the evidence, and the very fact that we know our material to be incomplete lays us under the greater obligation to examine thoroughly all that remains to us.
>
> I therefore intend to outline and analyze all of Aristotle's testimony and criticism bearing upon Plato and the pupils and associates of Plato, to observe in what way he distinguishes or omits to distinguish the doctrines which he ascribes to them, to determine specifically what consistency or inconsistency there may be in his treatment of them, to compare wherever possible his testimony and interpretation with relevant passages in Plato's writings, with the fragments which remain from the writings of Plato's pupils, and with the other ancient evidence concerning their doctrines, to estimate the validity of their criticism, and to decide not merely whether his interpretations are "right" or "wrong" but how and why he came to adopt them and formulate them as he did. In order to do this it will be necessary to interpret Platonic and Aristotelian texts, as well as many others, and to interpret them, furthermore, in their full philosophical intention; but there is no automatic canon in any case, and it is certainly unreasonable to disregard part of our evidence on the supposition that we are thus eliminating the danger of misinterpretation. I shall, however, avoid drawing any conclusions from such general concepts as the "temperament" or "tendency" of Aristotelian or Platonic philosophy and shall restrict myself to those for the support of which specific passages can be cited. Wherever to my knowledge interpretations have been adopted which differ from in a way what would be significant for the question in hand I shall try to give explicit reasons why I have not accepted those

interpretations. This may seem to make a tedious business still more tedious; but there can be no approach to common agreement on more general issues until scholars stop passing by in silence the discordant interpretations of specific passages on which any sound decision of those larger issues must depend. (Cherniss 1962a: xxi-xxii)

These words from Cherniss are not those of a dismissive scholar, but of a serious and careful one, judiciously weighing textual evidence from Aristotle in order to determine if scholars such as Shorey are too quick to dismiss or undervalue such testimony. To the methodological passage from Cherniss may be appended another lengthy one that reflects Cherniss' actual position on Aristotle on Plato:

The riddle of the early Academy is epitomized in the discrepancy between Aristotle's account of Plato's theory of ideas and that theory as we know it from Plato's writings. To explain that discrepancy, scholars have constructed the hypothesis of an oral Platonic doctrine. I have tried to show that that hypothesis is unsatisfactory not only because the evidence for Plato's one attested lecture fails to support it, but also because the inconsistency in Aristotle's testimony itself appears to contradict it; but the alternative hypothesis which I have proposed, namely, that the identification of ideas and numbers was not a theory of Plato's at all but the result of Aristotle's own interpretation,—this hypothesis also seems to assume the restriction of the whole enigma and the conditions of its solution to the testimony of Aristotle alone. Yet one might object that there were other members of the Academy, members who might be expected to have greater sympathy with Plato's teaching than had the founder of the Lyceum, who called the ideas "meaningless prattle." If, then, Aristotle deduced from the written or spoken words of Plato a doctrine which Plato had never meant to propound, would not such an ascription have been denied and such an interpretation opposed by these other members of the Academy, and especially by Speusippus and Xenocrates, the successors to the headship of the school? One might even expect that these two men, at least, would have maintained in tact the philosophical system taught by Plato, in which case their own doctrines could serve as a means of controlling directly Aristotle's reports and interpretation of that system....

Nor can these doctrines serve as a canon of Plato's teaching, for Speusippus and Xenocrates held metaphysical theories different from each other and each of them different not only from the theory of ideas in the Platonic dialogues but also from that discrepant theory of idea-numbers which Aristotle ascribed to Plato. Instead of being a control upon that ascription, then, these doctrines of Plato's successors only manifest anew, and reflect from another angle, the same enigma which it epitomizes.... So even the scholars who accept [Aristotle's] account as having reference to what Plato taught orally in the school usually recognize that his criticisms of this theory ascribed to Plato is somehow affected by his related criticism of Speusippus and Xenocrates, and they frequently assert that he has distorted Plato's doctrine in the direction of other Platonistic theories, especially that of Xenocrates. To admit so much, however, is in fact to admit that Aristotle's whole treatment of what is assumed to have been Plato's oral doctrine may have been determined by his concern with these Platonistic theories. (Chern iss 1962b: 31–32)

In light of quotations like these from Cherniss, to foist on Cherniss the "highly implausible"[6] argument that "both passages are irrelevant to understanding Plato since, if they were relevant, then Aristotle's testimony would also be irrelevant" is for Gerson to commit both a straw man fallacy and a violation of the Principle of Charity in Interpretation. Gerson's attribution error is compounded by the fact that, once again, he offers no quotations from Cherniss that Cherniss holds anything akin to the "exceedingly implausible"[7] view that Gerson ascribes to him. Nor does the above passage from Cherniss (nor any other passage I could find from Cherniss' works) suggest that Cherniss thought that the Idea of the Good in Plato's dialogues is "something of a hyperbolic joke." (Gerson 2014: 402) Careful students of the works of Cherniss know that Cherniss takes the matter under consideration seriously, as Cherniss is not given to such flippant interpretations of Plato's writings.

Moreover, in his description of Cherniss' objections, Gerson describes Cherniss' position on Aristotle's testimony as having to be "explained away," wherein the Forms are "reduced" to the level of "concepts," wherein the "distinct level of cognition and being in the Divided Line in *Republic* (510c-511a)…is trivialized," and wherein the "truly massive amount of material in the dialogues concerned with mathematics is written off as a kind of independent hobby of Plato…" (Gerson 2014: 401) While it is problematic enough to include such language in one's critique of another's position absent justification, it is even more problematic to do so in the *description* of a view the

---

[6] This locution is used by Gerson, as quoted above, to describe what Gerson refers to as "extreme Protestantism."

[7] This locution is used by Gerson himself, ironically enough, to describe Cherniss' position. (Gerson 2014: 402)

plausibility of which is yet to be considered on its own terms by reasonable parties.

Thirdly, the points about Robin absent Gerson's recognition of Cherniss' objections to Robin's work and Gerson's uncharitable description of Cherniss' objections to the reliability of using Aristotle's testimony as a means of understanding "Plato's philosophy" might be counted by some as merely unprofessional conduct in research. But Gerson has, as I have explained, implicitly offered a reason in favor of Aristotle's testimony about "Plato's philosophy" which can be turned against itself, thereby impeaching Aristotle's testimony. Furthermore, Gerson goes on to commit a logical error with regard to the *Phaedrus* and the *Seventh Letter* as he seeks to further discredit the Platonic Protestant approach and support his version of Platonic Catholicism. Gerson states:

> Finally, there are two texts which loom particularly large in the Catholic interpretive milieu and which, therefore, the unitarian Protestant approach is especially eager to discount. The first is the passage in *Phaedrus* (274b6-278e3) in which Socrates goes on at some length about the inferiority of written work to oral teaching. The second is the passage in Plato's 7th *Letter* (340b1-345c3) in which Plato tells his correspondent that there does not exist a document containing information about those matters in which Plato is most concerned. These texts lend support both to the idea that Plato had, as Aristotle testifies, an oral teaching and that this is at least as important as anything in the dialogues. (Gerson 2014: 401)

The difficulty with Gerson's reasoning here is that even if his interpretation of said passages is reasonably accurate, he misjudges what he is allowed to infer from them. More exactly, even if Gerson is correct in his interpretation about what the author of the *Seventh Letter* states regarding, presumably, Plato's never having written down "his philosophy," it does not follow from this, "as Aristotle testifies," that Plato had an unwritten "oral teaching." Gerson notes that said passages "lend support" to Platonic Catholicism." However, said passages also lend support to competing ways to approach Plato's works, one approach of which is sketched (and articulated and defended in Chapters 2 and 3 of this book) for the sake of exposing a bifurcation fallacy latent in Gerson's argument. If this possibility that Gerson fails to consider in Gerson (2014) is plausible, then Gerson's use of these passages to support Platonic Catholicism is at least neutralized to the extent that such passages support competing approaches to Plato's works as well as Gerson's.

Moreover, matters become worst for Gerson's reasoning about said passages. For given Gerson's interpretation of them, it not only does not follow that Plato had an unwritten esoteric oral teaching that was communicated to his students in the Academy, but it also fails to follow that this Aristotelian point about the oral teaching "is at least as important as anything in the dialogues." For while this assumption might be held in esteem by Platonic Catholics, it is contrary to any reasonable hermeneutical principle of which this author is aware. Just because it is convenient for Platonic Catholics to infer from said passages that the oral teaching to which Aristotle testifies "is at least just as important as anything in the dialogues" of Plato, this does not make it true. And it certainly fails to follow from any non-question-begging point that might be found in Gerson (2014). Thus even if the contents of said works are genuinely Plato's, and even if there exists no written document containing "Plato's philosophy," and even if Plato had an oral teaching, it would not follow straightaway that such oral teachings possess the level of importance as the dialogues in extracting "Plato's philosophy." First, this holds because Plato's oral teaching, if he had one, might not have been doctrinal or designed to teach what he believed. Secondly, Plato's oral teaching, even if it were doctrinal, would not (unless it were also published and genuinely Plato's) necessarily possess the hermeneutical authority as would Plato's writings—even assuming that Plato's writings were designed to communicate his philosophical beliefs. So the most that Gerson can claim is what he seems to claim, namely, that (in a rather attenuated sense) said passages might "lend support" to Platonic Catholicism. But said passages do not lend *unique* support to such an approach, as we will see below. Gerson's point is neutralized and cannot be used to uniquely support the idea that Plato had an esoteric oral teaching wherein he revealed his substantive philosophy in terms of his beliefs, doctrines, or theories. In combining the Mouthpiece Interpretation with Platonic esotericism (the view that Plato had unwritten teachings that he revealed only to his students), Gerson's Platonic Catholicism seems to face the following dilemma: "*either* one must go outside the dialogues to the 'unwritten teachings,' reported as they are especially by Aristotle in *Metaphysics* A6, or, in order to stay within the dialogues, one must reject Aristotle's testimony as, in some proportion, misinterpretation and fabrication." (Miller 1995: 226) As we shall see, the first horn of this dilemma is rendered problematic by Cherniss.

Cherniss addresses the matter of the alleged oral teachings of Plato in light of the *Seventh Letter* and evidence from the *Phaedrus*:

> Because Aristotle gave systematic lectures which are preserved and wrote dialogues which are not, it does not follow that Plato, whose dialogues we have, must have given lecture courses which have been lost. Even if the analogy were shown to be valid, however, the hypothesis itself is not thereby established; in order to stand, it must save *all* of the phenomena which it pretends to explain.
>
> Let us for the moment grant that Plato lectured to the school and in his lectures went beyond his writings in working out details and in resolving various problems connected with the general theory of ideas. Still, the identification of ideas with numbers and the derivation of ideas from two supreme principles are not such details. They concern the very foundations of the theory; and if in the lectures they had such importance as the modern hypothesis assumes, it is legitimate and necessary to ask why there is no mention of them in the later dialogues which treat of the ideas. The usual answer to this question, when it is recognized at all, is that Plato wrote the dialogues for the general public and consequently omitted them from any exposition of the more profound and technical aspects of his philosophy. This answer is sometimes bolstered up by citing the disparagement of written books at the end of the *Phaedrus* and the passage in the *Seventh Epistle* attributed to Plato in which the writer says there is not and never will be any composition of his dealing with the ultimate principles. This easy explanation, however, only makes the mystery still more obscure, for, if Plato felt, as the author of the *Seventh Epistle* says, that this doctrine was incommunicable in words, and if he did not put his ultimate philosophy into the dialogues because these were designed for the general public which he believed incapable of comprehending anything so profound, why is it that the one occasion which he is supposed to have chosen for an exposition of it in all its technical profundity was precisely a lecture given to a public audience which had no preliminary experience of the sort of thing he was likely to say?...Aristonexus himself makes it perfectly clear that the lecture was delivered before a public audience. What was thus publicly expounded was obviously not meant to be a secret or esoteric doctrine...of the *Seventh Epistle*. Those who cite from that *Epistle* the author's denial that he has written anything about ultimate principles usually take more lightly the sentence which immediately precedes this denial. Yet there the author says: "So much I can assert about *all* writers past and future who say that they know the subjects with which I am seriously concerned, whether because they have heard it from me or others or because they have found it out themselves: it is not possible, in my opinion, they understood anything about the matter at all." Whether authentic or not, this assertion is certainly directed against such publications as those of Hermodorus and Aristotle. Those who accept the *Epistle* as

authentic and say that Plato there warns us not to look for his ultimate philosophy in the dialogues should be at least consistent enough to admit that he also disowns his students' published reports of his lecture. Thorough consistency would, in fact, require an admission much more serious than this. For myself, I do not believe that Plato wrote this *Epistle*; but if I did, I should recognize that he himself has borne witness beforehand against anything which I might write about the real purport of his thought, and I should account it the madness born of stubborn insolence to seek to describe or even to discover the serious doctrine of a man who has condemned all those who ever have made the attempt or ever will. Sure the *Seventh Epistle* exacts a fatal price from anyone who would use it to support the hypothesis that Plato expounded orally in his school a philosophical system of ultimate principles more technical and more profound than that in his dialogues; but, the two-edged testimony of the *Seventh Epistle* aside, the real evidence for the lecture on the Good which I have set before you must itself, I am sure, appear to be incompatible with such a hypothesis. (Cherniss 1962b: 11–13)

Thus a closer study of Cherniss' work reveals that Cherniss has already addressed and refuted the points that Gerson makes concerning these passages from the *Phaedrus* and the *Seventh Letter*. The very least that Gerson could do is to address them straightforwardly while frequently quoting and citing Cherniss' works along the way in order to avoid misattributions. Readers deserve as much in a commentary entitled "Harold Cherniss and the Study of Plato Today" which is said to address directly Cherniss' position on such an important topic. They deserve more than Gerson's use of locutions such as "dismissing the Idea of the Good as something of a hyperbolic joke" in order to describe some of Cherniss' meticulous exegetical work on Plato's dialogues. What Gerson offers instead is a description of Cherniss' exegetical work that only once and quite briefly in a footnote actually quotes Cherniss and rarely cites Cherniss' work, but instead mostly offers his own often vague and uncharitable paraphrases of Cherniss' position. Instead, when Gerson attempts to counter Cherniss' detailed and exegetically-based philosophical objections to the use of the "Aristotle-as-a-Witness-to-'Plato's Philosophy'" theory, it can find little respect among serious and careful readers of Cherniss.

Yet another difficulty with Gerson's defense of the "Aristotle-as-a-Witness to Plato's Philosophy" theory is his claim that there is an "adherence to a conscious or unconscious assumption that Aristotle's testimony is to be ignored." (Gerson 2014: 403) Perhaps Gerson is

Appendices

correct that there are some scholars who ignore Aristotle as a possible witness to "Plato's philosophy." But it ought to be made clear that in an essay devoted primarily to Cherniss' objections to such a theory that Cherniss himself provides ample reasoning, sans mere assumption, for his objections to this approach to Plato. Specifically, Cherniss writes:

> Yet upon investigation one discovers that there are two and only two specific passages in the whole Aristotelian corpus which these scholars can or do adduce in evidence of their general statements...one of the two passages in which Aristotle is supposed to refer directly to the lectures of Plato—and a passage which, incidentally, has been widely used to reconstruct the content of those lectures—does not concern Plato at all and was not meant to be so understood. In the other, a passage of the *Physics*, Plato's "unwritten opinions" (ἄγραφα δόγματα) are cited; but, whether by this term Aristotle means to designate the published reports of Plato's lecture on the Good or just opinions which Plato had expressed in conversation with students and associates and which they may or may not have written down or collected, at least three conclusions must be drawn from this citation, and all of them contradict the statements which this passage is usually presumed to support. First, since the citation here is unique, Aristotle does *not* "commonly" refer to the teaching in the Academy as Plato's "unwritten doctrine"; second, he does not even here cite these "unwritten doctrines" as his source for the theory of idea-numbers; and, third, he mentions them only to assert their agreement with the *Timaeus*. He admits that in that dialogue and in the "unwritten opinions" the participant has different designations; but he implicitly denies that this is anything more than a difference in terminology, for he contends that whether the participant be called "the great and the small," as in the "unwritten opinions," or the material principle, as in the *Timaeus*, since it is in either case special position, the ideas in which it participates ought to be in place and Plato is faced with the difficulty of explaining why they are not. When we consider that it was just the discrepancy between Aristotle's reports and Plato's dialogues which suggests the hypothesis that Plato in his lectures taught a doctrine of ultimate principles which he omitted from his dialogues, it is startling to find that Aristotle himself, in the one passage which could be taken as a direct reference to such lectures of Plato's, dismisses as merely a verbal variation the discrepancy between the unwritten opinions and the dialogues and insists that what is taken to be one of the two ultimate principles of this supposedly recondite oral theory is identical with the participant concerning which we can read Plato's own words in the *Timaeus*. Startling as this is, however, it is useless to pretend that this passage in any way differentiates from the participant in that dialogue "the great and the small" of the "unwritten opinions." Not only would

> Aristotle's argument be pointless unless he took them to be identical; he *says* in so many words that by either name the participant is space. To be sure, his identification of the space of the *Timaeus* with his own conception of position, his assumption that the participant there is the equivalent of his own "material principle," his flat statement that Plato *says* that matter and space are the same—all these are misinterpretations or even misstatements of great consequence; and, since he misinterprets and misquotes the *Timaeus*, what he says of the "unwritten opinions" may be erroneous too. Even so, his misinterpretations of both expositions are likely to be of a similar kind, since he takes the meaning of both to be the same; and we can establish the general tendency of his interpretation,…In any case, the significance of the passage for the hypothesis of Plato's oral doctrine is that it justifies, or rather requires, the use of the *Timaeus* as a criterion for the possible nature of such a doctrine and for Aristotle's reports and interpretations of it.
>
> Consequently, this one passage itself would suffice to refute the widespread notion that for the theory of ideas or the Platonic metaphysics Aristotle always refers to Plato's lectures and discussions in the Academy and never to his published dialogues. (Cherniss 1962a: 16–17)[8]

This is part of the heart of Cherniss' objection to the use of Aristotle in attempting to decipher "Plato's philosophy." It is not "a conscious or unconscious assumption that Aristotle's testimony is to be ignored." (Gerson 2014: 403) Rather it is that Aristotle has so badly misinterpreted some of the ideas latent in Plato's dialogues that his key philosophical ascriptions to Plato are tainted by this fact, making Aristotle an unreliable witness to "Plato's philosophy." So Cherniss hardly ignores Aristotle and takes his testimony seriously. But when he does so, Cherniss discovers that Aristotle is a dubious witness.

If the most that can be said against Cherniss' objections is what Gerson offers, then Gerson does not do much, if anything, to either defeat or neutralize Cherniss' points of argument. How, in light of these factors, can one take seriously Gerson's claim that Gerson's own Aristotelianized Platonic Idea of the Good reduces "to absurdity Cherniss's position as exegesis"? (Gerson 2014: 402) Indeed, Gerson's uncharitable and inaccurate description of Cherniss' objections renders ineffective Gerson's attempt to reply to Cherniss' objections.

---

[8] Also see Cherniss (1962b: 38–48, 80–82).

An Alternative Approach to Plato

As we have seen, Gerson insists that the testimony of Aristotle, which Cherniss' objections have sought to impeach and Gerson has failed to either defeat or neutralize, is the "key witness" to "Plato's philosophy." But it is important to investigate, however concisely, an alternative approach to Plato's dialogues that Gerson and many other mouthpiece interpreters fail to take sufficiently seriously,[9] and one which holds that primary evidence generally outweighs secondary evidence when it comes to the Platonic Question. That Gerson would write that Aristotle is "the key witness" to "Plato's philosophy" seems to rest on the Platonically Catholic *assumption* that primary and secondary evidence for "Plato's philosophy" are on evidential par with one another—at least as concerns Aristotle's interpretation of Plato's dialogues. Indeed, recall Gerson's statement (quoted above) that, according to Platonic Catholicism, "the dialogues are not the ultimate authority for Plato's meaning."

Furthermore, if primary evidence is ever to be outweighed by secondary evidence along the lines implied by Gerson, then the burden of proof is on those such as Gerson to provide an argument why, at least in a particular circumstance, this is the case. Moreover, Gerson also bears the burden of justifying which kinds of secondary evidence can outweigh primary evidence, and how to weigh the quality of contradictory secondary evidences. Yet the most that Gerson does is to provide problematic reasons against Cherniss' objections, ones which are refuted by either a mere appeal to Cherniss' critical assessment of the Aristotle-as-a-Witness-to-"Plato's–Philosophy" hypothesis, or ones which can be either defeated or neutralized on other grounds. And if Plato is the author of the *Seventh Letter*, then it might be that adherence to the Mouthpiece Interpretation in light of the balance of evidential reasoning pertinent to the Platonic Question is an example of, to borrow Cherniss' words, quoted above, "…the madness born of stubborn insolence to seek to describe or even to discover the serious doctrine of a man who has condemned all those who ever have made the attempt or ever will." One would think that it is reasonable to

---

[9] Gerson takes up the topic of certain versions of such an approach in Gerson (2000: 201–210); Gerson (2002: 217–231). But therein Gerson does not address the version I outline here.

believe that, *other things being even approximately equal, primary evidence generally outweighs secondary evidence when it comes to attempting to understand an author's meaning*. In the case at hand, then, the writings of Plato outweigh those of Aristotle when the issue is that of attempting to discover whether or not Plato had a substantive philosophy that he desired to communicate in his dialogues.

These hermeneutical issues make it important to consider an alternative approach to Plato: the Socratic (Anti-Mouthpiece) Interpretation as it is articulated in earlier chapters of this book. It is a moderate version of the Anti-Mouthpiece Interpretation according to which it is primarily Plato's mentor, Socrates, who most influenced Plato and whose analytic method serves as a guide to understanding what Plato is up to in composing the dialogues. It eschews the "Plato says fallacy"[10] of ascribing to Plato this or that belief, doctrine or theory (i.e., substantive philosophy) found in the dialogues.[11] This version of the Anti-Mouthpiece Interpretation does not reduce to "absurdity" the principle of "*sola scriptura* by claiming that the dialogues alone cannot tell us what their author thinks…" (Gerson 2014: 398) According to this version of the Anti-Mouthpiece Interpretation, it is not that the dialogues "cannot" tell us what Plato thinks. Nor is it that the informational contents of the dialogues of Plato are always sufficient to interpret their contents well. Rather, it is that there seems to be no unproblematic manner by which to discern "*Plato's (substantive) philosophy*" from their contents as this discussion seems to indicate to be the inference to the best explanation of why Plato composed dialogues. Indeed, it seems reasonable to approach the dialogues with the real possibility that Plato, instead of subscribing to and desiring to expound, defend, and communicate the variety of often "highly implausible" views expressed in the dialogues, had no *substantive* philosophy in which to communicate in his writings. Alternatively, it is reasonable to think that even if Plato had a substantive philosophy, then Plato could have composed the dialogues without a desire to communicate it to others therein. Indeed, it is the set of ideas often

---

[10] This fallacy is dubbed such in Mulhern (1971).

[11] Gerson commits this fallacy throughout his essay on Cherniss. But see especially Gerson (2014: 407), where Gerson asserts without supportive argument that "…denied by Plato when he says…Plato's claim…Plato says about… Plato's explicit words…"

supported by implausible arguments found in the dialogues that Plato, like Plato's Socrates, wants his readers to critically examine. It is, moreover, a violation of the Principle of Charity in Interpretation to ascribe to Plato or to the historical Socrates any of the substantive views expressed by Plato's Socrates or by other characters in the dialogues. As such, it qualifies as a commission of a straw man fallacy to attribute such views to either the historical Socrates or Plato.[12]

Furthermore, the Socratic Interpretation does not construe the Platonic dialogues as communicating substantive philosophical beliefs, doctrines, or theories of Plato's. While the dialogues are dramatic works instead of treatises, they might be studied by readers to extract arguments and analyses from them in order to allow the reader to follow the philosophical dialectic and develop analytically various lines of argument on a particular subject matter in metaphysics, epistemology, ethics, etc.. This approach to Plato's works denies that there is sufficient evidence or reason to accept that the dialogues of Plato reveal, intentionally or not, of the positions expressed therein, which ones—if any—are Plato's own. This is because, according to this approach, it is not obvious that Plato composed dialogues for the purpose of communicating his substantive philosophy (if he even had a substantive philosophy). Instead, his intent may have been to provide various propadeutics for the study of philosophical issues such as the nature of human knowledge in the *Theatetus* and the *Meno*, the nature of justice, virtue, politics, poetry and education in the *Republic*, the nature of art and beauty in the *Hippias Major* and the *Ion*, etc.. For the general aim of the dialogues is to facilitate readers in achieving philosophical enlightenment on their own about such problems, to take up the torch of analytic philosophy where the dialogues leave off with the explicit aims of obtaining truth and avoiding error with regard to such problems that arise in the dialogues. So it is Plato's readers who bear the primary responsibility of doing philosophy analytically by following the arguments wherever they lead. This implies an active philosophical participation of readers in the manner of Socrates and some of his dialogical interlocutors. And this is the case in light of the fact that throughout Plato's dialogues there is often an inequality between

---

[12] By "believe" and its cognates is meant the Kripkean sense of "belief" according to which one sincerely assents to a proposition without ambiguity. (Kripke 1979)

interlocutors (Socrates over Glaucon, Thrasymachus and Adeimantus in the *Republic*; Socrates over Theatetus in the *Theatetus*, etc.), perhaps suggesting that certain positions are more or less plausible than others.

Insofar as textual evidence and the Platonic Question is concerned, the Socratic Interpretation holds that reliable secondary sources might be used to understand Plato's dialogues, but such sources must, absent strong justification to the contrary, be subordinated to the primary sources of Plato's own writings. That is, no secondary source can be used that would contradict the intent or informational contents of the dialogues, understood Socratically and in light of the plain sense of the contents of the dialogues. Caution must be used in consulting secondary sources so as not to permit them to determine on their own the interpretation of the dialogues.

Ironically, Aristotle can serve as a legitimate secondary source. However, it is not because, as Gerson and many other mouthpiece interpreters think, that Aristotle can assist us in better understanding "Plato's philosophy." Rather, it is because Aristotle can help us to see that certain ideas expressed in the dialogues, if interpreted in certain ways, are in and of themselves philosophically problematic regardless of whether or not Plato believes them. So long as we do not make the interpretive mistake of thinking that Aristotle is a key to unlock the content of Plato's own philosophy, Aristotle can assist us in picking up where the dialogues discontinue in philosophical reasoning. For instance, if the conception of Ideas found in certain of Plato's dialogues is taken to mean what Aristotle thinks it means, then that idea is dubious for reasons some of which we find expressed by Aristotle. But Cherniss cautions us for a variety of reasons to not commit the attribution error of assuming that Aristotle is accurate in his rendering of "Plato's philosophy." Hence interpreting the informational contents of Plato's dialogues is what Plato wants us to do: In reading and interpreting them, we are to carefully consider all possible philosophical options and follow the best arguments wherever they lead us about this or that topic found therein. In approaching Plato's dialogues, one ought never to presume that what we think we know is always the ways things really are. One does not want to become a prisoner in Plato's analogy of the cave in confidently believing that something is the case when it might not be such.

Conclusion

If Cherniss' critique of the Platonic Catholic approach to whether or not Aristotle is a reliable witness to the understanding of "Plato's philosophy" is correct, then Platonic Catholicism is deeply problematic. I have explained the problematic nature of some of Gerson's main replies to Cherniss' objections and have concluded that Cherniss' objections to the trustworthiness of Aristotle-as-a-Witness-to-"Plato's-Philosophy" hypothesis withstand Gerson's replies. However, for those who might think that it is too difficult to decide between these two Mouthpiece Interpretive approaches to Plato's dialogues in that, they might think, there is no decisive evidence one way or the other which would resolve the issue, a viable alternative to such approaches is to remain agnostic about them and to consider the Socratic Interpretation. No bifurcation fallacy need be committed with regard to this matter.

Gerson, a proponent of the Mouthpiece Interpretation of Plato's dialogues, attempts to prove the reliability of Aristotle's testimony about "Plato's philosophy." In so doing, he sometimes ignores the detailed objections set forth by Cherniss' rigorous exegetically-based work. Gerson is willing to see, moreover, in various of Plato's works alleged evidence of "Plato's philosophy," leading Gerson to commit the "Plato says" fallacy. Yet it is Gerson himself who accuses others of foregoing "the plain sense of the text of the dialogues" (Gerson 2014: 402) of Plato instead of adopting a more cautious stance on whether or not Plato even intends to communicate a particular set of substantive philosophical teachings in the dialogues. Evidence in favor of this charge is found above when Gerson derives some invalid inferences from the passages of the *Seventh Letter* and the *Phaedrus* concerning whether or not Plato ever wrote down anything of his alleged substantive philosophy. The "plain sense of the text of the dialogues" hardly requires the convoluted exegetical hoops that mouthpiece interpreters like Gerson want us to accept. Instead, it supports the plain sense adopted by the Socratic Interpretation of Plato's dialogues. It is an approach to Plato that refuses to give up the common sense hermeneutical principle of requiring primary textual evidence to outweigh, absent strong and uncontroversial justification to the contrary, secondary evidence.

Perhaps the irony of all ironies in the context of this discussion is Gerson's embracing of a form of Catholicism—even if only of the Platonic variety. For just as Martin Luther condemned Christian Catholicism for its selling of indulgences, its patronage to saints and depicting and essentially raising them to the spiritual level of Jesus of Nazareth who by testimony of the early Christians was and is God, etc., thereby significantly perverting the very message of the Christian writings, so too Platonic Catholicism, in seeking to justify a particular approach to the content of "Plato's philosophy," goes to great lengths to defend Aristotle's testimony which, if Cherniss' detailed exegetical analyses are correct, reveal the extent to which Plato's dialogues have been misunderstood particularly by those who essentially seek to Aristotelianize Plato and his dialogues. What the study of Plato's dialogues needs today is a Reformation of sorts (a Platonic Reformation), demanding that the Mouthpiece Interpretation either be adequately justified in some non-viciously question-begging sense or be rejected for the speciously-supported dogma that it has become amongst so many contemporary philosophers. Contrary to Gerson, then, Cherniss' detailed and well-reasoned work has not been a "baleful" influence on the study of Plato's dialogues.

References

Cherniss, Harold. 1962a. *Aristotle's criticism of Plato and the Academy*. New York: Russell & Russell.
———. 1962b. *The riddle of the early Academy*. New York: Russell & Russell.
Gerson, Lloyd. 2000. Plato *Absconditus*. In *Who speaks for Plato?* ed. Gerald Press, 201–210. Lanham: Rowman & Littlefield Publishers.
———. 2002. *Elenchos*, protreptic, and platonic philosophizing. In *Does Socrates have a method?* ed. G.A. Scott, 217–231. Philadelphia: Pennsylvania State University Press.
———. 2014. Harold Cherniss and the study of Plato today. *Journal of the History of Philosophy* 52: 397–409.
Kripke, Saul. A puzzle about belief. In *Meaning and use*, ed. A. Margalit, 239–283. Dordrecht: Reidel.
Lehrer, Keith. 2000. *Theory of knowledge*. 2nd ed. Boulder: Westview Press.
Miller, Mitchell. 1995. The choice between the dialogues and the 'Unwritten Teachings': A Scylla and Charybdis for the interpreter. In *The third way*, ed. F. Gonzalez, 225–243. Lanham: Rowman & Littlefield.
Mulhern, John J. 1971. Two Interpretive Fallacies. *Systematics* 9: 168–172.

Appendix II: The Concept of Art as *Mimêsis* in Plato's Dialogues

Most philosophers of Plato concur with the claim that, in the *Republic*, Plato condemns poetry and the mimetic arts *qua* mimetic arts. Yet, as Voula Tsouna points out, many ancients and contemporaries argue that Plato's dialogues themselves, in whole or in part, constitute some form of mimetic art. (Tsouna, 2013: 2–8) How can sense be made of the facts that, according to this view, Plato himself condemns mimetic arts and at the same time offers his dialogues which are themselves mimetic in nature?

Tsouna seeks to reconcile these seemingly conflicting facts about Plato and mimetic art in the *Republic* by distinguishing between different kinds of mimetic art forms and by arguing that Plato's dialogues do not constitute a harmful form of mimetic art as do poetry and certain other art forms such as painting, etc.. For, as Tsouna argues, Plato's mimetic art form, his philosophical dialogues, are not based on emotion but on reason and engage persons in a philosophical life that betters themselves and society. As she puts it of Plato's dialogues: They are "*awkward* objects of imitation. ... Plato's dialogues do not merely *represent* doing philosophy in a dialectical manner.... they *do* philosophy in that manner... They *draw* us *in* as participants to the conversation." (Tsouna 2013: 23) Moreover, Plato's dialogues do not deceive us about what is true (Tsouna 2013: 16) in a manner in which, say, *skiagraphia* or *trompe l'oeil* paintings do. (Corlett 2005: 88–89) So whereas harmful mimetic art seeks to hide truth, Plato's dialogues seek out truth. Additionally, "Plato's Socrates maintains an attitude of epistemic diffidence or at least of caution, which is quite unlike the attitude that he attributes to the poets. This is expressed, for instance, in his disclaimers that he knows anything about important things." (Tsouna 2013: 22)[13] Moreover, Tsouna writes of the *Republic* in particular, "unlike poems and plays, Plato's dialogues are, according to his own standards, devoted to realities and not to counterfeits (599a), and they stand as memorials of their author (599b)." (Tsouna 2013: 22)

---

[13] Also see Corlett (2005: 51–53).

Now this general line of reasoning is a plausible manner by which to reconcile the expressed condemnation of mimetic arts in the *Republic* with what transpires in Plato's dialogues as a whole and in the *Republic* in particular. What is of concern about Tsouna's approach to Plato is that she makes numerous attributions to Plato which find no plausible warrant from Plato's dialogues themselves.

This raises the quandary of the Platonic Question, one which is not the primary issue of Tsouna's article but which nevertheless underlies it. Indeed, Tsouna recognizes this very point when she writes: "Although my argument bears significantly on the broader issue of why Plato composes most of his works in the dialogue form, of course I do not pretend to exhaust that issue." (Tsouna 2013: 5) So it is clear that the Platonic Question is relevant to Tsouna's argument in attempting to resolve the apparent conflict within Plato's dialogue about mimetic arts.

Tsouna's Use of the Mouthpiece Interpretation of Plato's Dialogues

Several of Tsouna's locutions indicate her adoption of the Mouthpiece Interpretation of Plato's dialogues according to which some of the informational content of a Platonic dialogue is alleged or assumed to be Plato's own belief, theory, or doctrine in the sense that Plato is alleged to accept it as his own through the words he has placed in the mouths of this or that dialogical interlocutor. (Corlett 2005: 4–10, 19–38) For example, Tsouma states that "…Plato himself acknowledges the mimetic character of his enterprise…" (Tsouna 2013: 1) Furthermore, she writes of "Plato's argument," "Plato's position," and of how "Plato treats poetry" and "extends his criticisms" of poetry to painting. (Tsouna 2013: 1) Tsouna also writes of "Plato's own lights" and that "Plato suggests or says" with regard to "Plato's criticism of poetry" and how "Plato assesses" poets in the *Republic*. (Tsouna 2013: 5) Moreover, she even writes of "Plato's reason" for his censorship of the mimetic arts in said dialogue. (Tsouna 2013: 5) She follows this language of direct attribution of ideas in the dialogue to Plato with "his own argument" and "he uses *mimesis*" and "he could not deny that…" "Plato stands" to further describe what Plato allegedly believes or accepts. For Tsouna, "Plato's predominant imitation is Socrates" (Tsouna 2013: 11) "in the sense that he impersonates" him "in writing" (Tsouna 2013: 20), implying that Socrates is Plato's mouthpiece (though not his only mouthpiece throughout the dialogues). Later, Tsouna writes of "Plato's criticisms" against the poets, and of what "Plato *intended*…" (Tsouna 2013: 18) Again, she refers to "Plato's arguments" (Tsouna 2013: 24) and of what "Plato reserves for himself." (Tsouna 2013: 27) So it is clear that Tsouna has embraced some version of the Mouthpiece Interpretation of Plato's dialogues.

Yet it is precisely Tsouna's adoption of the Mouthpiece Interpretation which motivates her attempt to resolve the alleged problem posed above between Plato's alleged condemnation of the mimetic arts and the "fact" that Plato's dialogues themselves are mimetic. While she argues plausibly that Plato's dialogues are concerned with the attempt to reach truth and poetry and other mimetic arts are not so concerned with the acquisition of truth, and while she argues plausibly that the mimetic arts are concerned only with appearances and not with reality as are the Platonic dialogues, these points can also be used to support an alternative approach to Plato's dialogues which does not have to posit an alleged conflict, *prima facie* or otherwise, between the condemnation of the mimetic arts in Plato's *Republic* and more generally in Plato's dialogues as mimetic art as Tsouna suggests. Indeed, why not construe more simply, using William of Ockham's "Razor" as a hermeneutical guide, the expressed condemnation of the mimetic arts in the *Republic* and elsewhere in Plato's dialogues as just that, an expressed condemnation to be considered philosophically in order to discover if it withstands the test of reason? Why overly complicate the reading of Plato's dialogues with appeals to Plato's alleged theory of forms as Tsouna does? (Tsouna 2013: 16) While she is hardly alone in adopting the Mouthpiece Interpretation and its array of complex "doctrines" or "theories" of forms and who knows what else, the Socratic Interpretation of Plato's dialogues construes the words of Plato's Socrates and other interlocutors in Plato's dialogues as a search for truth regarding this or that matter under discussion.

Thus in Plato's *Republic*, the issue of how guardians ought to be educated in the ideal *polis* encounters the problem of censorship, a difficulty encountered by all who are serious about ethics, politics, religion, etc.. But it is problematic to attribute to Plato what cannot be substantiated absent the hermeneutical gymnastics concerning what this or that character in his dialogues (typically Socrates) is made to express. What mouthpiece interpreters such as Tsouna tend to do is to postulate "doctrines" or "theories" they find expressed in Plato's dialogues and then as either unitarians or developementalists (Corlett 2005: 6–8) piece them together and attribute them to Plato. But they seem to either fail to realize or refuse to admit that there is inadequate textual evidence in Plato's dialogues which warrants such attributions. (Corlett 2005: 19–38) And this is especially the case when it comes to the concept of art as *mimêsis* in the *Republic*! (Corlett 2005: 67–94)

Tsouna makes some statements that seem to soften her mouthpiece approach. For example, she recognizes the dialectical nature and purpose of Plato's dialogues in that they "*do* philosophy…" (Tsouna 2013: 23) Indeed, she writes that "they *draw* us in as participants to the conversation" (Tsouna 2013: 23), enticing "his audience to join the action." (Tsouna 2013: 26) But these statements, true as they are, must be taken together with her above-quoted statements attributing beliefs, doctrines, theories, etc. and even intentions to Plato, placing Tsouna within the category of the Mouthpiece Interpretation.

Some Problems with the Mouthpiece Interpretation of Plato's Dialogues

Yet there are several problems with the Mouthpiece Interpretation of Plato's dialogues, ones that undermine Tsouna's attempt to reconcile the problem that she sets out to solve. First, Tsouma makes much of the matter of how Plato's dialogues differ from the other mimetic arts he allegedly condemns. However, this is inadequate reason to attribute to Plato any belief, doctrine, theory or view expressed in his dialogues. Indeed, what Tsouma does not seem to consider is the distinct possibility that the Socratic Interpretation is justified in part precisely because it makes no sense, given a plausible principle of charity of interpretation with regard to Plato's dialogues, to think that Plato himself condemns the mimetic arts while, if Tsouna and various other scholars of Plato are correct, Plato offers us his own dialogues as mimetic. This is the case unless Plato himself were to offer readers of his dialogues some explanation as to why his mimetic dialogues are (however implicitly) justified while mimetic poetry and painting are not. To impute to Plato a set of conflicting positions such as these violates any plausible Principle of Charity of Interpretation. This fact ought to serve as a caution to Tsouna and other mouthpiece interpreters to seek a simpler explanation for the apparent conflict she seeks to address. For if the Socratic Interpretation is correct, then there is no need to see the conflict Tsouna sees. Rather, the reader ought to understand the expression of censorship of the mimetic arts in the *Republic* and elsewhere in Plato's dialogues as a view to be critically assessed on philosophical terms. Thus the genuine distinctions between Plato's dialogues as mimetic art and certain other mimetic arts forms is not an adequate means by which to develop an approach to Plato which attributes to him this or that belief, doctrine or theory when such an approach is unjustified by the Platonic texts themselves.

Furthermore, the appeal to Aristotle as "our most important external witness" to Plato's views (Irwin 1992: 77) runs afoul of various sorts of problems as was explained in both Chapter 3 and Appendix I. And this need not, as some think, lead to the inference that Plato is a skeptic (as if that were a philosophical vice!). (Annas 1992: 64) For from the supposition that we have inadequate textual or extra textual evidence of Plato's views it hardly follows that Plato was a skeptic. After all, Plato could have simply not wanted to reveal his views in the dialogues or to anyone else, perhaps out of fear of his mentor's fate for practicing philosophy in ancient Greece where freedom of expression was not a robust right.

Thus any version of the Mouthpiece Interpretation which construes the words of any of Plato's characters in his dialogues as representing or speaking for Plato himself is problematic. Moreover, that there might be a view, theory or doctrine of art as *mimêsis* in the *Republic* or in some other or all of Plato's dialogues is also problematic insofar as it is unclear both that such expressions amount to either a unified or developed belief, view, theory or doctrine and that Plato himself subscribes to any such expressions about the mimetic arts. (Corlett 2005: 72–84) As John Fisher writes:

> Moderns who demand a theory of art from Plato expect too much, and those who construct one from other elements of his philosophy can only be partially successful, can only create a partial theory... To invent

> Platonic theories is harmless and edifying, provided that we do not believe them to be Plato's. He had no theory of art in any way remotely suggesting a modern theory of art, which is always what is expected of him. (Fisher 1982: 99)

The epistemic burden of proof lies with mouthpiece interpreters of Plato's dialogues who either naively assume or dogmatically assert that "Plato says" this or that in any of his dialogues. This point applies just as well to other alleged beliefs, views, doctrines, or theories of Plato's as it does to the allegation that Plato has a belief, view, doctrine or theory of the mimetic arts. Tsouna's attempt to reconcile Plato's alleged condemnation of poetry and other mimetic arts in the *Republic* with the fact that Plato himself composes dialogues with mimetic features is yet one more attempt by mouthpiece interpreters to make sense of nonsense, namely, the idea that Plato wrote dialogues to propound this or that view to which be subscribes. Indeed, it might be argued by mouthpiece interpreters that Tsouma's attempt to reconcile the facts in question just is an attempt to provide evidence in favor of the Mouthpiece Interpretation. However, this argument runs afoul of question-begging as it assumes what must be proven by mouthpiece interpreters: that Plato's beliefs, views, doctrines or theories are intentionally expressed by Plato via this or that character in his dialogues. Mouthpiece interpreters must come to grips with the fact that several attempts to justify their position have met with failure on logical grounds as well as internal textual grounds and external evidence.

Conclusion

While there is some plausibility in Tsouma's attempt to reconcile the condemnation of the mimetic arts in Plato's *Republic* and Plato's own use of mimetic art forms in the very production of his dialogues, in the end her attempt assumes a version of the Mouthpiece Interpretation which is not necessary in order to address the apparent conflict by way of the more straightforward Socratic Interpretation of Plato's dialogues. And unless there is sufficiently good reason to interpret otherwise, a simpler, more straightforward and plain reading of Plato's dialogues still registers as the most plausible approach to his remarkable corpus of writings. In short, Plato's dialogues are philosophical works which intend to draw readers into the doing of analytic philosophy so that we can be better for the rest of our lives, as Plato's Socrates put it on various occasions.

References

Annas, Julia. 1992. Plato the Sceptic. In *Oxford studies in ancient philosophy* (Supplementary Volume), ed. James C. Klagge and Nicholas D. Smith, 43–72. Oxford: Oxford University Press.

Corlett, J. Angelo. 2005. *Interpreting Plato's dialogues*. Las Vegas: Parmenides Publishing.

Fisher, John. 1982. Did Plato have a theory of art? *Pacific Philosophical Quarterly* 63: 93–99.

Irwin, Terrence. 1992. The intellectual background. In *The Cambridge companion to Plato*, ed. Richard Kraut, 51–89. Cambridge: Cambridge University Press.

Tsouna, Voula. 2013. *Mimesis* and the Platonic dialogue. *Rhizomata* 1: 1–29.

Selected Sources

Allen, R.E. 1972. Law and justice in Plato's *Crito*. *The Journal of Philosophy* 69: 557–567.
———. 1980. *Socrates and legal obligation*. Minneapolis: University of Minnesota Press.
———., Translator. 1984. *The dialogues of Plato*, Vol. 1. New Haven: Yale University Press.
Annas, Julia. 1981. *An introduction to Plato's <u>Republic</u>*. Oxford: Oxford University Press.
———. 1992. Plato the Sceptic. In *Oxford studies in ancient philosophy* (Supplementary Volume), ed. James C. Klagge and Nicholas D. Smith, 43–72. Oxford: Oxford University Press.
———. 2006. Ethics and argument in Plato's Socrates. In *The virtuous life in Greek ethics*, ed. B. Reis, 32–46. Cambridge: Cambridge University Press.
———. 2017. *Virtue & law in Plato & beyond*. Oxford: Oxford University Press.
Barker, Andrew. 1977. Why did Socrates refuse to escape? *Phronesis* 22: 13–28.
Benn, Stanley. 1958. An approach to the problem of punishment. *Philosophy* 33: 325–341.
Bentham, Jeremy. 1948. *An introduction to the principles of morals and legislation*. New York: Hafner.
Bertman, M.A. 1971. Socrates' defence of civil obedience. *Studium Generale* 24: 576–582.
Beversluis, John. 2006. A defence of dogmatism in the interpretation of Plato. In *Oxford studies in ancient philosophy*, ed. David Sedley, vol. 31, 85–112. Oxford: Oxford University Press.
Bobonich, Christopher. 2008. Plato's politics. In *The Oxford handbook of Plato*, ed. Gail Fine, 311–335. Oxford: Oxford University Press.
Bostock, David. 1990. The interpretation of Plato's *Crito*. *Phronesis* 35: 1–20.

Brickhouse, Thomas C., and Nicholas D. Smith. 1984. Socrates and obedience to the law. *Aperion* 18: 10–18.
———. 1994. *Plato's Socrates*. Oxford: Oxford University Press.
———. 2002a. The Socratic *Elenchos*? In *Does Socrates have a method?* ed. Gary A. Scott, 145–157. Pennsylvania State University Press: University Park.
———. 2002b. The problem of punishment in Socratic philosophy. *Aperion*: 95–107.
———. 2006. Socrates and the Laws of Athens. *Philosophy Compass* 1: 564–570.
———. 2007. Socrates on how wrongdoing damages the soul. *The Journal of Ethics* 11: 337–356.
———. 2010. *Socratic moral psychology*. Cambridge: Cambridge University Press.
———. 2012. Reply to Rowe. *The Journal of Ethics* 16: 325–338.
Brittain, Charles. 2008. Plato and Platonism. In *The Oxford handbook of Plato*, ed. Gail Fine, 526–552. Oxford: Oxford University Press.
Burnyeat, Myles, and Michael Frede. 2015. In *The Pseudo-Platonic Seventh Letter*, ed. Dominic Scott. Oxford: Oxford University Press.
Calvert, Brian. 1987. Plato's *Crito* and Richard Kraut. In *Justice, law, and method in Plato and Aristotle*, ed. S. Panagiotou, 17–33. Edmonton: Academic Printing and Publishing.
Cherniss, Harold. 1944. *Aristotle's criticism of Plato and the academy*. Baltimore: Johns Hopkins University Press.
———. 1945. *The riddle of the early academy*. Berkeley: University of California Press.
———. 1962a. *Aristotle's criticism of Plato and the academy*. New York: Russell & Russell.
———. 1962b. *The riddle of the early academy*. Russell & Russell: New York.
Colson, Darrel D. 1986. On appealing the Athenian Law to justify Socrates' disobedience. *Aperion* XIX: 133–151.
———. 1989. *Crito* 51a-c: To what does Socrates owe obedience? *Phronesis* 34: 27–55.
Congleton, Ann. 1974. Two kinds of lawlessness: Plato's *Crito*. *Political Theory* 2: 432–446.
Cooper, John M., and D.S. Hutchinson. 1997. *Plato: Complete works*. Indianapolis: Hackett Publishing Company.
Corlett, J. Angelo. 1989. Is Kripke's puzzle really a puzzle? *Theoria* LV: 95–113.
———. 1996. *Analyzing social knowledge*. Totowa: Rowman & Littlefield Publishers.
———. 2001. Making sense of retributivism. *Philosophy* 76: 77–110.
———. 2003. Making *more* sense of Retributivism. *Philosophy* 78: 277–285.
———. 2005. *Interpreting Plato's dialogues*. Las Vegas: Parmenides Publishing.

———. 2006a. The philosophy of Joel Feinberg. *The Journal of Ethics* 10: 146–151.

———. 2006b. *Responsibility and punishment*. In Library of ethics and applied philosophy, vol. 9, 3rd ed. Dordrecht: Springer.

Davis, Michael. 1992. *To make the punishment fit the crime*. Totowa: Rowman & Littlefield Publishers.

Deane, P. 1973. Stylometrics do not exclude the *Seventh Letter*. *Mind* 82: 113–117.

Dixit, R.D. 1980. Socrates on civil disobedience. *Indian Philosophical Quarterly* 8: 91–98.

Dybikowski, J. 1974. Socrates, obedience, and the law: Plato's *Crito*. *Dialogue* 13: 519–535.

Dyson, M. 1978. The structure of the laws' speech in Plato's *Crito*. *The Classical Quarterly* 28: 427–436.

Farrell, James M. 1978. Illegal actions, universal maxims, and the duty to obey the law: The case for civil authority in the *Crito*. *Political Theory* 6: 173–189.

Feinberg, Joel. 1979. Civil disobedience in the modern world. *Humanities in Society* 2: 37–59.

———. 1980. *Rights, justice, and the bounds of liberty*. Princeton: Princeton University Press.

———. 1992. *Freedom and fulfillment*. Princeton: Princeton University Press.

———. 1995. The classic debate. In *Philosophy of Law*, ed. Joel Feinberg and Hyman Gross, 5th ed., 613–618. Belmont: Wadsworth Publishing Company.

———. 2003. *Problems at the roots of law*. Oxford: Oxford University Press.

Fisher, John. 1982. Did Plato have a theory of art? *Pacific Philosophical Quarterly* 63: 93–99.

Fiske, Susan T., and Shelley E. Taylor. 1991. *Social cognition*. 2nd ed. New York: McGraw-Hill.

Gallop, David. 1998. Socrates, injustice, and the law: A response to Plato's *Crito*. *Ancient Philosophy* 18: 251–265.

Gerson, Lloyd. 2000. Plato *Absconditus*. In *Who speaks for Plato?* ed. Gerald Press, 201–210. Lanham: Rowman & Littlefield Publishers.

———. 2002. *Elenchos*, protreptic, and platonic philosophizing. In *Does Socrates have a method?* ed. G.A. Scott, 217–231. Philadelphia: Pennsylvania State University Press.

———. 2005. What is Platonism? *Journal of the History of Philosophy* 43: 253–276.

———. 2014. Harold Cherniss and the study of Plato today. *Journal of the History of Philosophy* 52: 397–409.

Gill, Christopher. 1996. Afterword: Dialectic and the dialogue form in late Plato. In *Form and argument in late Plato*, ed. Christopher Gill and Mary Margaret McCabe, 283–311. Oxford: Oxford University Press.

Gomme, A.W. 1958. The structure of Plato's *Crito*. *Greece & Rome* 5: 45–51.

Goodspeed, E.J. 1916. *The story of the new testament*. Chicago: University of Chicago Press.

Grant, F.C. 1933. *The growth of the Gospels*. New York: Abingdon Press.
Grant, M. 1977. *Jesus: An historian's review of the Gospels*. New York: Charles Scribner's Sons.
Greenberg, N.A. 1965. Socrates' choice in the *Crito*. *Harvard Studies in Classical Philology* 70: 48f.
Grice, Paul. 1971. Meaning. In *Philosophy of language*, ed. Jay Rosenberg and Charles Travis, 436–444. Englewood Cliffs: Prentice-Hall.
Guthrie, W.K.C. 1969. *A history of Greek philosophy*. Vol. 3. Cambridge: Cambridge University Press.
———. 1975. *A history of Greek philosophy: Plato: The man and his dialogues*. Cambridge: Cambridge University Press.
Hampton, Jean. 1984. The moral education theory of punishment. *Philosophy and Public Affairs* 13: 208–238.
Hart, H.L.A. 1968. *Punishment and responsibility*. Oxford: Oxford University Press.
Irwin, Terence. 1986. Socratic inquiry and politics. *Ethics* 96: 400–415.
———. 1995. *Plato's ethics*. Oxford: Oxford University Press.
———. 2008. The platonic corpus. In *The Oxford handbook of Plato*, ed. Gail Fine, 63–87. Oxford: Oxford University Press.
James, Gene G. 1973. Socrates on civil disobedience and rebellion. *The Southern Journal of Philosophy* 11: 119–127.
Kahn, Charles. 1989. Problems in the argument of Plato's *Crito*. *Aperion* XXII: 29–43.
Kant, Immanuel. 1965. *The metaphysical elements of justice*, (Trans. John Ladd). London: Macmillan.
Kennedy, J.B. 2010. Plato's forms, pythagorean mathematics, and stichometry. *Aperion* 43: 1–30.
Kenny, Anthony. 2006. *What I believe*. London: Continuum.
Keyt, David. 2008. Plato on justice. *Philosophical Inquiry* 30: 37–53.
Koester, Helmut. 1990. *Ancient Christian Gospels: Their history and development*. London: SCM Press.
Kraut, Richard. 1984. *Socrates and the state*. Princeton: Princeton University Press.
———. 1992. The defense of justice in Plato's *Republic*. In *The Cambridge companion to Plato*, ed. Richard Kraut, 311–337. Cambridge: Cambridge University Press.
———. 2003. Justice in Plato and Aristotle: withdrawal *versus* engagement. In *Plato and Aristotle's ethics*, ed. R. Heinaman, 153–167. London: Ashgate.
Kretzmann, Norman. 1988. *Lex Iniusta Non Est Lex:* Interpreting St. Thomas Aquinas ("Laws on Trial in Aquinas' Court of Conscience"). *American Journal of Jurisprudence* 33: 99–122.
Kripke, Saul. 1979. A puzzle about belief. In *Meaning and use*, ed. A. Margalit, 239–283. Dordrecht: Reidel.
Lehrer, Keith. 2000. *Theory of knowledge*. 2nd ed. Boulder: Westview Press.

Levinson, M., A.Q. Morton, and A.D. Winspear. 1968. The *Seventh Letter* of Plato. *Mind* 77: 309–325.

Lewis, V.B. 2000. The rhetoric of philosophical politics in Plato's *Seventh Letter*. *Philosophy & Rhetoric* 33: 23–38.

Mackenzie, M.M. 1981. *Plato on punishment*. Berkeley: University of California Press.

Martin, Rex. 1970. Socrates on disobedience to the Law. *The Review of Metaphysics* XXIV: 21–38.

McCabe, M. M., "Plato's ways of writing," in Gail Fine, The Oxford handbook of Plato (Oxford: Oxford University Press, 2008), pp. 88–113.

McLaughlin, Robert J. 1976. Socrates on political disobedience: A reply to Gary Young. *Phronesis* 21: 185–197.

Miller, Mitchell. 1995. The choice between the dialogues and the 'Unwritten Teachings': A Scylla and Charybdis for the interpreter. In *The third way*, ed. F. Gonzalez, 225–243. Lanham: Rowman & Littlefield.

———. 1996. 'The arguments I seem to hear': Argument and Irony in the *Crito*. *Phronesis* 41: 121–137.

Mulgan, R.R. 1972. Socrates and authority. *Greece & Rome* 19: 208–212.

Mulhern, John J. 1971. Two interpretive fallacies. *Systematics* 9: 168–172.

———. 2000. Interpreting the Platonic dialogues: What can one say? In *Who speaks for Plato?* ed. Gerald A. Press, 221–234. Lanham: Rowman & Littlefield Publishers.

———. 2011. *Plato's putative mouthpiece and ancient authorial practice: A reply*, 17. New York/New York: The Society for Ancient Greek Philosophy/Fordham University.

Murphy, Jeffrie G. 1974. Violence and the Socratic theory of legal fidelity. In *Violence and aggression in the history of ideas*, ed. Philip P. Wiener and John Fischer, 15–33. New Brunswick: Rutgers University Press.

———. 1987. Does Kant have a theory of punishment? *Columbia Law Review* 87: 509–532.

Murphy, David. 2011. A certain Socrates swinging around there and claiming...' Characters' utterances and authors' views in Plato's practice, 22. New York/New York: The Society for Ancient Greek Philosophy/Fordham University.

Nails, Debra. 1995. *Agora, Academy, and the conduct of philosophy*. Dordrecht: Kluwer Academic Publishers.

———. 2011. The structures of Plato's dialogues, 22. New York/New York: The Society for Ancient Greek Philosophy/Fordham University.

Nozick, Robert. 1981. *Philosophical explanations*. Cambridge: Harvard University Press.

Panagiotou, S. 1987. Justified disobedience in the *Crito*? In *Justice, law, and method in Plato and Aristotle*, ed. S. Panagiotou, 35–50. Edmonton: Academic Printing and Publishing.

Peterson, Sandra. 2011. *Socrates and philosophy in Plato's dialogues*. Cambridge: Cambridge University Press.

Plato, see Cooper, John M., and D. S. Hutchinson, (Eds.), *Plato: Complete works*.

Popper, Karl. 1962. *The open society and its enemies: Volume 1: The spell of Plato*. New York: Harper Torchbooks.
Press, Gerald, ed. 2000. *Who speaks for Plato?* Lanham: Rowman & Littlefield Publishers.
Price, A.W. 2008. Reasoning about justice in Plato's *Republic*. *Philosophical Inquiry* 30: 25–35.
Quandt, Kenneth. 1982. Socratic consolation: Rhetoric and philosophy in Plato's *Crito*. *Philosophy and Rhetoric* 15: 238–256.
Quinton, Anthony M. 1954. Punishment. *Analysis* 14: 133–142.
Rawls, John. 1955. Two concepts of rules. *The Philosophical Review* 64: 3–13.
———. 1971. *A theory of justice*. Cambridge: Harvard University Press.
———. 1999. *The law of peoples*. Cambridge: Harvard University Press.
Ray, A. Chadwick. 1980. The tacit agreement in the *Crito*. *International Studies in Philosophy* 12: 47–54.
Reshotko, N. 2006. *Socratic virtue*. Cambridge: Cambridge University Press.
Rosen, F. 1973. Obligation and friendship in Plato's *Crito*. *Political Theory* 1: 307–316.
Rowe, Christopher. 2003. Reply to Richard Kraut. In *Plato and Aristotle's ethics*, ed. R. Heinaman, 168–176. London: Ashgate.
———. 2006. Interpreting Plato. In *A companion to Plato*, ed. Hugh Benson, 13–24. London: Blackwell Publishing.
———. 2012. Socrates on reason, appetite, and passion: A response to Thomas C. Brickhouse and Nicholas D. Smith. *The Journal of Ethics* 16: 305–324.
Ryberg, Jesper. 2004. *The ethics of proportionate punishment*. Dordrecht: Kluwer Academic Publishers.
Santas, G.X. 1979. *Socrates*. London: Routledge & Kegan Paul.
Shields, Christopher. 2008. Plato and Aristotle in the academy. In *The Oxford handbook of Plato*, ed. Gail Fine, 504–525. Oxford: Oxford University Press.
Soper, Philip. 1996. Another look at the *Crito*. *The American Journal of Jurisprudence* 41: 1–21.
Stephens, James. 1985. Socrates on the rule of law. *History of Philosophy Quarterly* 2: 3–10.
Strauss, Leo. 1984. *Studies in Platonic political philosophy*. Chicago: The University of Chicago Press.
Streeter, B.H. 1924. *The four Gospels: A study of origins*. London: MacMillan and Company Limited.
Taylor, A.E. 1963. *Plato: The man and his work*. London: Methuen & Co., Ltd.
Tsouna, Voula. 2013. *Mimesis* and the Platonic dialogue. *Rhizomata* 1: 1–29.
Vlastos, Gregory. 1974. Socrates on political obedience and disobedience. *Yale Review* 63: 517–534.
———. 1991. *Socrates: Ironist and moral philosopher*. Ithaca: Cornell University press.
Wade, Francis C. 1971. In defense of Socrates. *The Review of Metaphysics* XXV: 311–325.

Weinrib, Ernest J. 1982. Obedience to the law in Plato's *Crito*. *The American Journal of Jurisprudence* 27: 85–108.

Weiss, Roslyn. 1998. *Socrates dissatisfied: An analysis of Plato's Crito*. Oxford: Oxford University Press.

West, E.J.M. 1989. Socrates in the *Crito*: Patriot or friend? In *Essays in Ancient Greek Philosophy III: Plato*, ed. J. Anton and A. Preus, 71–84. Albany: State University of New York Press.

White, James Boyd. 1996. Plato's *Crito*: The authority of law and philosophy. In *The Greeks and Us*, ed. R.B. Louden and P. Schollmeier, 97–133. Chicago: The University of Chicago Press.

Woozley, A.D. 1979. *Law and obedience: The arguments of Plato's Crito*. London: Duckworth.

———. 1980. Socrates on disobeying the law. In *The Philosophy of Socrates*, ed. Gregory Vlastos, 299–318. Notre Dame: University of Notre Dame Press.

Young, Gary. 1974. Socrates and obedience. *Phronesis* 19: 1–29.

Young, Charles M. 2006. Plato's *Crito* on the obligation to obey the law. *Philosophical Inquiry* XXVII: 79–90.

Index

A
Annas, J., 1, 7, 9, 39, 65, 229
Apology, 11, 22, 24, 26–29, 56, 58, 112, 114, 121, 134–136, 138, 140, 143, 145, 147, 155, 156, 158, 160, 161, 163, 164, 174, 175, 200
Aristotle, vii, xi, 2, 12, 59–66, 69, 71, 72, 78, 90, 108–111, 201, 203–224, 229

B
Beversluis, J., 1, 37, 39, 62, 63, 73–81, 84
Brickhouse, T.C., xi, 10, 11, 19, 99–109, 111–119, 153, 158, 161–164, 171, 185

C
Compensation (Compensatory Justice), 187–197
Cooper, J.M., xi, 21, 30, 110, 114, 152, 172
Crito, 11, 21, 89, 101, 113, 123, 128, 133–165, 169, 200, 208

D
Developmentalism, 1, 16, 17, 36–38, 134

F
Feinberg, J., 129, 130, 137, 138, 141, 171, 181

G
Gallop, D., ix, 138, 139
Gerson, L., ix, 12, 33–37, 59–62, 80, 87, 201, 203–224
Gorgias, 2, 22, 56, 114, 123, 125, 128, 133, 145, 149–151, 164, 169, 175–177, 187–191, 195

I
Irwin, T., 1, 40, 68–73, 128, 129, 134, 229

K
Kahn, C., 29, 99, 112, 135, 143
Kraut, R., 1, 122, 130, 134

L

Laws, 2, 7, 22, 48, 49, 60, 69, 70, 89, 114, 121, 123–128, 137–140, 143, 144, 147, 148, 151, 152, 154–156, 160, 162, 178–182, 185, 187, 190–195

M

McCabe, M.M., 19, 20, 22–26, 44–46, 56, 57
Moral education, ix, xiii, 11, 169, 171–173, 175, 177–179, 181, 183, 185, 197, 200
Mouthpiece interpretation, vii–x, 1–7, 9–12, 15–21, 24, 25, 27, 28, 30, 31, 33, 34, 36–38, 40, 42–45, 48, 49, 51–57, 59, 61, 62, 66–81, 83–88, 90–93, 97, 99, 102, 104, 111, 112, 116–119, 121, 130, 135, 153, 160, 199–201, 205, 206, 214, 219, 220, 223, 224, 226–230
Mulhern, J.J., xi, 4, 20, 30, 63, 64, 109, 135, 220

N

Nails, D., 4, 17, 18, 22, 38, 86, 97, 114

P

Peterson, S., 24–30, 35, 114
Press, G., ix, xi, 39
Principle of Charity in Interpretation, 58, 82, 129, 134, 139, 208, 212, 221
Protagoras, 22, 23, 114, 175, 184
Punishment, viii–xi, xiv, 2, 10, 11, 82, 123, 125, 126, 131, 136, 142, 149, 153, 169–186, 188–194, 196, 197, 200

R

Rawls, J., 127, 138, 159, 170, 171, 191
Republic, 2, 4–7, 12, 17, 22, 24, 25, 27, 39, 43, 48, 49, 51, 60, 67, 70, 103, 114, 115, 121, 123–126, 128, 129, 138, 150, 177, 178, 183, 207, 208, 212, 221, 222, 225–230
Retributivism, xi, 169–185

S

Seventh Letter, 2, 31, 44–58, 74, 76, 86, 90, 116, 213, 215, 216, 219, 223
Smith, N.D., ix, xi, 10, 11, 19, 99–109, 111–119, 153, 158, 161–164, 171, 185
Socratic (Anti-Mouthpiece) Interpretation, viii, ix, xiv, 2, 3, 11, 15, 16, 18, 30, 31, 33, 36, 37, 40, 45, 49, 54, 58, 59, 74, 76, 78, 80, 84, 87, 92, 93, 98, 112–119, 121, 153, 199, 201, 205, 220–223, 227–230

T

Theaetetus, 2, 4, 20, 22, 24, 27, 56, 70, 73, 92, 103, 114, 115
Timaeus, 56, 89, 217, 218

U

Unitarianism, 16, 134

V

Vlastos, G., 2, 5, 6, 21, 25, 28, 29, 114, 136, 140, 145, 155, 156, 158

W
Woozley, A.D., 21, 113, 133, 136, 153, 172

Y
Young, C., ix, xi, 41–43, 133, 157

The manufacturer's authorised representative in the EU is Springer Nature Customer Service Centre GmbH, Europaplatz 3, 69115 Heidelberg, Germany. If you have any concerns regarding our products, please contact ProductSafety@springernature.com

Printed and bound by CPI Group (UK) Ltd, Croydon, CR0 4YY

23/03/2026

02076675-0014